SAVING LAK

SAVING
LAKE
TAHOE

AN ENVIRONMENTAL HISTORY

OF A NATIONAL TREASURE

MICHAEL J. MAKLEY

UNIVERSITY OF NEVADA PRESS

RENO AND LAS VEGAS

University of Nevada Press, Reno, Nevada 89557 USA

Copyright © 2014 by University of Nevada Press

All rights reserved

Manufactured in the United States of America

Design by Kathleen Szawiola

Library of Congress Cataloging-in-Publication Data

Makley, Michael J.

Saving Lake Tahoe : the environmental and political history of a national treasure /

Michael J. Makley. — First edition.

pages cm

Includes bibliographical references and index.

ISBN 978-0-87417-934-7 (pbk. : alk. paper) — ISBN 978-0-87417-935-4 (e-book)

1. Tahoe, Lake (Calif. and Nev.)—History. 2. Natural history—Tahoe, Lake (Calif. and Nev.)

3. Tahoe, Lake (Calif. and Nev.)—Environmental conditions. 4. Tahoe, Lake, Region (Calif.

and Nev.)—-History. 5. Tahoe, Lake, Region (Calif. and Nev.)—Politics and government.

I. Title.

F868.T2M348 2013   979.4'38—dc23

2013041105

FIRST PRINTING

22 21 20 19 18 17 16 15 14 13

5 4 3 2 1

FOR RANDI, MOLLY, MATT, AND BRIE

CONTENTS

Illustrations follow page 94

||||||||||||||||||||||||||||||||||||||||||||||||||||||||||||||||||||||||||||||||||||||||||||||||||||||||||||||||||||||||||||||||||||||||||||||||||||||||||||||||||||||||||||||||

In the weeks before delivery of this manuscript for publication, stories about Lake Tahoe headlined Internet sites, television news, and the pages of the *New York Times:* "Conservationists File Suit over Lake Tahoe Compact," "Giant Goldfish Found in Tahoe," "Nevada Governor Favors Abandoning Tahoe Pact," "Lake Tahoe's Clarity Best in Ten Years."

Because of Lake Tahoe's awe-inspiring beauty, scientific findings and political disputes over it are newsworthy. Yet there is no single source that puts stories about the lake in context or ties them together. *Saving Lake Tahoe: An Environmental History of a National Treasure* is intended to fill that void. It charts the events that have shaped the area, beginning with logging companies clear-cutting the forests in the 1870s. It discusses the complications, past and present, in attempting to rehabilitate and protect a delicate ecosystem governed by multiple authorities. The book explains the passionate fights between those who seek to preserve environmental qualities by regulating development and those advocating for the rights of business and property owners, and it reviews groundbreaking efforts to utilize science in establishing policies of governance.

The Tahoe story holds personal interest for me: I grew up at the lake, moving there in 1959, and have lived there most of my life. I have known a number of key actors in its modern history, some of whom assisted in the compilation of this study. Larry Schmidt was foremost in helping out. His father, Andrew Schmidt, led the US Forest Service team that helped develop the Tahoe Regional Planning Agency, the agency charged with protecting the lake for the past forty years, and wrote a comprehensive account that documents the Forest Service's role at the lake as well as TRPA's early history. Larry Schmidt provided me with cartons of his father's research as well as several tapes of interviews with principals involved in the lake's mid-twentieth-century governance. Larry Schmidt's own career spanned several decades as a Forest Service hydrologist, and he introduced me to two agency figures who played critical roles in the

Tahoe story and agreed to be interviewed: former US Forest Service associate chief Doug Leisz and renowned physical geologist Robert G. Bailey, who produced the Lake Tahoe Basin capabilities map—and for whom "the Bailey system," devised from it, is named.

Other important players in these events who took time to provide their perspective in interviews include former Washoe Indian Tribal chair Brian Wallace and Washoe traditionalist Art George; former Lake Tahoe Forest Service supervisor and TRPA executive director Bill Morgan; Robert Twiss, US government and UN planning adviser who has acted as a State of California consultant on Tahoe for more than forty years; Bob Richards, who led scientific experiments on Lake Tahoe for thirty-five years; retired Lake Tahoe Forest Service hydrologist Bill Johnson; former spokesperson for TRPA the late Dennis Oliver; Rochelle Nason, who served as League to Save Lake Tahoe executive director for eighteen years; Steve Teshara, who for many years represented the Tahoe Gaming Alliance and other lake-basin businesses; Tahoe Area Sierra Club representative Laurel Ames; Bob Kingman of the Sierra Nevada Conservancy; Bob Ferguson of Lahontan Water Quality Control; Robert Stewart, former administrative assistant to Nevada governor Mike O'Callaghan; and current League to Save Lake Tahoe executive director Darcie Goodman-Collins.

Bill Johnson and Bob Richards were gracious as well in making available photos from their private collections. Flavia Sordelet provided access to photos from the League to Save Lake Tahoe collection. Jessica Maddox assisted me at University of Nevada, Reno, Special Collections, and Kim Roberts was especially helpful in taking the time to find Special Collections pictures that are not replicated online.

In addition, University of Nevada Press director Joanne O'Hare offered valuable suggestions, design and production manager Kathleen Szawiola provided guidance regarding photos and supervised the graphic planning and design of the book, and senior editor Matt "Becks" Becker directed the project, advising me throughout. As in my last project, I was fortunate to have Annette Wenda as copy editor: adding, deleting, and rearranging text to ensure it conveyed what was intended and correcting the format of the notes so they made some sense. Others who provided important information or avenues of research include McAvoy Layne, Guy Rocha, Susan Searcy, Joyce Cox, Scott Baez, Trisha Leonard, Peggy Cocores, and John Brissendon.

As in all my writing ventures, Matthew Makley was my primary consultant, and Randi Makley provided counsel. This work would be significantly less developed without their assistance.

SAVING LAKE TAHOE

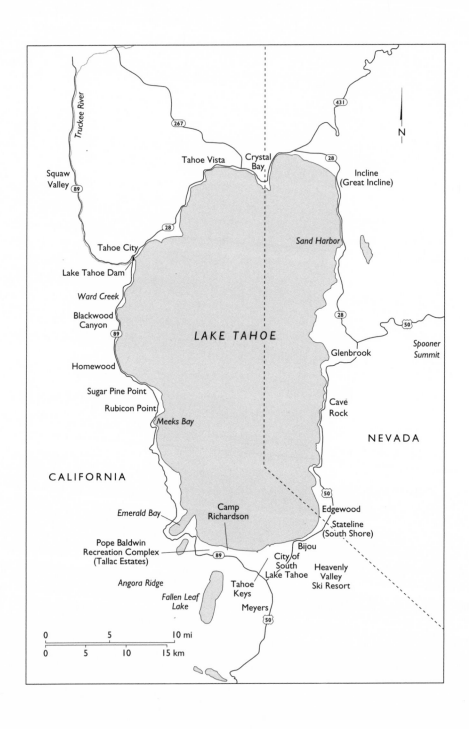

Truckee River

Squaw
Valley (89)

(267)

Tahoe Vista   Crystal
Bay

(431)

(28)

Incline
(Great Incline)

(28)

Sand Harbor

Tahoe City

Lake Tahoe Dam

Ward Creek

Blackwood
Canyon

(89)

LAKE TAHOE

(28)

(50)

Glenbrook

*Spooner
Summit*

Homewood

Sugar Pine Point

Rubicon Point   *Meeks Bay*

Cave
Rock

NEVADA

CALIFORNIA

(50)

Emerald Bay

Camp
Richardson

Edgewood

Stateline
(South Shore)

Pope Baldwin
Recreation Complex
(Tallac Estates)

(89)

Bijou

City of
South
Lake Tahoe

Heavenly
Valley
Ski Resort

Angora Ridge

Tahoe
Keys

*Fallen Leaf
Lake*

Meyers   (50)

0   5   10 mi

0   5   10   15 km

N

Influential Americans from Mark Twain in the nineteenth century to Presidents Carter, Reagan, and Clinton in the twentieth have acclaimed Lake Tahoe a national treasure. Executive orders, congressional bills, and Supreme Court decisions have dealt with the lake. Poets and artists have sought to capture its essence, and twice we nearly destroyed it.

In the nineteenth century, when virgin lands were thought to be going to waste, entrepreneurs clear-cut the area's forests. The loss of vegetation caused erosion on the surrounding mountains, carrying silt into the lake that reduced its clarity more than sevenfold.

A hundred years later, with the forests regrown and the water's purity restored, Tahoe's scenic values and recreational activities attracted annual visitors by the millions. The resultant urbanization again caused immense environmental damage, most apparent in a dramatic escalation of building, traffic congestion, air pollution, and the deterioration of lake clarity—this time more than 30 percent. It is only because its waters began with unmatched purity that Lake Tahoe maintains its unique, scenic grandeur.[1]

Saving Lake Tahoe argues that the lake's heritage must take precedence over the unrestricted use of private and commercial properties. To what extent property owners and business interests should be allowed to develop their lands at the expense of the lake's ecological health has been disputed for more than fifty years. To substantiate the thesis that the Lake Basin, 75 percent of which is publicly owned land, can be effectively protected only by overarching governance and regional environmental standards, this book looks at the interaction through the years between human activities and Tahoe's natural ecosystems. It recounts ecodisasters and near disasters and political successes and failures. It tells why and how a new type of government entity, a bistate regional agency, was formed and the innumerable problems it has incurred.

Much has been done in the modern era in attempting to mitigate human damage at Lake Tahoe. Both the Environmental Protection Agency (EPA) and the State of California have designated the lake an Outstanding National Resource Water, giving it special protections. California and Nevada passed bonds, and the federal government sold public southern Nevada properties to raise money to buy environmentally sensitive lands at Tahoe. In the recent past, $1.55 billion has been expended, and some of America's most astute scientific and political minds have been employed, in attempting to renew Lake Tahoe's health and protect its picturesque splendor.

Americans' discovery of the area and the impact it had on the Native people have aspects that are familiar. For thousands of years, in the snowless months, the Washoe Indians lived at the lake. When the Americans arrived, the Washoe were a small tribe of perhaps two thousand members, utilizing systems developed through the millennia. The Indians selectively harvested, burned, pruned, and thinned plants and fished and hunted, sustaining the region's bounty. Protected by the massive Sierra Nevada to the west and the desert of the Great Basin to the east, 150 years after the Lewis and Clark expedition and nearly 100 years after missions were established in California, the Washoes continued to pursue their traditional lives undisturbed.

Americans, arriving in the late 1850s, found a pristine lake, seventy-two miles in circumference and more than sixteen hundred feet deep, surrounded by ancient pine forests on basin-forming mountains. Within three decades, the newcomers had removed the forests, fenced out the Washoes, and over-fished the lake—leading to the ultimate extinction of the once abundant native trout.

Owing to the manner in which it was done, the clear-cutting of the forests was not fatal to the lake. The number of roads built, none with impervious surfaces, was limited. Log skids were built that prevented cuts from digging deeply into the mountainsides. Flumes and trains used in transporting the timber utilized trestles that protected canyons and drainages. After the cutting, limbs, needles, and other forest debris were left and served as ground cover, limiting soil loss. Most important, once the timber magnates had taken the trees, they abandoned the region, and the populace largely ignored it.[2]

In the first half of the twentieth century, human neglect allowed the forests to grow back and the lake's transparency to return. In the 1960s, the lake's health and beauty reestablished, entrepreneurs created a "year-round play-ground," featuring gambling, summer sports, and skiing. The tourism and population explosion resulted in the lake being loved nearly to death.

The States of California and Nevada governed the area, sharing jurisdiction with five counties, the City of South Lake Tahoe, two towns, the US Forest Service, the Department of Housing and Urban Development (HUD), the US Coast Guard, and more than sixty other agencies. With consensus rarely sought, the authorities' rulings were generally fragmented and at times conflicting.

In December 1969, the US Congress created a unique government entity to deal with the Tahoe Basin: the Tahoe Regional Planning Agency, the country's first regional organization charged with coordinating planning between states.

TRPA was intended to supplement and coordinate the lake basin's ineffective regulating bodies. Under its compact, the agency ultimately claimed sweeping authority to regulate land, air, and water quality. Scientists developed environmental analyses that were adopted into ordinance form. From the beginning, no one was pleased with TRPA decisions.

Disputes flared within the agency; the TRPA Governing Board often rejected the findings of the TRPA staff. At the same time, local government representatives resisted the authority of the regional officials; Nevada's gaming industry, supported by state representatives, fought against any outside entity regulating its growth; environmentalists opposed economic user groups—with each confronting TRPA; and the States of Nevada and California battled. A number of disputes were argued and appealed through state and federal courts.

Some of these events have been discussed in the three principal works used to guide this study: Andrew Schmidt's *The Role of the United States Forest Service and Other Federal Agencies in the Evolving Political, Social, and Economic Microcosm of the Lake Tahoe Region: An Historical Brief* (1979); environmental historian Douglas H. Strong's seminal book, *Tahoe: An Environmental History* (1984); and his revised and shortened *Tahoe: From Timber Barons to Ecologists* (1999). As well as updating these narratives, *Saving Lake Tahoe* provides some aspects of the lake's history heretofore neglected. It approaches the subject from a somewhat different perspective as well. In particular, it focuses on the complex and many times volatile interactions of individuals and political groups that have dramatically affected the area's ecosystem. An example is the account of what was the most far-reaching and arguably the most important of the court cases regarding the lake.

In 2002 the US Supreme Court ruled against the contention that a thirty-two-month building moratorium on home construction violated the regulatory taking sections of the Fifth and Fourteenth Amendments to the US Constitution. The Court found that there was a difference between takings of property and regulating its private use. The plaintiffs' attorneys had been seeking millions of dollars in compensation from TRPA for landowners forbidden to build on their properties during the lengthy moratorium. TRPA was represented by John G. Roberts, later to become the Supreme Court's chief justice. The significance of the case is emphasized by amicus briefs from a dozen parties. Environmental groups, the US government, and twenty states supported TRPA. Conservative litigation organizations, the National Home Builders Association, and the American Farm Bureau backed the plaintiffs.

Through the years, scientists and regulators have worked to restore and sustain the health of Tahoe. Efforts included building the first tertiary wastewater treatment plant in the country and transporting sewage out of the basin; limiting the amount of impervious surfaces and restricting building in stream environments and on steep slopes to reduce silt, nitrogen, and phosphorus entering the lake; restoring wetlands; rechanneling streams; establishing environmental thresholds; limiting casinos and other large projects; and funding pollution-reducing transportation systems. At each juncture, the answer to Tahoe's ecological problems seemed at hand. Although each fix has been beneficial, and the lake remains unique in its beauty, after a half century the goals of reversing environmental deterioration and improving lake clarity remain elusive.

Lake Tahoe's spectacular setting is a visual record of its geologic history. The lake basin was formed millions of years ago from faulting that caused it to drop between its western and eastern crests. Uplifting action and volcanic eruptions followed, and, within the past 2 million years, glaciation and additional volcanic action further altered its appearance. Great ice blocks and lava flows at the mouth of the North Shore's Lower Truckee River raised the water level several hundred feet before the ice melted and the volcanic rock was worn down. The conclusion of the last glacial epoch, some 10,000 years ago, finalized the area's basic 500-square-mile form.

On the West Shore's glaciated topography, sheer cuts down towering mountains reveal the paths over which the 1,000-foot-deep glaciers moved, their moraines creating small pristine lakes and, in one case without a terminal moraine, spectacular Emerald Bay.

Stream-cut, dissected granitic lands on the East Shore are interrupted by Cave Rock, a 350-foot volcanic mass sweeping up from the lakeshore, its jutting lines illustrating the force of a volcanic eruption. On the North Shore, displacement of rock layers created precipitous slopes that plunge far below lake level. Its later volcanic flows formed stepped cliffs and fantastic underwater canyons, amphitheaters, and grottos. In the south, glacial deposits produced a large delta valley and massive marshes that acted as filters, trapping silt and nutrients before they could reach the lake. Twenty feet below the lake's surface, in the southwest, submerged stumps are remnants of trees that lived for 100 to 350 years along a much lower shoreline thousands of years ago.[1]

Lake Tahoe's remarkable clarity is due to the integrity of its 511-square-mile drainage. Quite small in area in relation to the size of the lake, the surrounding mountains' soils are predominately granite, which has low mineral content and hence few nutrients; other of the rock is volcanic, which is moderately fertile but has deep soils that allow water to infiltrate into the bedrock. The purity of the water draining into the lake limits algal growth, inhibiting the greening process. When the first Americans viewed the lake, in the mid-nineteenth century, it was pristine. In mid-November 1844, Angeline Morrison was in the first party of Americans to enter the lake basin—a group of six riders crossing the Sierra Nevada after separating from the Elisha Stephens emigrant train. In a dangerous setting, trying to cross the massive range before the heavy snows, she could not help noting "awe and wonder" at the scene. She wrote, "We came out on the shores of a magnificent lake, verily an ocean, as blue as a sapphire in a setting of mountains."[2]

From the lake's edge to the surrounding summits, forests, hundreds of years in the making, filled the land. In 1879 D. L. Bliss, a timberman, reported that many of the trees they were cutting stood well over 100 feet high and 8 feet in diameter; one, he remarked, was 11 feet in diameter and 1,000 years old. In 1863 Samuel Bowles, a touring newspaper publisher, described the ancient trees as "forests to which the largest of New England are but pigmies."[3]

Those early-day arrivals were seeing a lake and landscape cultivated by the Washoe Indians, whose creation story begins in the area. Every year for millennia as soon as melting snow allowed, the Washoe Indians traveled from their winter homes in the valleys adjoining the Sierra Nevada to Tahoe's lakeshore. The various clans, coming from as far away as current-day Susanville in the north and Bridgeport in the south, spent the summer months hunting, fishing, tending plants, and celebrating, the elders taking time to meet and plan the use of hunting and plant resources for the following fall and winter. The Washoes saw themselves as caretakers of the land, water, and animals. The Americans could not have been more different. The integral elements of the Native people's daily lives, the newcomers thought of as commodities. The Americans created an ecodisaster because it was widely acknowledged that the exploitation of natural resources was necessary for the improvement of the country.

In 1860 news spread of the discovery of the Comstock Lode in Virginia City, Nevada, thirty-two miles northeast of Tahoe. Its silver fissure veins, streaked with gold, extended thousands of feet underground, allowing its mines to become the richest in the world. Mining was believed to create "clean money," meaning that taking ore from the earth was a benefit that harmed no one. The resultant environmental damage and the devastation of the areas with supporting resources were completely overlooked.

The Tahoe Basin became the most valuable of the Nevada industry's hinterlands. Its natural stores, including trout, dairy grasses, sheep forage, hay, and timber, in the Americans' view God given and untapped by the Indians, appeared to be inexhaustible.[4]

The timber was the most important of the resources. Tahoe's forests were marked for destruction when geologists determined that the Comstock's silver deposits would probably continue thousands of feet underground. In 1865 the mineralogist of the California State Geological Survey wrote that the ore would likely be found "at as great a depth as it is possible to extend underground workings."[5]

It was discovered early on that following veins in the unstable clay and porphyry soil required a system of wood supports to secure the walls of the mines. A twenty-eight-year-old German native, Phillipp Deidesheimer, engineered an invention he called square sets. The sets were twelve-inch-thick posts locked in six-by-five-foot quadrangles and notched at the corners so they could be continuously connected in whichever direction the veins led.

By 1875 the *Territorial Enterprise,* Virginia City's leading newspaper, reported that as an example of the amount of lumber used in square sets, one mine, the Consolidated Virginia, was consuming six million feet per year. It commented that the Comstock Lode would be "the tomb of the forests of the Sierra." By 1878 the *Nevada State Journal* reported that the previously dense forests were becoming a thing of the past. In time, the paper predicted, they would be completely wiped out. "It is too bad to have those beautiful groves cut away," an editorial said, "but the Comstock must have timber and wood, and the trees must go."[6]

Few questioned that Tahoe's forests would be processed into lumber. The ore coming out of the Comstock would earn a total of some four hundred million dollars. It was financing the building of the West and benefiting the development of the entire United States. William Ralston used it to finance California businesses from furniture and watch factories to a wool industry and the state's first wineries. The Hearst newspaper empire was funded with Comstock money. Longtime US senator J. P. Jones founded and developed Santa Monica using Comstock silver. E. J. "Lucky" Baldwin utilized his mining proceeds to build hotels—including one featuring a casino at Tahoe—and procure land for the Santa Anita Race Track, and Southern California holdings including a forty-six-thousand-acre tract that later became the Los Angeles suburb of Baldwin Hills and parts of Arcadia, Pasadena, and Monrovia.

Comstock wealth was used for the construction of transcontinental and western railway systems as well as many of San Francisco's important buildings. It provided money for the wealthiest of its bonanza kings, John Mackay, to build a transoceanic telegraph cable system that crossed the Atlantic and Pacific Oceans, allowing the company to boast that "the sun never sets on the Mackay system."[7]

The primary forces that might oppose action such as clear-cutting forests in a market economy are social or natural resistance; neither existed at Tahoe. No Americans lived at the lake to oppose the destruction, and instead of natural resistance the lake basin readily lent itself to logging. Steep mountainsides allowed for skidding logs downhill. Lumbermen easily controlled the outlets to lakes to feed flumes that carried the timber out of the mountains. On the flats, yoke of oxen hauled logs on immense wagons. Later trains, utilizing movable tracks, hauled the logs. In all instances, once at Lake Tahoe, steamers towed booms of logs across the lake to shoreline sawmills and transport centers.

In that era, the government wanted to populate the West, and Congress had passed laws that encouraged individual families to cultivate properties. Under the Preemption Act of 1841 and the Homestead Act of 1864, settlers could purchase up to 160 acres at $1.25 per acre. Under both these acts, corporations would pay a fee, and the claimant would transfer the land to the company. In 1878 the Timber and Stone Act established a law wherein individuals could purchase similar amounts of public domain forests at a similar cost. Because of widespread abuse, the Timber and Stone Act required the purchaser to swear the timberland was for his own use. But 160 acres was not enough land to make a profit working timber, so even with the oath individuals sold the lands to the timber industrialists.

Charles H. Chamberlain, receiver of the land office at San Francisco, testified to the Public Lands Commission that the timber law did not work. He told commissioners, "I think that a man who takes the timber land intends to sell it immediately to the best advantage." The problem with enforcing the law, according to Chamberlain, was that cutting timber was not an offense the courts sought to punish.

Throughout the 1870s, because the government had not surveyed the land, the forests could not be policed. B. C. Whitman, an attorney from Virginia City, explained that therefore authorities would not sell the land, and companies went ahead and cut on it. No one objected because the wood was used for development and improvement. The explanation was simple: "In Nevada the wood was not cut for export, but for actual necessities in carrying on the business of the country."[8]

A few years later, William A. J. Sparks, commissioner of the US General Land Office, commented that he had no confidence in the officials charged with regulating sales in Northern California. "The register and receiver and some of the special agents appear to have been the only persons in the vicinity who were ignorant of the frauds," he said.[9]

On the Comstock in the early 1870s, William Sharon, a Bank of California agent, managed the affairs of a cabal commonly referred to as the Bank Ring or Bank Crowd. The group of wealthy California investors created vertical integration in the Nevada Comstock mining industry, controlling most of the productive mines, seventeen ore mills—almost all foreclosed upon after missing loan payments to Sharon's bank—and transportation in the form of the newly constructed Virginia and Truckee Railroad. At the time, Sharon, one of the wealthiest men in the West, was occupied managing the bank; running the Bank Ring enterprises; fighting numerous lawsuits; battling to reduce taxes on mining; attempting, generally successfully, to control the San Francisco mining stock market; and running a campaign to become Nevada's US senator while dogged by an antagonistic press. It was apparent that the mines, hoisting works, and mills required wood in ever-increasing quantities. Sharon suggested to two lieutenants, D. L. Bliss, who became the titan of business at the lake, and Henry M. Yerington, for whom a Nevada town is named, that they set up a business to supply it.

At the time, Bliss was working for the Sharon group; his own Virginia City bank had been appropriated when the Bank of California opened its Comstock

offices. Yerington had sold his Merrimac Mill on the Carson River to the Bank
Ring and was directing the Sharon-run Virginia and Truckee Railroad.[10]

In 1871 Bliss and Yerington began buying timberland, and in 1873 they officially formed the Carson and Tahoe Lumber and Fluming Company (CTLFC),
the first enterprise to log the Tahoe Basin. The company needed capital to pursue what would become a multimillion-dollar business—its beginning crew
numbered some five hundred—so Bliss and Yerington got another Bank Ring
principal, the wealthy D. O. Mills, to join them as a primary investor.[11]

After acquiring seven thousand acres of timber along the lake's South and
East Shores, the fledgling company purchased much of Glenbrook. Until
recent times, during summer months, Washoe Indians lived at Glenbrook,
which was valued for its fish and berries. Americans had turned it into a travel
hub, accessed by the lake as well as toll roads from the South Shore and over
the summit into Nevada. The purchase included a water-powered sawmill built
in 1861 at the mouth of a stream at the lake's edge. As early as 1863, the *Sacramento Daily Union* had identified the area's possibilities: "As soon as the new
road, which is now being rapidly pushed forward, is completed, this timber
will readily find its way to a good market." The new owners built two additional
mills and purchased additional acreage from the Central Pacific Railroad on
the North and Northwest Shores, eventually utilizing fifty thousand acres.[12]

Other companies were also buying land, and within a few years nearly all
the forests around the lake had been taken up. In 1879 the hugely successful
Bliss and Yerington testified before the Public Lands Commission, which was
investigating the use of land in the West. Bliss, giving management's version
of purchasing and consolidating small land claims, was forthright: "We have
adopted the practice of buying the land, cutting off the timber, and then abandoning it, in order not to have to pay taxes on the land." He said that the CTLFC
paid $3.00 to $3.50 an acre in buying from timber owners who had paid $1.25.
Bliss suggested the government should devise a system of valuing the land and
selling it by section in unlimited quantities, saying he would just as soon pay
the government as the middlemen.

The CTLFC engaged in logging, milling, and transportation. Their early
advantage came with their ability to build flumes in which streaming water
carried logs from mountain passes to the valleys below. Formed of two-inch-

thick planks shaped like the letter V, flumes were built atop trestle works that in crossing ravines might stand 75 feet above the ground. Extending as far as fourteen miles, they could cost five hundred thousand dollars to build.[13]

Because of the expense of transporting the timber, Yerington explained to the land commissioners that owners of small claims could not succeed. "They can't make it win, because a flume costs half a million dollars. . . . Our wood is scattered over an area of 50 by 70 miles; we have about 75 miles of flume that cost about one and a half million of dollars." He said that originally, people feared the Bank of California–backed company would come to monopolize the market. Now, he asserted, both the buyers and the "little fellows" were glad they were there. The CTLFC could sell at half previous rates while buying wood from small operations that could not get their own lumber to market. Later in the hearing, he confidently added, "We have got all the timber lands that we want, and it don't make any difference to us what laws you pass on the subject."[14]

In 1875, two years into their operation, the CTLFC dramatically enhanced their transport capabilities by replacing a steep, laborious wagon road with an eight-and-a-quarter-mile railway built from Glenbrook to its flume at the top of Spooner Summit. At the same time, the company contracted with Matthew C. Gardner, for whom Gardnerville, Nevada, is named, to provide additional timber from the lake's Southwest Shore.

After securing the CTLFC contract, which called for 12 million feet of logs a year, Gardner, who owned several thousand acres of South Shore timberland, built a short-line railroad. Besides the cars for hauling timber, the train featured a kitchen car and sleeping cars for the lumberjacks. Gardner moved the track from stand to stand as timber in an area was depleted.

At Camp Richardson, below Gardner Mountain, where Washoe Indians caught spotted trout in a clear water creek, Gardner ran tracks out into the lake on a long trestle pier. Pilings were driven into the water every few feet to support the weight. There, a train could dump the timber to be hauled across the water. In August 1875, the *Carson Daily Appeal* reported that Gardner was hauling logs to the lake's edge: "Only a short mile from here is the breakwater. You hear the shrill whistle of the old 'Ormsby' locomotive as it invades these piney solitudes."[15]

In the late 1880s, with Gardner having logged his land and gone bankrupt, the CTLFC utilized a trestle pier, reaching 1,800 feet into the lake, to complete a timber-hauling rail system at Bijou, mid–South Lake Tahoe. Grinding stones and other evidence reveal the area to have originally been a major Washoe Indian trailhead leading south and east to Carson Valley. The CTLFC overran the Indians' trails with a network that included thirteen miles of railroad and sixteen miles of wagon haul roads, as well as a two-mile V flume and at least twenty-eight railroad or wood camps.[16]

Securing wood at top dollar for the Comstock mines led to immense waste. The wood for square sets had to be clear, and "40 to 50 foot topped tree sections, along with other parts of a felled giant, were left to rot because of a knot or two."[17]

Once cut and hauled to the lake, utilizing steamships and 100-foot barges, the cargo was towed to Glenbrook, where the mills drew the timber from the water directly onto saw carriages. Once the logs were cut into the desired lengths, the short-line railway transported them up Spooner Grade. The trains wound their way, crossing ten trestles and passing through a 487-foot tunnel. Atop Spooner Summit, the company's main flume carried the logs and lumber to their yard on the outskirts of Carson City for transport to the Comstock on the Bank Ring's Virginia and Truckee Railroad.

Five years after the CTLFC began operations, in 1878, Walter Scott Hobart organized the Sierra Nevada Wood and Lumber Company on Tahoe's north shore. Hobart had served as president of the water company that built a pipeline from Marlette Lake in the Sierra to bring fresh water to Virginia City. He hired Captain John Bear Overton as the company's general manager. Overton later created the Comstock's first electrically powered process mill to work low-grade ore.[18]

Hobart acquired ten thousand acres of forestland on the northeastern side of the lake as well as the southeast near the Bliss and Yerington holdings. Overton engineered a nearly vertical 1,400-foot lift. The double-track narrow-gauge tramline was powered by a 40-horsepower steam engine embedded in a granite-walled powerhouse. It was called the Great Incline of the Sierra Nevada, giving its name to present-day Incline Village at the same location. Yoked oxen hauled lengths of timber, much of it rafted by steamer, from the shore at Sand Harbor to be carried by locomotives and milled at the Great Incline sawmill. In a twenty-minute climb, the tram could carry three hundred cords of wood or its equivalent in lumber to the summit. A V flume carried the wood down the other side of the mountain on its way to the Comstock. Hobart's instructions for logging the area were for Overton "to take everything worth felling along the shoreline and back up the slopes to the northwest of his sawmill" to the boundary of the next company.[19]

With the establishment of the wood companies, stands of massive pines and old-growth cedars, junipers, and sugar pines were stripped from the land. In July 1873, the *Truckee Republican* reported that forty-man logging camps of French Canadian lumberjacks were averaging one tree dropped every three minutes, saying, "The great forest kings are crashing in every direction."

In 1881 a *Reno Evening Gazette*'s account noted the result of the companies' activity on that year's harvest, saying, "Trees are scattered, and the work is expensive." By the mid-1880s, all the forests that circumscribed the shore had been removed. Despite the cost, the companies continued cutting up the mountains and to the far reaches of Lake Valley until all accessible trees were gone.[20]

They removed twenty-eight million cords of firewood and upwards of a billion board feet of lumber from the lake basin. Only 950 acres of old growth remained: some left around resorts or scattered homes, the rest in areas of terrain too extreme to log.

Historian Grant Smith, who grew up on the Comstock, commented: "No later visitor could conceive of the majesty and beauty fed into the maws of those voracious sawmills." In 1855 surveyor George H. Goddard, traveling along a low ridge, had reported, "The country is so heavily timbered that we saw nothing of the lake and very little of the mountains." Thirty years later, the view was composed of stumps and slash.[21]

The industry had destroyed the lake basin's climax ecosystem in exchange for the Comstock's gold and silver. Few questioned the trade-off, for developing the mines had substantially increased the wealth of the country.

In another case of ecodestruction in the era, Lake Tahoe's large native trout, the Lahontan cutthroat, met a fate similar to that of the forests. That Americans drove them to extinction was only partly owing to the era's value system. Conflicting jurisdictional decisions and, when regulations were passed, lack of funding for enforcement were more critical elements in causing the native's demise.

Mackinaw trout killed the last of the cutthroat, the culminating insult to a species threatened from the time of the Americans' arrival. At the end of the nineteenth century, mackinaws—monstrous, razor-toothed predators that in Tahoe grow to nearly four feet long and well over thirty pounds—were imported from the Great Lakes. They are rapacious, eating anything that fits in their mouths. Whether the mackinaw feasted on the Lahontan or, as has also been speculated, a mackinaw-carried epizootic caused their destruction, it was a mere matter of years from the mackinaw's introduction to the native trout's disappearance.

The Lahontan cutthroat, named for red slashes beneath the jaw, can be traced back seventy thousand years to the time when the Great Basin desert was filled by two giant lakes, Bonneville and Lahontan. Natural selection favored the cutthroat, which was larger and longer lived than its competitors, and it prospered. As the climate changed and the landscape became desert, the Lahontan cutthroat survived only in Pyramid Lake—the thirty-mile-long, nine-mile-wide sink northeast of Reno—and its tributary, the Truckee River. From there it made its way into Lake Tahoe.[1] The habitats contained in the two lakes, and the river between, were mature ecosystems, largely unchanged from year to year, allowing the cutthroat to continue to thrive.

The human abuses to the lake that severely affected the fish involved overfishing and the clear-cutting of the forests that allowed large quantities of sediment and silt to flow into the lake. Meanwhile, the lake's tributaries and its one outlet, the Truckee River, were dammed, diverted, and polluted, ruining spawning beds.

In the early 1870s, ten years after Americans came in numbers to Tahoe, they undertook attempts to sustain the fish population. They introduced artificial breeding in an attempt to preserve the Lahontan cutthroat and imported other fish to further counter losses. In 1895 the US Fish Commission reported on attempts to introduce mackinaw into the Sierra. From a commercial standpoint, the commission pointed out that the species was the "most valuable of the so-called trouts." In 1893 mackinaw fishermen in the Great Lakes had earned more than six hundred thousand dollars.[2]

In November 1894, the US Fish Commission sent one hundred thousand mackinaw eggs to California, and sixty-five thousand were placed in the Lake Tahoe hatchery. But local resort owners blocked the experiment to plant the voracious predator at Tahoe. Harry O. Comstock, whose Tahoe career would span some seventy years, led the effort to foil the introduction, just as years later, as a director in the Lake Tahoe Protective Association, he led a fight to prevent power companies from taking Tahoe water.[3]

The opposition caused the fish managers to change plans. They distributed the mackinaw fry southwest of Tahoe in the Tallant Lakes, a string known as "paternoster lakes," because they are strung out in the mountains like rosary beads. These, like other lakes in the 136,335 acres of wilderness, much of which is now known as Desolation Valley, previously had no fish.[4]

The planted fish were not heard of for several years. But at the beginning of the twentieth century, Tahoe fishermen caught trout with scars on their sides and bites taken from their tails. An occasional eight- or nine-pound mackinaw was taken, although it was not generally recognized as one of the Great Lakes' plants. In May 1902, using seines to gather trout from which to take spawn, hatchery workers captured a number of similar-size mackinaw. These first specimens were believed to have gained the lake by following Meeks Creek, the West Shore stream that cuts through granitic bedrock down the gorge to Tahoe. It was tougher to explain a catch a year later: a two-and-a-half-foot mackinaw caught in the lake and presented to President Theodore Roosevelt as he passed through Truckee. In 1905 a fisherman trolling with heavy tackle hauled in a twenty-eight-and-a-half pounder and in 1909 a thirty-one pounder was taken, and it became apparent that mackinaw had been growing in the lake before the plants made their way from the Tallants.[5]

Unbeknownst to Comstock and his associates, they had lost the war against the predator's introduction nine years before their battle to keep them out. In 1885 the US Fish Commission had sent one hundred thousand mackinaw eggs to Nevada. Having lost twenty-five thousand eggs in transit, the commission sent another thirty thousand eggs in 1889. George T. Mills, Nevada's fish commissioner, although not announcing where the original consignment had been planted, said that most from the second were placed in Tahoe. In May 1896, another forty-eight thousand, given their start at the Carson City hatchery after being shipped from Michigan, were planted in the lake.[6]

This was not the first time that conflict of authority and lack of communication came into play in the bistate lake, and it was far from the last. The state line divides the lake so that approximately 65 percent of its waters are in California and 35 percent in Nevada, but knowing the geographic bounds does not clarify the states' rights. Five different lake-basin counties, many special districts, a city on the South Shore, two towns to the north, and sixty local agencies also claim power. These entities have diverse interests and are frequently at odds.

The reason H. O. Comstock had fought against adding a predator to the lake was that laws to protect the native fishes had been largely ignored, there had been widespread destruction of fish habitat, and the numbers of cutthroat and native royal silver trout were already dramatically reduced. In pre-American times, Washoe Indian fishing leaders regulated Tahoe and its tributaries, designating areas to be fished, culling parasitic fish, and monitoring the numbers to be taken. The tribe's management guaranteed a stable fish population and bountiful yearly harvests.[7]

In 1844 explorer John Frémont named the lake's only outlet the Salmon Trout River after feasting on two- to four-foot trout boiled, fried, and "roasted in the ashes." He noted that the plentiful fare, provided by friendly Paiute Indians, had a flavor "superior" to any other fish. The river was soon renamed the Truckee in honor of a pioneer company's Paiute guide, and all early reports echoed Frémont's evaluation, earning it a reputation as the finest of the West Coast's trout streams.[8]

In the 1860s, the lake provided similar fare in seemingly unlimited quantities, and Virginia City provided a ready market. The fish for sale on the Comstock from "the cold depth of Lake Tahoe" weighed up to twenty pounds and were variously described in newspapers as delicious, enormous, or of superior quality.[9]

More than twenty commercial fish operations plied their trade in the summers, with the fish being sent to Carson and Eagle Valleys as well as Virginia City. In Carson City, in 1867, a vendor advertised the delivery of 250 pounds of fish averaging 8 pounds each. After describing anglers taking fish from 5 to 30 pounds, a reporter from San Francisco wrote that two men working for a Tahoe hotel had just brought in 81.5 pounds of fish, the result of one day's labor.[10]

Into the 1880s, Tahoe trout remained plentiful. Although the *Carson Morning Appeal* tongue-in-cheek labeled them a "nauseating drug," commenting, "Our people are getting very tired of them," distant venues featured them on their menus.[11] With the completion of railroad lines and the development of a local ice industry, tons of the famous trout were carried west to the Palace Hotel and the Lick House in San Francisco and east to Salt Lake City, Denver, Chicago, and New York.

In 1881 the *Tahoe Tattler* newspaper editorialized: "Fishing has been going on at the lake for over 20 years, and the supply is inexhaustible if trout are taken by hook and line only." Of course, killing fish had never been limited to hook and line. From the early days, commercial fishermen had used oversized traps, basket nets, and even cartridges of giant powder that blasted trout to the surface. As early as 1862, Martin K. "Friday" Burke and partner "Big Jim" Small, of Friday's Station House, were selling fish taken up in half-mile-long seines.[12]

In April 1866, even as the lake's fame for fishing was spreading, the *Daily Alta California* warned of a problem: "We regret to say that unscrupulous men are wantonly and barbarously destroying, by wholesale, in an illegitimate manner, these delicious fish." The state passed laws later that year declaring seines, nets, spears, weirs, fences, baskets, traps, or other implements, except hook and line, unlawful and forbidding fishing from August through January. But the laws were ineffectual, as there was no funding for enforcement.[13]

In 1872 a writer for the *Sacramento Daily Union* used the logic of the day to present an optimistic perspective regarding the future of the lake's trout. "The genius of the Indian was never equal to lessen the supply [of fish]," he commented before noting Americans' outright slaughter of trout, which on the Truckee were being fed by the bushel to hogs. "But cultivated man triumphs over nature," the reporter observed, and while hitherto man's efforts had been in diminishing the fish, the time had come "to return for his shortcomings fourfold as an atonement, and this his genius enables him to do." The newsman saw a reversal of the trend with the requirement that fish ladders be built at dam sites, the introduction of new species imported from the East, and fish hatcheries being established. Unfortunately, the solutions were hit and miss.[14]

Beginning in 1871, the California Fish Commission hatched and planted many millions of fish. Tahoe's own fish provided hundreds of thousands of spawn per annum in the 1870s and millions each year by the mid-1890s. Truckee and Lake Tahoe hatcheries eventually shipped fish throughout California.[15] Parent fish, leaving the lake to spawn mid-April through mid-June, were trapped, and hatchery workers stripped the fish of their eggs and milts. Mixed in waterless pans to produce fertilization, the eggs developed into alveus, or embryo fish, and then fry. When the fry had been swimming for about two weeks, distribution began.

The spawn survival rate was low in the early years. Problems involved ending incubation too soon, transportation that jarred the alveus, and the failure to keep them cool while moving through the extreme heat of California's Central Valley. By the 1890s, the process had improved markedly. In 1894 the commission produced and successfully transported well over 4 million healthy Tahoe cutthroat fry for distribution. One of the program's goals was increasing the number of cutthroat in Tahoe itself. The lake received 1.5 million of the plants, and another 350,000 were placed in nearby Donner Lake and the Truckee River.[16]

The Tahoe experiment was unsuccessful, as the fry were merely prey for the nonnative species that now inhabited the lake. A few years earlier, an eminent zoologist, Dr. Carl Eiggemann, speaking at the Academy of Sciences in San Francisco, accurately forecast the fate of the hatchery trout. He told of the voracious little bullhead, five or six inches in length, that feed greedily on smaller fish. One bullhead was captured with the tail of a young trout sticking out of its mouth. It had been unable to swallow the prey because its stomach was already filled with four others. Professor Eiggemann concluded that even if some trout survived to spawn in the lake, their young would be subjected to the same danger.[17]

The commission attempted to stock the lake by importing thousands of nonnative salmon and trout. The majority died out, although three species other than mackinaw survived: kokanee, brown trout, and rainbow trout.

The entire time officials were attempting to stock the lake, the problem of illegal taking of fish persisted. Throughout the 1870s, newspaper articles in San Francisco and Sacramento condemned the stealing that used prohibited traps, spearing, and other devices. The violators' work was variously labeled as "a terrible destruction," "a wanton destruction," "a slaughter," and "wholesale destruction." As late as 1881, B. B. Redding, the California fish commissioner, commented, "I do not know what I can do about the spearing of fish in Lake Tahoe. We have no officers there."[18]

Two years later, a new commissioner, A. B. Dibble, visited the lake and found that "fish laws were constantly being violated." On the West Shore, at the mouth of the creek at Sugar Pine Point, where the Washoes traditionally fished, Dibble and Truckee judge John Kizer found some nine hundred trout that had been trapped. The officials confronted General William Phipps, an old veteran of the Plains Indian wars, at his cabin. Phipps proclaimed that no authority had the right to stop him from taking a few spawning eggs since he had "saved this hyar great country of ours from the clutches of the red man." Phipps demonstrated his fury by using a brace of Colt revolvers to blast holes through his cabin's ceiling and walls. The authorities responded coolly to the display, giving Phipps forty-eight hours to release the fish or go to jail.[19]

As their means of livelihood was destroyed by Americans, some Native peoples joined the slaughter. It was several times reported that, because fishing laws were waived for Indians, some were providing white sponsors with fish to sell. Damming rivers and then spearing the fish trapped in the holes was called by one old Washoe man "shooting fish." In 1870 a correspondent reported to the *Daily Alta California,* "Indian in the foreground, murdering at a furious rate; white man in the rear and tolerably well concealed, making a nice thing out of this arrangement. If something be not done to check this sort of thing soon, there will be no trout for Indian or anyone else."[20]

In January 1884, a Sacramento correspondent commented on local reactions to the situation: "Parties who live in the neighborhood of the lake, especially those who have watering places and summer resorts, are interesting themselves in the matter, and will render the [Fishing] Commission valuable service in that direction." Certain white residents seem to have used disproportionate measures as a means of correcting the situation: penalizing people who used legal methods of fishing to feed their families. At the Tallac Hotel, on the lake's South Shore, while guests were tallying trout catches "by the hundreds each day," Washoe Indians, described as "friendly tribesmen" who had their encampment nearby, were "forbidden to spear and net trout in streams flowing to the lake."[21]

In the mid-1870s, Nevada governor L. R. Bradley decried the fact that lumber companies were dumping tons of sawdust into the Truckee River. The governor complained of vast numbers of dead fish, ruined downstream irrigation systems, and a sawdust delta or dam at the river's terminus at Pyramid Lake on the Paiute Indian Reservation.

Truckee booster C. F. McGlashan led a committee of businessmen to investigate the claims. McGlashan concluded that natural causes and overfishing by the Paiute Indians caused the extreme loss of fish. He did not mention the large number of Lahontan cutthroat being taken illegally by white commercial fishermen on the reservation at Pyramid Lake, transgressions that continued into the twentieth century.[22]

McGlashan wrote that the sawdust dam was composed of sand and sediment, "with only a light, superficial coating of sawdust." He believed that the sawdust problem had been blown out of proportion. But he also found another danger to the fisheries: imperfect fish ladders. Because the fish spawned in gravel beds above the mills, obstructions were fatal. McGlashan was certain the mill men would build new ladders if provided with an improved design.

McGlashan concluded as well that an act prohibiting the discharge of sawdust into the river would sound a death knell for the timber industry. It would force improvements costing the mills at least $590,000 and some $50,000 per year thereafter to dispose of the waste. He forwarded his findings to Washington, DC, warning Congress of bankruptcies and ruination.[23]

Of course, McGlashan was wrong regarding the sawdust. It continued to pollute the Truckee, and, despite efforts to restock the river each year, between the contaminants and barriers, the number of native trout diminished drastically. In the fall of 1879, the California fish commissioners agreed to restock the river with five hundred thousand fry but also issued an admonishment to keep sawdust out of the water.[24]

In 1880 fish commissioners noted that there were no Lahontan trout in the upper half of the Truckee River; they were unable to get to their spawning beds. In 1884 it was reported that the mill men were willing to assist in the matter of preserving the trout, telling the commissioners to order all necessary ladders, and "they will cheerfully foot the bills." However, they noted that because no fish had come upriver for four or five years, there did not seem to be any necessity for the action. Regardless, the fish commission ordered the ladders be built. By November 1887, six ladders were finished, and it was believed that if the dams on the Nevada side built similar structures, trout could come up above the sawdust to spawn.[25]

Nevada officials continued to focus on the sawdust, not fish ladders. In February 1887, Reno had charged that diseases, including a scarlet fever epidemic, were caused by sawdust in their drinking supply. In 1889 a California legislative delegation traveled to investigate. Shortly thereafter, they passed an amendment making it a misdemeanor to place into a waterway "any lime, gas, tar, cocculus, indicus, sawdust or any substance deleterious to fish."[26]

Stream users first complained of companies disregarding the law just days after it took effect. From that time forward, county officials heard the grievances but did not enforce the statute. In 1894, five years after the amendment passed, the mills, arguing that "shavings" were not included in the law, continued to use the river to wash waste downstream.

The Truckee Lumber Company mill, controlling the dam at the top of the river, was the most egregious of the violators. When a lawsuit finally detailed their transgressions, they agreed to put in a burner to dispose of their waste. A year later, in August 1895, deputies investigating another mill witnessed

Truckee Lumber Company workers again pouring debris into the river. The workers said the burner had broken down.[27]

In 1896 California gave up planting fish in the Truckee. The deterioration of what had been the West Coast's premier fishing river made the effort fruitless.

For years the Floriston Pulp and Paper Company, built on the river, dumped waste, including acid, into the water. In the early twentieth century, three power plants were built on the river, more diversions removed water from it, and a major oil spill at the Southern Pacific Railroad yard sent oil flowing down it. In 1904 a fourth power company plant became operational on the river. In 1905 still another dam, the Derby Diversion Dam, was constructed to remove Truckee water for the federal government's Newlands Water Project. The river was serving many purposes; trout habitat was not one of them.[28]

Originally, California law allowed trout fishing in April, and fishing in early spring was a prime attraction at Lake Tahoe. So as not to interfere with spawning season, the state later moved opening day to May 1. In order to further protect cold-water fish and those at high elevation, El Dorado and Placer Counties passed special ordinances that kept trout in and around Tahoe from being taken until June 1. In mid-May 1909, a sheriff arrested two commercial fishermen at Ward Creek near Tahoe City. The court fined each twenty-five dollars for taking fish before opening day. "Market" fishermen protested and continued to test the counties' ordinances until finally, in May 1912, twenty-four commercial fishermen were arrested at one time.

Interest was high when the following day the first of the offenders was brought to court in Auburn, California. Superior Court judge James E. Prewett summarily dropped the charges, citing the state law that gave residents the right to fish in *all* public waters. Three years later, after a study found that 16,313 trout were caught at Tahoe in May 1915, and that nearly half were females about to spawn, the state revised the law, moving the lake's trout opening to June 1.[29]

But by the time the law took effect in 1916, the Lahontan cutthroat demise at Tahoe was irreversible. Record trout were still taken in the lake, ten pounders, twenty pounders, and a thirty-three pounder caught in 1924 by a seven-year-old Washoe. But all these were mackinaw. After prospering during seventy thousand years of evolution, including thousands as a primary food source of the Washoe Indians, Lake Tahoe's native cutthroat had been driven to extinction.[30] The misperception that the natives were limitless or that man was clever enough to replenish depleted stores was partly to blame. Lack of coordination between jurisdictions and local governance inefficiencies were more significant, ensuring the loss. Those local government failings would continue for another fifty years.

In the "Age of Enterprise," the late nineteenth and early twentieth centuries, with shifts in technologies and economic markets, giant corporate organizations rose, concentrating wealth and power. Practical engineers created cross-country railroads and telegraphs, streetcars, and roadways and supplied electricity to modernize the country. As with its forests and fish, at Tahoe development-minded Americans saw the immense body of water as a resource, one that engineering ingenuity could tap. The *San Francisco Daily Alta* commented, "Nature seems to have located this spacious reservoir in a convenient position, overlooking the agricultural valleys and rich mining regions of California."[1]

In this case, the governing entities' battles over legal authority would prevent environmental disaster, keeping the lake from being reduced to a high Sierra reservoir. Clashes involved the federal government, California and Nevada, a multinational banking syndicate, other businesses, local residents, Nevada landowners, and succeeding presidential administrations: one accused of overuse of its regulatory power, the other exhibiting abuse created by its intimate connection with business.

In 1864, before Tahoe's name change came into common use, the Lake Bigler Canal Company sought to use the lake's water for mining and irrigation in California's Placer County. The canal company's failure set the stage for a more grandiose and fully developed scheme. New proponent Alexis Von Schmidt was a vigorous and confident civil engineer.[2]

The Prussian-born Von Schmidt arrived in San Francisco with the '49ers and became successful in several important endeavors. He ran a dredging business, using a ship-to-shore dredging machine that he devised; he helped develop San Francisco's cable car system; and he surveyed and mapped California lands and Spanish land grants. In 1857 Von Schmidt helped found the San Francisco Water Works, instituting the first regular supply of water to the city.

He invented a water meter and, as the chief engineer for Spring Valley Water Company, supervised construction of the first Pilarcitos dam and tunnel.

In 1872, in the midst of developing his plan to use Lake Tahoe to supply water to much of Northern California, he was retained to establish, once and for all, the disputed boundary line separating California and Nevada. His line proved to be off by several miles—a not uncommon occurrence for surveys in that era. After correcting a third of it, with no further funding provided, Von Schmidt abandoned the project, and the boundary remained "kinked" for another twenty years.

While he was surveying, Von Schmidt's proposal to build a 163-mile aqueduct to tap Tahoe's water, backed by millionaire magnates and California's interior counties, passed the state assembly on a vote of forty-nine to twenty-seven. His plan was to dam the Truckee in two places. He calculated that the first dam could raise the lake level six feet, yielding 13.5 million gallons. Then lowering the water twelve feet from the six-foot raised level would produce 162 million gallons of usable water.

He would construct the second dam 3.75 miles downstream. It would divert the water from the Truckee into a canal running through Squaw Valley to a point where a 5-mile tunnel was to be blasted through the volcanic Sierra rock. On the west side of the range, the plan called for utilizing the route of the North Fork of the American River and pipes, with diversions for hydraulic mining and mills, to service Sacramento, Fairfield, Vallejo, Oakland, and San Francisco. Costs had been precisely calculated, including the Vulcan Iron Works' estimate of manufacturing the pipe, totaling $6,386,758.40. Von Schmidt projected the total cost to be $10,396,258.[3] How close the proposal came to being implemented is evidenced by the state assembly vote and the granting of a franchise to lay pipes by the San Francisco Board of Supervisors and the City of Oakland.

Those opposed to the project included San Francisco mayor T. H. Selby, who rejected a thirty-year bond issue of $6 million, calling it a mortgage on works the municipality would never own. The *San Francisco Chronicle* added its objection, saying that Von Schmidt's scheme could bankrupt the city. It editorialized sarcastically, "Might it not be a good plan to confiscate the city altogether—sell her off at a tax sale—give Sacramento and Oakland their just proportion of the proceeds, and hand the balance to the Tahoe Water Company."[4]

Nevada's legislature and California capitalists with Nevada interests also opposed the proposal. Virginia City's *Territorial Enterprise* famously proclaimed Von Schmidt's company would need twenty regiments of militia to undertake the robbery of the lake's water.[5]

Von Schmidt got only as far as building the timber crib dam on the Truckee below the lake. He completed it in 1870, but in that same year the California Legislature awarded a twenty-year franchise for exclusive use of the Truckee River to the Donner Lumber and Boom Company, capitalized by Central Pacific Railroad magnates Mark Hopkins and Leland Stanford. The Donner Company spent $25,000 building a crib structure at the lake's outlet and eventually claimed ownership of the Von Schmidt dam. The dispute would be settled in court in favor of the railroad-company men, who for many years charged tolls to carry logs to mills in the town of Truckee.[6]

By the turn of the century, a new scheme to use the lake's water was introduced at the federal level. Rather than allow the water to be "wasted," the Truckee-Carson Project, which in 1919 was renamed the Newlands Project—posthumously honoring Nevada senator Francis J. Newlands—sought to irrigate portions of the Northern Nevada desert, utilizing the Truckee River as one of its sources. The project, which built the Derby Dam on the Truckee east of Reno as well as a number of reservoirs and canals, was an engineering success but, having failed to account for the desert's mineral salts, was limited in its agricultural worth. Originally projected to reclaim four hundred thousand acres, the project's arable land proved to be less than sixty thousand acres, sustaining only forage crops like alfalfa.[7]

At Tahoe the key issue for the Newlands Project, as the Von Schmidt venture before it, involved the dam at the lake's outlet. Its use, the subject of negotiations and court cases, was also directly affected by the attitudes and actions of the first four presidents of the twentieth century: McKinley, Theodore Roosevelt, Taft, and Wilson.

In 1900, with the demand for water increasing in the American West, both major political parties had irrigation projects in their party platforms.

Still, eastern and midwestern congressmen, supported by McKinley, opposed investing in the arid lands. When the president was assassinated in 1901, Roosevelt brought a decidedly different attitude to the office. His affinity for the West, as well as his philosophy of "the greatest good for the greatest number," caused him to promote conservation and "homemaking" by creating family farms throughout the region. With the new president behind the policy, Congress passed the Reclamation Act of 1902. The Newlands Project was the first venture completed under the act.

The twenty-year franchise awarded to Hopkins and Stanford's Donner Lumber and Boom Company had not specified a termination date for collecting tolls, and the company was still collecting for fluming timber seven years after their franchise expired in 1890. In 1903, assuming prescriptive rights to the river, the company demanded rents from the downstream users. When the users refused to pay, Donner Lumber and Boom threatened to open the dam gates and release all the water.

The owners of two power plants below Truckee, H. and M. Fleishhacker, paid Donner Lumber and Boom forty-five thousand dollars to purchase the dam and avert the possibility of a discharge. The sale included fifty-four acres near the lake outlet and littoral rights so the Fleishhackers might cut a new channel.[8]

Federal government officials did not think the Fleishhacker deal was lawful, and soon after the purchase the Department of the Interior served notice that they claimed rights to the water stored in Tahoe as well as the tributaries that fed it. The government's declaration did not take into account other parties with long-standing claims to the water: basin residents and those dependent on the water of the Truckee. Reno residents used the river for their domestic supply, while power companies used it for generating hydroelectricity and the Paiute Indians relied on the fishery at the river's terminus, Pyramid Lake.[9]

In 1908 the US Supreme Court found that the Paiutes' rights to water were established at the time their reservation lands were drawn, giving them the seniormost claim. But the ruling was ignored. With fresh water being choked off before reaching the lake, the Indians' way of life underwent a devastating change. The lessened flow stopped members from earning a fishing livelihood and caused many families to abandon the reservation. The Paiutes' claims regarding Truckee water continued into the twenty-first century when the tribe finally won their proprietary rights.[10]

The new Federal Reclamation Service was blocked in efforts to control the crib dam in two separate incidents by wealthy landowners fearful of water-level fluctuations causing damage to their properties and by a syndicate of English and New York bankers. In the early years of the twentieth century, American corporations were beginning to extend their businesses around the world, and British and other European nationals and their firms were investing in the United States. The bankers' syndicate purchased all the power plants on the Truckee River in 1902. Called Truckee General Electric, the company later became Sierra Pacific Power.[11]

Having found that reliable flows of Truckee waters for farmlands could not be maintained, in February 1909 the Reclamation Service began condemnation action to gain ownership of the dam. Director Frederick H. Newell commented that had he known the difficulty in turning the lake into a reservoir, the Nevada farming project would never have been approved.[12]

In March 1909, in one of his first actions as president, William H. Taft replaced Roosevelt's secretary of the interior, conservationist James R. Garfield, son of the assassinated president James Garfield, with Richard Ballinger. The new secretary had a decidedly different perspective than Roosevelt and Garfield, saying in a speech that the conservationists were all wrong: "You are hindering the development of the West. In my opinion, the proper course is to divide it up among the big corporations and let the people who know how to make money out of it get the benefits of the circulation of money."[13]

Ballinger directed that an agreement be written to purchase the dam, giving the electric company everything it might want. Government concessions included a guaranteed water flow the company requested; a perpetual franchise for the company to divert water at any point along the river; the right to construct reservoirs, powerhouses, roads, and transmission lines on any public land east of the Tahoe-Truckee watershed; and, in furthering a new scheme to tap the lake, the right to divert water from a second point. The idea was to bore into the lake's rim fifty feet below its surface and build a tunnel to a reservoir to hold water for the company to sell. Last, the government agreed to pay any damage claims brought against the power company by interests along the river.

Two Roosevelt conservationist holdovers, chief forester Gifford Pinchot and the secretary of agriculture, James Wilson, vehemently opposed the proposal. Pinchot argued that the government could not award perpetual rights and pointed out that the contract would allow the company power over large sections of public domain. He stated unequivocally that Ballinger was favoring private trusts in water-power issues. Attempting to avert a public brouhaha, Taft appointed a commission to take the Ballinger plan under advisement.

When the committee upheld the plan and it came up for reconsideration in 1911, Congressman William Kent, a Tahoe property owner, became involved. A major landowner in Marin County, California, Kent established a long personal environmental legacy: he wrote the bill that created the National Park Service, and in California he donated land for Mount Tamalpais State Park and redwood lands for what later became Muir Woods National Monument. Roosevelt suggested the area be named for Kent, who demurred, proposing it honor the naturalist John Muir. At Tahoe Kent later donated a three-hundred-foot beach and twenty-three acres of West Shore land, the William Kent Campground and Recreation Area, for public use. Supported by other Tahoe residents, Kent pressed for a congressional investigation of Ballinger's proposal. He won a continuance until the case was presented to George Wickersham, Taft's attorney general.[14]

Wickersham would later gain his place in history by methodically applying the Sherman Antitrust Act to a number of industries, including the breakup of Rockefeller's Standard Oil. In this instance, Wickersham found the Ballinger contract to be legal, and the conflict escalated.

Kent rallied nationwide support, enlisting the National Conservation Association to fight against the project. The California press supported Kent, trumpeting the rights of the Tahoe residents. A *San Francisco Chronicle* front-page headline read: "Secret Deal with U.S. Puts Tahoe in Syndicate's Clutch." The California Legislature quickly passed a law against any appropriation of the state's water. The governor then telegraphed the president, who discontinued negotiations between the government and the company.[15]

The Pinchot-Ballinger quarrel continued on other fronts, evolving into a national political tsunami. When Taft exonerated Ballinger of obstructing justice in an antitrust case in Alaska, Pinchot publicly rebuked Taft, having the charges read into the *Congressional Record*. Taft promptly fired Pinchot. A year later, under questioning by a congressional committee, Ballinger's anticonservation views came to the fore, and he resigned. The Pinchot firing alienated the progressives in the Republican Party and was a major factor in leading to the split between the Taft and Roosevelt factions in 1912. With Taft as the incumbent Republican and Roosevelt running as the Bull Moose Party candidate, Woodrow Wilson, the Democrat, won.

While the 1912 election was being contested, problems in the Sierra led to the rejection of another Reclamation Service plan for the Tahoe dam. Snowpack measurements in 1911–12 had been less than 25 percent of normal. In the spring, the entire flow of the Truckee was diverted at the new Derby Dam below Reno. Dead and dying fish, attempting to find a way upstream, clogged the last two-mile section of the river. The surface-water level at Pyramid Lake dropped, beginning a yearly decline that, over the next fifty-six years, totaled 86.1 feet. The Paiute Indians' concerns with their fishery were ignored, as the government, following the national policy toward Native peoples that began with the Dawes Act in 1887, pressured them to take up family farms. Even diverting the last of the river water, there was not enough for irrigation, and Nevada farmers advocated for a direct means of opening the dam at the lake.[16]

In September Truckee General Electric, in collaboration with Reclamation Service director Newell, hired workers to dredge the channel and cut the rim of the Lake Tahoe Dam some 4 feet. Among other things, this action would have lowered the lake enough to obstruct the boat entrance to the West Shore jewel, Emerald Bay. Tahoe property owners filed an injunction that again frustrated Truckee water users.

The conflict devolved into a California versus Nevada battle. Newspapers in Sacramento and San Francisco argued that Tahoe's outlet was in California; those in Carson City and Reno said because it was a bistate issue, the federal government, whose Newlands Project, wanting more water for Nevada, needed to adjudicate. The dispute resulted in several dramatic actions. The property owners formed the Lake Tahoe Protection Association, incorporating the first environmental preservation group at Tahoe. The *San Francisco Call* announced that the association "proposes to make a fight to prevent interference with the waters of Lake Tahoe by power corporations or others."[17]

Whereas the California Conservation Commission recommended that the state bring suit against Nevada in federal court to ensure equitable water apportionment, the Nevada Legislature gave its consent for the federal government to use the lake's water as needed for its purposes. The confrontational attitudes forced Wilson's interior secretary, Franklin K. Lane, to meet at Truckee with California representatives and Tahoe property owners. Lane brokered a compromise wherein the Reclamation Service and the power company could replace the old rock-filled timber crib dam with an eighteen-foot concrete slab and buttress dam with seventeen vertical gates. The agreement stipulated that, even with the increased capacity, no more than the normal flow of water would be taken.[18]

In 1919 the Reclamation Service, soon to be renamed the Bureau of Reclamation, stirred up a hornet's nest by suggesting that, in order to store additional water, the lake level could be raised six feet above normal. Adding insult to the potential injury, the service requested that shoreline property owners sign quitclaims relieving the federal government of penalties for any damage to their properties that the increased level might cause. Congressman Kent again led the opposition and, supported by the Lake Tahoe Protection Association and others, took the objections to Interior Secretary Lane. The proposed work was shelved until legal rights could be adjudicated, and the US District Court appointed Nevada Supreme Court judge George F. Talbot as a special master to resolve the case.[19]

In July 1924 Judge Talbot issued his decree. Continuing federal policy to make Indians into farmers, it did not set aside water for Pyramid Lake. Instead, it allocated enough water so the Paiutes could irrigate 3,130 acres, while the Newlands Project farmers were provided rights for the venture's entire 232,800 acres "to the extent the amount would allow."[20]

Throughout the 1920s and 1930s, drought conditions afflicted the eastern Sierra and western Nevada. At nearly the same time the "Talbot Decree" proposal was released, the lake's water level fell below its natural rim. Project farmers threatened Tahoe property owners with crop-damage suits, convincing the owners to allow water to be pumped from the lake. Four gasoline-powered pumps were placed east of the Lake Tahoe Dam, a quarter mile from the natural waterline. The pumps were surrounded by a horseshoe-shaped barrier of sandbags that created a holding pond. Pumping began on August 2, continuing for three months. The lake's natural level is 6,233 feet. On December 1, 1924, the level was 6,222.88 feet, close to its all-time recorded low.[21]

In 1929 nearly 34,000 acre-feet of water was pumped from Tahoe. As drought conditions intensified the following year, and Tahoe property owners fought against the taking of more water, a group representing Nevada water interests, including the power company and others, took direct action. On July 24, they sent a steam shovel, a forty-man crew, and a guard from the Reno City Police to the power-company land adjacent the dam. They began digging a diversion ditch around the dam.

Local residents rallied to the scene. A local deputy sheriff stopped the digging with a temporary warrant, charging the workers with disturbing the peace. Once the excavation was halted, amid renewed rumors of possible dynamiting, locals stood guard at the site. The second night of the standoff, local vigilantes, after stealing the magneto from the steam shovel, tried to fill in the ditch. The dangerous situation was finally resolved when the Placer County sheriff from Auburn arrived with a court injunction to halt any digging. Subsequently, an agreement allowed the pumping of 24,000 acre-feet of water, and the trench was backfilled.

Officials and scientists had begun several studies of the Truckee River operations and storage in 1929. With the drought and ongoing disagreements over pumping from the lake, negotiations between the federal government and river users utilized the studies to develop the "Truckee River Agreement" of 1935. The agreement recognized Tahoe's natural rim and allowed a maximum of 6.1 feet of storage above that level. Moreover, it confirmed the established water-flow rates as modified by the season and Lake Tahoe's water level. It also paved the way for additional reservoir storage to reduce demands for releases at the Lake Tahoe Dam. The agreement stipulated that no additional outlet from the lake would be permitted and that the dam "shall not be disturbed or altered by any of the parties hereto without the approval of the Attorney General of the State of California."

As years passed, the agreement continued to be debated and refined. In 1944 the court-ordered Orr Ditch Decree incorporated the Truckee River Agreement and finally established user water rights based on the suit filed in

March 1913. The court appointed a water master empowered to enforce the decree. The Orr Ditch Decree recognized the Pyramid Paiute Tribe's claims to Truckee water as the most senior, allotting them irrigation water for another 2,745 acres. Following precedent, the decree did not account for Pyramid Lake, providing no water to protect or restore it.[22]

Beginning in the 1950s, the Bureau of Reclamation proposed, and the US Army Corps of Engineers built, additional reservoirs capturing waters from tributaries of the Truckee. Even with improvements in storage and management, conflicts and litigation continued unceasingly in the second half of the century. Nevada and California continued battling over distribution of water from the rivers the two states shared. In 1955 Congress passed a law granting the states the right to enter into a compact over the issue, and negotiations began.

In February 1967, Pyramid Lake's surface level reached its lowest point in modern history, 94.3 feet lower than its original level. In 1968, with President Lyndon Johnson calling Indians "the forgotten Americans" and the Indian-rights movement beginning, the tribe filed the first in a series of lawsuits to reduce Truckee River water diversions. In the next decade, the Endangered Species Act and Clean Water Act added requirements to water allotments, and the cumulative reports on the damage to Pyramid Lake fisheries became difficult to ignore.[23]

In 1970 the California Legislature ratified the Lake Tahoe Interstate Compact, delineating the use of the lake's water by the two states. Walter Hickel, secretary of the interior, argued against approval because it did not consider Paiute Tribe concerns about Pyramid Lake. Further, it limited the federal government's alternatives in future Paiute-rights litigation.

In November 1970, President Richard Nixon fired Hickel, who publicly disagreed with him and supported antiwar students after the killings at Kent State. But even with his dismissal, and Nevada's 1971 ratification of the agreement, Hickel's objections held sway in congressional opposition to the water compact. In the mid-1970s, the Paiute Tribe won an eight-million-dollar Indian Claims Commission case that included lower Truckee River lands taken without treaty. Even with the settlement, Paiutes continued the fight for water for Pyramid.

In an extraordinary event in 1987, Joe Ely, a twenty-five-year-old Paiute leader, and tribal attorney Bob Pelcyger traveled to Washington, DC, and, by lobbying Democratic senators and initiating a national media campaign, they stopped Nevada senator Paul Laxalt from pushing through ratification of the California and Nevada Interstate Compact, inducing the lawmakers to include Pyramid Lake's health in any agreement.

In 1990 Congress passed a law providing some sixty-five million dollars for the restoration of the Pyramid's fishery and for tribal economic development. Seventeen years later, negotiations produced a more flexible operating system that included reservoir-stored water dedicated to sustaining the lake.[24]

The agreement also sanctioned an equitable apportionment of waters shared between the states, retaining two-thirds of Tahoe's annual surplus water for California's tourist and recreation industries while guaranteeing Nevada allocations from the Truckee and Carson Rivers. Because the states had overcome their mutual mistrust in negotiations, California and Nevada had finally resolved their water issues. Still, suspicions and lack of trust remained, and, in other political disputes over Tahoe, each state would act unilaterally out of self-interest.[25]

The fact that in the nineteenth century Americans ignored Lake Tahoe's grandeur as they destroyed its mature ecosystem emphasizes the changing values that led to similar results seventy-five years later. In the twentieth century, boosters promoting its reestablished beauty brought Tahoe worldwide acclaim. But the sheer numbers of those visiting, and the infrastructure needed to accommodate them, again led to ecodisasters at the lake.

In the first half of the twentieth century, while the forests were reestablishing themselves, resorts enhanced their properties. Meadows were turned into golf courses, and pleasure piers were built for the convenience of boaters. The Tahoe Tavern, in one of the remaining old-growth forests, brought trainloads of white sand from Monterey Bay to create a beach.[1]

Tahoe promoters publicized the lake's attractions: campgrounds, tent cabins, or lodges with full amenities and nightly entertainment. The area offered fishing, hiking, boating, horseback riding, and golf, as well as winter sports.

In the 1920s, when skiing became popular in the western United States, Truckee and Tahoe's North Shore were at the center of the action. In 1926 the Southern Pacific Railroad began running the Snowball Special, bringing skiers from California's Bay Area to the lake. At Truckee the pullback, the only ski tow in America, ran alongside a ski jump. Near Tahoe Tavern, at North Shore, seven-time national champion Lars Haugen designed a sixty-meter ski jump, and national meets were held there throughout the 1930s.[2]

In that era, Nevada, needing to expand its economic foundation, had liberalized its laws. Gambling, declared illegal in 1910, was again legalized in 1931. In 1927 Nevada had reduced its residency requirement to obtain a divorce to three months. In 1931, after two other states followed suit, Nevada reduced its requirement to six weeks. Tahoe was a serene place to wait for vows to be annulled.[3]

Because California did not outlaw gambling until 1911, a year after Nevada, gambling had a history as part of early-day resort entertainment at the lake. In the closing days of the nineteenth century, at the South Shore, mining magnate and land developer Lucky Baldwin built a three-and-a-half-story lakefront casino. Advertised as "the marvel of the century," the gambling palace featured five hundred electric lights, a stage for theatricals, a ladies billiard room, a bowling alley, and ten thousand dollars' worth of French plate mirrors.

Once gambling was declared illegal, it slowed but did not end the activity at the lake. In the 1930s and 1940s, it was reported that North Tahoe's Old Buckhorn Inn offered gambling "if the county climate was suitable," and the Tahoe Tavern had slot machines that could be hidden away when the county sheriff called to say he would be making a raid.[4]

In 1937, with gambling again legalized on the Nevada side of the lake, the Cal Neva Casino at Crystal Bay was such a moneymaker that when it burned down, the owner, developer Norman Biltz, approved blueprints while the ruins still smoldered. With construction going on around the clock, the sizable establishment was rebuilt, and Biltz was welcoming guests thirty-one days after its destruction.

At South Shore's Stateline, Nevada, several small board-and-batten or log buildings housed casinos. The Stateline Country Club, originally developed by Cal Custer, a Southern California rumrunner, offered big-name entertainment and a restaurant where for $2.50 you could dine on filet mignon or Louisiana frog legs. More typical were casino coffee shops serving breakfast all day and where, for a silver dollar, you could get an inch-thick tenderloin with all the trimmings.

In 1944 Harvey and Llewellyn Gross, the former owners of a Sacramento meat-retailing business, opened a modest South Shore casino, Harvey's Club. Their building contained three slot machines, two blackjack tables, and a six-stool lunch counter where Mrs. Gross offered meals prepared at her home. Into the 1950s, the most successful of the neon-lit "gameries" was the former Custer operation, purchased by the Sahati brothers and renamed Sahati's State Line Country Club. It featured high-stakes gambling and Sally Wickman's "bosomy" chorus line.[5]

After World War II, wave after wave of people moved west: in 1950 Nevada's population was a mere 160,000; by 1980 it would be more than 800,000. In the same time period, California gained 13 million people. At midcentury

Americans took to the road. Taxes were used to improve highways, leisure time expanded, and automobiles offered new, improved models each year.

Bill Harrah owned a Reno casino that, beginning in 1948, had grossed more than $1 million a year. Realizing that Tahoe was seventy miles and a mountain pass closer to California's population centers, Harrah risked his Reno profits, investing in the basin. In 1955 he snapped up two small casinos adjoining Harvey's Club, later selling them to the Grosses for $5.25 million—an unheard-of sum for the era. The Grosses tore them down to expand their operation.

Harrah moved across the highway, buying Sahati's and two adjoining casinos. Within four years, he built his new casino: the world's largest single structure devoted to gambling. It included ten acres of parking and the $3.5 million "South Shore Room," an 850-seat theater and restaurant that would bring the biggest names in show business to the lake.[6]

At the same time, basin ski resorts began to develop. Originally, jumping was the main skiing activity, but in the 1940s Wayne Poulsen began developing Squaw Valley, just northwest of the lake, with downhill runs in mind. Purchasing land from Southern Pacific, he and his guests climbed the hills using skins on their skis. When his wife, Sandy, used twenty-two kick turns to ski down from one of the peaks, Poulsen named the run—destined to gain fame in Olympic lore, KT-22. In 1948 Poulsen brought in Alex Cushing from New York as an investor, and Cushing soon squeezed Poulsen out to take charge himself.

In 1953 at South Shore, Chris Kuraisa bought the Bijou Park Skiway, a two-rope tow area, for $5,700. He made more than $5,000 in profits that first year, selling lift tickets for $1, while his wife sold sandwiches and drinks. The following summer, he enlisted several investors, secured Forest Service permits, and, cutting trees and helping erect chair-lift towers on the face of the mountain, opened Heavenly Valley.[7]

In 1954 Squaw Valley had a chair lift and two rope tows. As an advertising gimmick, Cushing applied to host the 1960 Winter Olympic Games. Against all odds, he won them, built the necessary facilities, and brought the Games to the lake. This singular event sparked Tahoe's becoming a worldwide destination. With the spectacle of the Games televised daily, Tahoe's remarkable scenery was on continuous display. With the area gaining renown, money became readily available to build and upgrade tourism facilities. With tourist visits to the lake escalating exponentially, California renovated the highways into the basin, and local jurisdictions improved their roadways. Developers built motels, subdivisions, and apartment and condominium complexes. In the five years after the Games, Tahoe's number of year-round residents doubled to twenty-nine thousand.[8]

Problems associated with the growth affected the lake's ecosystem. With two hundred of the basin's five hundred square miles taken up by the lake itself, changes in the small watershed have disproportionate impacts. Disturbances to the plants and soil facilitate accumulations of nitrogen and phosphorus that are carried in steams feeding the lake, enhancing algal growth. Much of the basin's lands have at least a 10 percent slope, exacerbating erosion, as do grading and covering natural soils for roads, buildings, and parking lots in flat areas.[9]

Historically, local governments control land use, passing laws to balance economic, cultural, and environmental interests. Lake Tahoe's political geography, composed of the two states and numerous other authorities, created situations where consensus proved impossible.

Typifying the failure of the coordination of governing institutions was the construction of four illegal breakwaters at Crystal Bay, on the North Shore, in the mid-1960s. Breakwaters disrupt the natural flow of the lake, causing the proliferation of algal blooms. When the work was begun, officials at the Nevada Health Department thought their opposition had stopped the project. But the US Plywood Company, doing the work, could show a permit to build from the US Army Corps of Engineers. The federal agency, in this instance, was concerned only with navigation safety and so gave the work its approval.

Charles "Chic" Martin, executive director of the protectionist group the Lake Tahoe Area Council (LTAC), was furious that illegal structures were increasing the value of violators' holdings by damaging the public domain. "The punishment in these cases does not fit the crime," Martin said, "for once a fill is in, it cannot be removed or the damage repaired. It becomes a permanent liability to the lake."[10]

The US Forest Service had long been interested in acquiring land in the Tahoe Basin to protect the forests and to provide for public use. It began buying cut-over and burned-out lands in 1911 and controlled a quarter of the basin by 1920. But almost all lakefront land was in private hands, and, hoping to secure recreation lands, in 1948 the Forest Service had begun a purchase of several large tracts of land on the southwest shore. The properties included what are now nearly ten thousand feet of Baldwin and Pope Beaches, the Tallac Estates, and the north shore of Fallen Leaf Lake.

Ray Knisley, who became a key player in Tahoe environmental politics for the next half century and was a trustee for the Anita Baldwin Estate, proposed and helped coordinate the sale. Knisley knew the Baldwins as far back as 1915 when, as a youngster, he worked summers for them. When Lucky Baldwin had purchased the vast acreage from Fallen Leaf Lake to Lake Tahoe in 1880 to build his hotel and casino, he insisted the forests and groves "never be surrendered to the woodsman's axe."

The Baldwin family had honored their patriarch's wishes, and the property was kept in its natural state, with the old-growth trees left untouched. After World War II, when the heirs needed money to settle the vast estate, they sold to the Forest Service, ensuring the old-growth trees would be maintained. The Pope family, who owned the adjacent property, had been in the timber business in the East from early colonial times. The Pope descendants had considered subdividing their property into home lots and perhaps a hotel. Still, Knisley said, in the end they were "as anxious to preserve the native timber for future generations as the Baldwins."[11]

Shortly after the Baldwin-Pope acquisitions, the Forest Service pursued a trade that involved land leased as summer tracts for Camp Richardson, a shorefront resort property between Pope and Baldwin Beaches. Ray Knisley was also involved in this complicated exchange. He was the son-in-law of Cora Richardson, the resort owner, who offered to sell her property to the government. The deal involved not only the Richardson interests but also El Dorado and Placer Counties and more than 255 summer-home permittees in adjoining lands.

The Forest Service worked for seventeen years to broker the exchange. In the end, Mrs. Richardson received money, the permittees acquired title to their homes, and the Forest Service gained the resort property. The transaction secured for public use the Pope-Baldwin recreation complex, stretching from Pope Beach through Camp Richardson to Baldwin Beach.[12]

Federal land acquisition has delays inherent in its process that cause problems if there is competition for land made available on the market. When Congress passed the Land and Water Conservation Act in 1968, providing a guaranteed annual authorization that reached $600 million for purchasing valuable lands, the system ensured the actions would be deliberate. Congress has to enact legislation authorizing the acquisition of each designated parcel and, in a separate action, appropriate money from the fund. Recognizing the problem, the Nature Conservancy, a nonprofit group devoted to preserving America's natural areas for the public, assisted the Forest Service when a valuable 48-acre parcel was offered in 1969. It acquired 900 feet of shoreline adjoining the west edge of Baldwin Beach as well as 14 acres of meadow behind the beach and 30 acres of timber farther from the shore. The conservancy then held the property until 1971, when the Forest Service was able to procure Land and Water Conservation Act funding.[13]

For all their successes, the Forest Service also had failures. Shortly after the recreation complex purchases, some 750 acres of marshland at the mouth of the Upper Truckee River, at South Shore, were offered to the Forest Service for $75,000. The marsh was the largest wetland in the entire Sierra Nevada, and two Washoe ethnographic sites were located along its feeder streams. Present-day Trout Creek, named mathOcahuwO'tha, or "river of the white fish," led into the eastern portion of the marsh; the Upper Truckee River, Lake Tahoe's main tributary, called ImgiwO'tha, or "river of the cutthroat trout," fed the rest. In the marsh, the Truckee, moving to the lake, spread and slowed, filtering nutrients as sediments settled into the grasses. Forest Service representatives rejected the offer because they saw no reason to acquire a swamp.[14]

In December 1956, Tahoe Keys, Inc., seeing an opportunity that the agency had not considered, purchased the Upper Truckee marsh and surrounding land for $201,476. The company rechanneled the river directly into the lake and excavated the land at its mouth, creating 150-foot-wide boating canals. Over four years, using vast amounts of dredge fill, it created fingers of land between the canals for a proposed two-thousand-home subdivision. Each of the home sites would have its own dock and boat access to the lake. In the early 1960s, the Dillingham Corporation of Hawaii, expanding to the mainland, acquired the Keys, projected upon completion to be worth $150 million.

The effects of the development were devastating. The inflow of the colder, denser Truckee River water directly into the lake established new currents while depositing its sediment in the lake. Although Dillingham invested in research to find chemical or mechanical treatments, it was unsuccessful at preventing massive amounts of turbid materials from being continuously discharged into the lake.[15]

The homes' lawn-fertilizing agents added to the natural nutrients and sediments being fed into the lake. Invasive, exotic weeds, like the noxious Eurasian water milfoil, were somehow introduced and quickly spread in the canals' warm temperatures. By the 1970s, a vehicle dubbed "the Tahoe Keys Dragon" was needed to cruise the canals, cutting the vegetation. The foreign species changed microenvironments, helping create a gradual warming of the entire lake whose temperature over thirty years increased nearly a full degree.[16]

The Forest Service's failure to secure a property in the mid-1930s allowed the development of another ecological disaster. The agency was unsuccessful in its attempts to buy the steep mountainside of Incline and Incline Beach. At the time, Incline's clear-cut forests were recovering with second-growth pine and fir. Some 16,000 acres were offered for $350,000. When the federal government bogged down in red tape, eccentric multimillionaire George Whittell bought the properties, along with most of the lake's East Shore, for about $1.5 million.[17]

Whittell originally intended to develop the land but, falling in love with it, instead built Thunderbird Lodge, a villa on a point over the lake, and left the rest undisturbed. Beginning in 1970, years after Whittell's death, Nevada senator Alan Bible, chairman of Appropriations, began pressing for Land and Water Conservation Fund moneys for acquisition of the property. In his twenty years in the Senate beginning in 1954, the Nevada Democratic senator helped create eighty-six parks, historic sites, and national monuments. Now he procured $8.1 million originally allocated to fifteen other states and, combining it with $3.7 million from appropriations, added more than 11,000 public acres in Nevada, including wide swaths of Tahoe's shoreline.

Unfortunately, Whittell had previously sold the Incline property for $5 million. Within months the buyers resold what would become Incline Village for $25 million to their own Crystal Bay Development Company.[18]

The most important geometric property for hillside erosion and mass movement in shorezones is steepness of slope. Vegetation is the major element that keeps polluting sediment from being carried into the shorezone. On hills the velocity of water varies as the square root of the slope so that it will flow down a sixteen-degree slope twice as fast as down a four-degree slope. Kinetic energy can be figured as the square of velocity: when speed is doubled, cutting power is increased four times, the quantity of a certain size of material transported is increased thirty-two times, and the volume of particles that can be transported increases sixty-four times. Owing to the fact that most of Incline's land was a precipitous mountainside and two of the lake's eleven most important tributaries flow through it, the area's development had a devastating impact on the lake.[19]

Incline is the primary basin population center in Nevada's Washoe County, which reaches from North Shore Stateline to Marlette Lake. Noting the water and sewage problems that would be engendered by the steepness of the terrain, the Washoe County Planning Commission rejected the Incline plan. County commissioners, however, overrode the decision, and what environmentalist William Bronson called a "mountain-scarring desecration" proceeded. The *Nevada State Journal* commented that the project would "eventually become a $300,000,000 chunk of real estate to gladden the heart of the Washoe County assessor."[20]

A dozen years later, scientist Antony Orme reported that significantly increased erosion was "creating a noteworthy plume of sediment at the mouths of Incline and Third Creeks." Shortly thereafter, scientists found that the plumes were so extreme that the eggs deposited during kokanee salmon runs into the creeks were buried, dramatically reducing the production of young fish.[21]

Like Washoe County, the other Tahoe Basin counties repeatedly subordinated planning to growth. Ordinances were often overridden by variances or simply ignored. The counties' population bases and seats of government were well outside the basin, and 1960s policies regulated only so far as they did not interfere with revenue-generating tourism and development.[22]

In El Dorado County, Paul Brace, director of planning, had developed an effective master plan. His plan for Tahoe established a valuable green-belt boundary between community and forestlands. When Brace protested Board of Supervisors variances in 1963, they fired him. The action, which prompted the grand jury to issue a stinging criticism of the board, was all too typical of basin counties' political priorities.[23]

The errors and unrestrained construction projects led to the deterioration of the lake's clarity. The standard for its transparency was set in 1873 when scientist John LeConte measured visibility using a method devised by Angelo Secchi in the Mediterranean eight years earlier. LeConte sank a white dinner plate until it was no longer visible. Generally, any depth over 16 feet is adjudged to be clear. LeConte found the dish visible at 108.27 feet.[24] In the following years, the logging, begun shortly before LeConte's test, produced high levels of erosion, decreasing transparency. In the late twentieth century, sediment core samples, which accumulate in layers, showed Comstock sediment included sawdust, pine needles, and charcoal from burned slash. In 1959 University of California at Davis scientist Charles R. Goldman, whose work would gain worldwide recognition, began studying the lake, and in 1968 he reintroduced "Secchi dish" experiments.

Goldman's initial tests showed that the new forests had arrested silt flows, allowing the sediment to settle to the lake bottom. His first Secchi dish tests revealed visibility to 102 feet. But the effects of urbanization had initiated a second period of deterioration. In July 1968 Goldman published an article titled "The Bad News from Tahoe." Yearly measurements after 1968 confirmed Goldman's early findings, showing that pollutants were entering the water at an alarming rate. The following year, Goldman's tests, run by his associate Robert C. Richards, averaged a depth of transparency to 93.7 feet.

Richards went on to conduct the Secchi dish observations for thirty-five years. Testing was done year-round in the same place at the same time every ten days, and in a number of years a second observer recorded remarkably similar results.[25]

By 1973 visibility was reduced to 85.6 feet, and Goldman commented in the *Christian Science Monitor* that unless the effects of land development were stopped, "I will be recording the death of a lake." Thereafter, the loss of clarity averaged more than a foot a year until in 1997, the level measured at its all-time low: a 64.1-foot average. In the first years of the twenty-first century, transparency has stabilized at a still luminous level, averaging a little more than 70 feet since 2001. One problem in regaining clarity is that the modern era includes long-lasting perturbation—buildings, roads, and other impervious surfaces—that were not part of the Comstock damage.[26]

In the late 1950s, observers began noticing the impact of urbanization. Individuals formed two organizations that would begin to find solutions for the emerging problems. William D. Evers, a San Francisco attorney who owned property at Rubicon Beach, served as the first president of the Tahoe Improvement and Conservation Association, formed in September 1957. The goal of the group was planning regarding building and infrastructure. At its inception, this association claimed one hundred members preceded the League to Save Lake Tahoe, whose motto is spread on the popular bumper sticker "Keep Tahoe Blue." Evers hoped to work closely with a group formed some months earlier, the Nevada-California Lake Tahoe Association.[27]

The Nevada-California association, forerunner of the Lake Tahoe Area Council, had formed in January 1957. The association was funded by the foundation of businessman and naturalist Max C. Fleischmann. Fleischmann, a partner in the Fleischmann Yeast Company, had lived parts of each year at his Tahoe home, near Glenbrook. At age seventy-four, shortly before his death, he formed a $192 million charitable trust. Over the next twenty-eight years, his wife, until her death, and friends who served as board members distributed moneys to nonprofits involved in religion, education, medical research, and the environment.

The first Fleischmann Tahoe grant was for a planning survey for the entire basin. Business leaders and civic organizations greeted the idea of regional planning with widespread interest. But soon realizing that an outcome of the survey might be to control growth, thereby restricting profits, a large number of the businesspeople withdrew.[28]

The LTAC evolved from the association in an attempt to create a bistate agency to sponsor further research and coordinate administering Tahoe affairs. Waterweeds had proliferated in the shallows of the South Shore in the early 1950s. Effluents, along with disturbed soil, and several drought years had been identified as the cause. Due to high water tables, malfunctioning septic tanks were common. Even more damaging, several of the large South Shore resorts were pumping sewage to the lake or its tributaries.

Using a Fleischmann Foundation grant, the LTAC initiated a study of erosion and sewage facilities in the basin. That effort featured the work of the young limnologist Goldman. Limnology, the study of bodies of freshwater, was a relatively new field, and Goldman was developing the first courses at the University of California at Davis. Just after being hired in 1959, he had begun studying Lake Tahoe along with a smaller lake in undeveloped land near Mount Shasta, Castle Lake, which would serve as a comparison.

Goldman measured algal growth rates, finding that Tahoe was remarkably sterile. In limnology terms, it was oligotrophic—a deep, clean-water—lake, illustrating that it had recovered from the clear-cutting of its forests eighty years earlier.[29]

Goldman's work for the LTAC on what came to be known as the *McGauhey Report* was crucial. P. H. McGauhey, from the University of California, and four other eminent authorities on pollution control and sanitary engineering studied chemical nutrients from effluents entering the lake. The original plan was to develop a tertiary treatment process whereby wastewater would be processed and allowed to flow into the lake. The scientists believed that wastes would be trapped on the lake bottom by the thirty-nine-degree water. Goldman conducted bioassay studies that showed that treated effluent would mix in the water, leading to heightened eutrophication, or greening, eventually killing the lake.

In the meantime, a new South Shore sewage facility, built in 1960, was immediately overtaxed. On Labor Day 1961, two million gallons of effluent overflowed from the plant and found its way into the lake. The North Shore was also having problems because its system lacked the necessary capacity. Needing additional funding, utility district officials were reluctant to limit the number of new hookups, and so problems worsened.

The *McGauhey Report* concluded that nutrients contained in the effluents were reaching the lake. Noting that certain shoreline areas were already showing signs of eutrophication, the engineers concluded that the effluent needed to be exported from the basin and that an effective solution would require an agency representing the entire basin.[30]

In September 1963, the LTAC brought national attention to the sewage problem when it convinced President Kennedy's Water Quality Control Advisory Board to meet at Tahoe. Meanwhile, California's governor, Edmund G. Brown, and Nevada's governor, Grant Sawyer, joined in a pledge to correct the sewage problem. Anthony Celebrezze, US secretary of health, education, and welfare, who would enact the Civil Rights Act of 1964, warned the states that if they did not remedy the problem, the federal government would take action. Instead, the states raised hundreds of millions of dollars for effluent removal. In a case where local governing bodies could not solve a critical problem, the federal government and the states acted. It heralded an ongoing involvement in the lake's political business.[31]

On November 30, 1965, at a Sacramento ceremony, the state officially recognized California's newest city, South Lake Tahoe. Reporters clustered
around Mayor Brad Murphy and the new city council members. "What are
you going to do to stop polluting the lake?" asked a *San Francisco Chronicle*
newsman.

"We've already done it," answered the mayor. "We have built the most modern sewage treatment plant in the United States." Murphy had made a campaign pledge not to allow further "hodgepodge" development. When asked
about such problems, he conceded, "We've become incorporated five years too
late," but he proclaimed now the city would take leadership in protecting the
lake's beauty.[1]

Unfortunately, the mayor's assurance was more than he could deliver. The
council, composed of business owners and contractors and later land developers and real estate agents, touted local sovereignty and generally disregarded
safeguards to the region. Their inability to protect the lake, along with other
local governments' failures, was inadvertently leading toward a comprehensive
regional government.[2]

The issues of sewage and the possible deterioration of the lake's beauty
would not go away. A week after the incorporation ceremony, the city council
received a letter from the director of the South Tahoe Public Utility District
(STPUD), complaining that the economy of the South Shore was endangered
by the environmentalists in the LTAC who had written the Lahontan Regional
Water Quality Control Board, which controls water issues in California east
of the Sierra Nevada crest, requesting a moratorium on building in the basin
until sewer capacity was expanded. The previous August, an engineering firm
had concluded that the system was working at full capacity, and by the following summer, if building continued, the plant would completely fail. The city
council disagreed and approved developments continuing apace.[3]

In early-December 1965, Mayor Murphy was again asked about the sewage issue because of a report concerning Supreme Court justice William O. Douglas. Justice Douglas, a noted conservationist, told a gathering of newspaper editors in Denver that conditions at Lake Tahoe were a "national disgrace." He reportedly said that raw sewage was being discharged into the lake for the convenience of gamblers.

Mayor Murphy said that the justice was either amazingly misinformed or intentionally misrepresenting conditions at the lake. Alluding to the new five-million-dollar plant, he added, "We have about 15,000 permanent residents along the south shore who must provide services for an estimated 200,000 summer visitors. . . . We think we're doing pretty well."[4]

At that time, the El Dorado County Health Department threatened Tahoe Keys with a building shutdown if the company did not receive clearance by December 15, 1965. The health department had continually advised management that stop orders would be issued for the Keys' dredging projects because of emissions into the lake. In five years, the Dillingham Corporation had spent fifty thousand dollars in unsuccessful attempts to find a successful treatment. On December 12, warning that a shutdown would have cost the community a five-million-dollar payroll and promising that they would continue efforts to alleviate the impact of the pollutants, the Keys received clearance for continued dredging.[5]

The basin's five counties had established a joint planning commission several years earlier in an effort to devise a plan for development while protecting the environment. A June 3, 1963, editorial in the *Sacramento Bee,* running a five-part series on Tahoe's problems, touted a blueprint for the "1980 Plan" produced by the commission. The plan outlined how to meet the needs related to rapid growth that would exist by 1980, but the *Bee* commented that its success would depend on its acceptance by the counties' officials.

The 1980 Plan recommended zoning regulations and natural resource management for the region. Along with a proposal that state and federal agencies buy undeveloped lands for open space, an important recommendation was that urban development be located in the coastal plain, avoiding slopes of more than 10 percent.

El Dorado County realized that if management plans were not implemented, "the state will move in and assume control of many Basin functions," and its commissioners voted to adopt the 1980 Plan. Placer County also provisionally accepted it, although at a commission meeting in December 1965, one commissioner commented that the Tahoe Regional Planning Commission (TRPC) was merely a "paperwork outfit" without authority. The county then proved the point by ignoring the plan's recommendations and approving the Twin Peaks Ski and Golf Club, with 224 home sites at Ward Creek.[6]

The Nevada counties rejected the 1980 Plan outright, and Washoe County's environment-damaging development at Incline Village proceeded as designed.

Robert Pruitt, of Douglas County, Nevada, which comprised lands from South Shore Stateline to Spooner Summit on the East Shore, explained his county's objection to the plan. He posited that open areas at the lake were preserved by low taxes. Any increase in taxes to comply with basin-wide plans would force owners to develop their properties to pay for the increase. In this context, his quote to the local newspaper can be understood: "Douglas County had no plans to delegate authority to anyone who plans to change the thought structure of the county."[7]

The City of South Lake Tahoe also ignored the joint county commission's call for voluntary regulatory compliance. Disregarding a recommendation that building heights be limited to forty-five feet, the city council adopted an ordinance allowing high-rise development along both sides of Highway 50, the town's main artery.[8]

One California project, a bridge across the mouth of Emerald Bay, which had been first proposed in the mid-1950s, was an ongoing source of contention. The California Division of Beaches and Parks looked unfavorably on the project from the time it was proposed. It had secured influence in the area with the help of Harvey West, a Placerville lumberman. West had operated a mill at Tahoe Valley during World War II and owned 177 acres at Emerald Bay that he wanted to sell. The California State Park Commission expressed its eagerness to buy the land but needed to find matching funds. Over the objections of the El Dorado County Chamber of Commerce, which argued that the county needed the land for private development so it would remain on its tax roles, West kept the property off the market.

The lumberman then donated half the value of the property to the state, and California purchased the balance for $150,000. By 1954 the state had also secured the adjoining lands, creating the spectacular Emerald Bay State Park, contiguous with the 744-acre D. L. Bliss State Park, half of which had been donated by the Bliss family in 1929. These acquisitions gave the Division of Parks land that circumscribed the bay.[9]

Local governments, businesses, and an important agency leader, state highway engineer W. L. Warren, opposed the parks' position regarding the bridge. When a state senate committee came to the South Shore to discuss the proposal, in March 1960, the *Tahoe Daily Tribune* reported that the $4 million project had 100 percent support of the residents and organizations around the lake.

The South Shore Chamber of Commerce president gave his group's unqualified endorsement, saying it would not detract "one iota" from Emerald Bay's beauty. "The view from a low level bridge," he commented, "would furnish the visitor a more spectacular vista of Emerald Bay than from the present roadway." But protectionists as well as the California parks' leadership fought the proposal, and it stalled in the state legislature.[10]

By 1962 the California Division of Highways had combined the bridge proposal with a project to build a four-lane freeway around the lake's West Shore. Along with the others, the Forest Service, summer residents on the West Shore, and the LTAC, which was about to change its name to the League to Save Lake Tahoe, opposed the proposal.

Despite the opposition, the California Highway Division adopted the freeway route in 1964, but construction was temporarily prevented by the Forest Service, which refused to grant a right-of-way through the Pope-Baldwin Recreation Area.[11]

In November 1965, the State of California spent $8.3 million purchasing two thousand acres of prime recreation land, including one and a quarter miles of beach, on the lake's West Shore, to create a park later named Ed Z'berg Sugar Pine Point State Park, after the California legislator who led much of the state's action on Lake Tahoe in the 1960s and early 1970s.[12]

In 1966 the California Division of Highways again moved to undertake the four-lane construction around West Shore. At hearings through 1967, the park commission and the league continued to raise objections, saying the preservation of the lake should not be subordinated to rapid transit.[13]

The following summer, Doug Leisz, El Dorado Forest Service supervisor who later became the Far West regional forester and then the Forest Service's associate chief in Washington, DC, invited California Highway Division engineer Warren and his wife to picnic with Leisz and his wife at Emerald Bay. Among other issues, Leisz wanted to discuss the bridge across Emerald Bay. The couples traveled together from Placerville, and, at Emerald Bay, Warren's wife questioned building a bridge that would ruin such an idyllic scene. Warren saw her point.

The El Dorado County General Plan, presented in 1968, continued to call for the bridge to be built. But with the strong opposition of the state's chief engineer, and funds diverted for other traffic improvements, consideration of construction was deferred. In 1973 the commission finally rejected the proposal for the four-lane freeway, officially "un-adopting" the route, and the bridge never again came close to being approved.[14]

With various entities pursuing different and at times opposing goals, in a meeting in December 1964 the LTAC, joined by the five counties' joint commission, had suggested that a regional approach was needed to meet the basin's needs. In 1965 the California and Nevada Legislatures approved the idea, creating a study committee.

The underlying question involved individual property rights versus the communal good: because damage may last decades, or in the most severe instances ruin a resource, at what point must a government act against individual rights in order to protect the rights of the community? The nine-member committee, composed of local and state representatives, held public hearings that led to its final report, issued in March 1967. Its finding was radical: it postulated that Tahoe development required the creation of a bistate regional authority for basin-wide planning and permitting. The proposal would need to pass both states' legislatures, be approved by the US Congress, and be signed into law by the president.

Edwin Z'berg, chair of the Committee on Natural Resources in the California Assembly, took up the cause. Z'berg later crafted legislation that established open space, funded state park acquisitions, created a workable system of state timber management, and established off-road vehicle policies. He was unstinting in his support of Lake Tahoe, which he called a "fabled resource."[15]

Z'berg authored a bistate regional authority bill based in large part on the joint study report. His bill added a provision intended to protect the California side of the lake until the bistate agency gained efficacy: the creation of a temporary agency, the California Tahoe Regional Planning Agency (CTRPA), with the same powers as the bistate agency. The CTRPA idea passed the California Legislature and was formed as the rest of the bill was being considered.[16]

Z'berg's bill was vehemently opposed by local interests and by Nevada legislators, led by Douglas County assemblyman Lawrence Jacobsen. The assemblyman questioned the "philosophy" of the Z'berg bill. Calling it "frightening," he claimed that California's "big state pressures" forced the bill on local people. The Douglas County contingent, composed of Douglas County commissioners, planners, and property owners, believed the problem needed to be worked out locally. Charles Meneley, the acting chair of the Douglas County Commission, demanded a solution that "is not in the shadow of some California attitude nor influenced by out-of-basin residents." The county district attorney expressed concern over zoning regulations, stating that to gain Nevada approval, any bill would be required to exempt existing casinos from new regulations.[17]

There were also a number of Nevadans and Nevada-based groups supporting a Z'berg-type bill, including former state assemblyman, recently named a "Distinguished Nevadan," Ray Knisley; the League of Women Voters; members of the northern Nevada Regional Planning Commission; the Tahoe-Douglas Chamber of Commerce, composed of Douglas County residents at the lake; and state senator Coe Swobe, who would be the lead legislator in negotiations regarding the proposed bistate compact. The proponents emphasized the need to work across county and state lines. W. S. Meneley, who had served as president of the joint counties' planning commission and whose brother, on the Douglas County Commission, opposed the proposed agency, commented that he and his brother were friends as long as they did not discuss the Tahoe Basin.

Meneley pointed out that recommendations by the joint commission were often frustrated by lack of county enforcement or county veto. In emphasizing why the regional agency was needed, he said, "Once the [lake's] beauty is destroyed there is no possible method of recovery."[18]

The arguments against the proposal were mirrored on the California side of the lake, with the City of South Lake Tahoe and the counties in opposition to the state proposal. The city council members saw layers of government being added to what they believed should be local jurisdiction. They argued that the joint commission should continue in its role of coordinating basin policy. The proposal went unheeded, it being apparent to all objective observers that the commission was a toothless entity, powerless to secure compliance with its proposals.[19]

Across the lake, the North Lake Tahoe Chamber of Commerce petitioned Governor Ronald Reagan to veto the Z'berg bill. But Reagan, early in his governorship, was establishing a governmental role in protecting natural resources. Although when he became president his administration worked against many environmental interests, as governor he signed legislation establishing the state's Air Resources Board to set motor vehicle emissions standards and worked to block federal dam projects on the Feather and Eel Rivers.

The outwardly conservative governor was developing a reputation as a communicator of broad goals who was passive regarding day-to-day business and, although not vetoing the compact, was not forthcoming in support of it either. The *San Francisco Examiner* laid blame for the bill stalling in the California Senate in part on his "embarrassing silence" on the issue. Years later his good friend Paul Laxalt, at the time his counterpart as newly elected governor of Nevada, said Reagan was brand new to politics, and although he had a fundamental philosophy, "When it came to what you were going to do with the degradation of Lake Tahoe or something, he was just lost." Reagan eventually made clear that if the agreement allowed state and local governments to achieve desirable objectives, it would obviate intervention by a higher level of government, and he advocated for a modified form of the Z'berg bill.[20]

Reagan and Laxalt had much in common and later worked together on the national level. Laxalt, as a US senator, was the chair for all three of Reagan's campaigns for the presidency, and during the Reagan administration the Nevadan was given the nickname "first friend." Ironically, the two men who pushed through the regional agency for Tahoe were both proponents of property rights and limited government. When each man was elected governor, limnologist Goldman and representatives of the league met with them, showing them photographic evidence of damage being done to Tahoe. Laxalt said that Tahoe rose to the top of their agendas. "Actually, Tahoe was a ticking bomb that I don't think any people—other than the environmentalists in the area—were aware of," said Laxalt. "And there was [Goldman] conducting tests for the University of California. He came with all these alarming levels about what was happening to Tahoe. . . . So we both dug into it . . . and we came to the conclusion that the scientists over in California were probably right. And if they were, we couldn't hazard in any degree adding to the problem. . . . So we finally decided, which was very unconservative, to go to a metro-type government."

The governors paid a political price for taking such an extraordinary measure. "We had difficulty," said Laxalt, "certainly not with the moderates and liberals—we had difficulty with the conservatives. My people thought I'd gone off the side of the cliff or something, and Ron's felt the same way about him."[21]

In the end, Laxalt, like Reagan, disregarded his political allegiances, commenting, "The lake is not going to go gray on my watch." Laxalt worked for a year to promote the lake-wide regulatory concept, encouraging legislators to adopt a bill. He asked Senator Swobe to negotiate the bistate compact, and Swobe and California's secretary of resources, Ike Livermore, acted as the governors' go-betweens. At several points, Swobe thought the idea would fail, but he said, "Whenever we needed it, Reagan and Laxalt, who were both so charismatic and were both so convinced that this was the way to go, they'd just step forward and work their magic. If it hadn't been for Reagan and Laxalt, it never would have happened."[22]

In California, early in the 1967 legislative session, although opposition to the concept was "bitter and widespread," conservationists made concessions that allowed an amended bill to pass in August. It authorized a much weaker agency than the Joint Study Committee or Z'berg's bill proposed. Control of the agency would be shifted back to local entities, with the Governing Board, originally to be composed of six local, eight state, and one federal representative, changed to six local, four state, and no federal members. Six months later, Nevada state senator Swobe shepherded enabling legislation through his state's legislature.

The Nevada version further reduced regional authority. Worried about possible restrictions on gambling, as predicted one of its provisions grandfathered in the rights of businesses and casinos to disregard new regulations. It established rules that deemed projects approved if the states disagreed on them or were not acted upon within sixty days of their application. It also limited the agency's budget to $150,000 a year. The broad powers originally intended for the agency were being weakened to favor local jurisdictions and interests associated with the promotion of economic growth.

California's Z'berg was unequivocal in criticizing the new version, saying that by virtue of its structure and composition it would be "bowing to the same monied gambling interests and wealthy land speculators" who were causing the problems. Just as the counties had to worry about state intervention, Z'berg warned that failure by the states would inevitably lead to intervention by the federal government.[23]

Despite his objections, those representing Tahoe's economic interests and local governments quickly introduced the Nevada proposal into the California Legislature. Z'berg and his committee refused to accept it. They voted four to two against the bill. Z'berg immediately came under attack from various sources, including Governors Laxalt and Reagan. He was vilified as "the one man standing in the way of legislation to protect Lake Tahoe." Reagan urged the legislator to "begin to act responsibly for the benefit of all concerned."[24]

The Sierra Club's legislative advocate, Michael McCloskey, offered a unique solution to the impasse: in return for accepting the structural weaknesses in the bistate agency, the California Legislature would maintain CTRPA as a failsafe system. CTRPA could continue to establish and enforce its own standards on the California side of the lake, thereby balancing the actions of the bistate agency. Z'berg had previously argued that California would be better off regulating the two-thirds of the lake on its side of the state line than accepting an ineffective bistate agency. In large part, McCloskey's proposal did just that, and Z'berg's committee accepted the compromise. With the California agency remaining in place, the TRPA legislation passed out of committee, and Reagan signed it in August 1968.[25]

Nevada adopted the recommendations for a regional compact that same year, and the state formed the Nevada Tahoe Regional Planning Agency (NTRPA). The Nevada organization was designed to make planning decisions for its portion of the basin until the US Congress approved the regional compact. Unlike CTRPA, the soon to be disbanded NTRPA had little impact. It developed population density and land-use proposals, but their plans could not be carried out because the agency had no enforcement power.

Many years of fractional problem solving adopted on the basis of short-term, generally economic, needs had failed. Now steps toward addressing issues of the entire microcosm of the region had been taken. A governing entity, new to the United States, was to be created. The trouble was just beginning.

In March 1970, with congressional ratification of the bistate compact and President Richard Nixon's signature on the bill, the Tahoe Regional Planning Agency experiment convened. The agency's mandate was to protect the lake. Never before had the federal government authorized two states to join in such a legal relationship to administer a shared area. The agency's formation indicated that the states were willing to work together to "maintain equilibrium between the natural and manmade environments." It would be a rocky relationship.[1]

On March 19, 1970, with a nonvoting federal representative still to be named, ten members, five from each state, took an oath to serve as the original governing body of TRPA. It seemed the perfect time for the new agency to begin safeguarding the lake. At the beginning of 1970, Nixon had declared it would be the year of the environment. In April, led by US senator Gaylord Nelson, twenty million Americans rallied coast to coast for the first Earth Day. The US Environmental Protection Agency was established later that year, and the Resource Recovery Act and the Clean Air Act were passed. But environmentalists' hopes for TRPA were quickly dashed.

Doug Leisz, who served many years as the presidential representative to the regional agency, later commented that the original compact was "deliberately underfunded" and "designed to fail." Moreover, because the interests most closely associated with Tahoe's economic growth had played a major role in the legislation creating the agency, the same local leaders previously making decisions now formed the majority: six of the ten board members represented the counties and the City of South Lake Tahoe. The composition predisposed the board to favor further economic development over protecting the environment.[2] J. Allen Bray, an Oakland businessman who served as the board's first chairman, said, "In many cases the objectives of the non-local politicians was antithetical to the [locals'] objectives. . . . The objectives of the local politicians were compatible with the objectives of the casino [interests]."[3]

Three months earlier, the planning firm Livingston & Blayney had compiled a study listing problems associated with growth in the basin. The day before being sworn in, the members received the report. It listed deterioration of water quality, air pollution, and other negative impacts. It also outlined budget and staffing requirements, recommending a staff of eight and clerical help.

The new TRPA Board chose Justus K. Smith as executive officer to head the agency's planning staff. With an extensive background as a planner, including the last seven years as executive director of the Denver Regional Council of Governments, Smith was selected from more than six hundred applicants. He proved to be a take-charge, assertive leader. He was a tall man with a stern, unrelenting aspect. He faced what appeared to be an impossible mandate. He was to present an interim plan, offering solutions to the basin's problems, within 90 days and a comprehensive regional plan within 180 days.

Smith proposed hiring a working staff of ten, but the local representatives rejected it, saying they would be duplicating county duties. Placer and El Dorado Counties had filed suits contending that, because representatives were not elected, the agency was imposing taxation without representation. They were withholding payment of their assessments, $93,750. Smith was directed to hire a skeleton staff: a single planner, a development administrator, a draftsman, and two clerks. By the time the staff reported in June, developers besieged the agency with development proposals, the comprehensive general plan loomed, and the interim report was due.[4]

A major question hung in the air: should private basin lands that needed to be protected from development be purchased or dealt with through regulations? The new agency and federal administrators pointed their fingers at each other. In July 1970, four months after its creation, the TRPA Board passed a resolution requesting that the federal government allocate funds to acquire lands in the basin. Federal administrators, on the other hand, preferred that the agency put in place restrictive regulations. Nevada's Senator Bible proposed a third, more contentious, alternative: a bill directing the secretary of the interior to look into making Tahoe a national lakeshore, a protected area under National Park Service jurisdiction.[5]

In the meantime, the TRPA Board was deciding which new proposals would be approved. They appointed an Advisory Planning Commission to assist in reviewing projects. Smith headed the APC, composed of representatives of the five counties, the City of South Lake Tahoe, the Lahontan Water Board, the Nevada Bureau of Environmental Health, and four laypersons. But relations between Smith and the TRPA Board and Smith and the APC were thorny: local officials saw the agency's task as planning *growth;* Smith thought they were charged with saving Tahoe from urbanization.

The agency's success would be, in large part, dependent on its ability to gain the acceptance of local governing units and inspire them to assist in implementing its goals. Smith ignored such considerations, relying on professionalism to accomplish an essentially political task. As differences arose with local officials, he began pursuing his own course.[6]

Smith had invaluable assistance from one quarter, the US Forest Service. It was logical that the agency would help, since national forestlands constituted the largest single bloc in the basin, some 50 percent that would grow to 65 percent by 1979. The Forest Service offered a team to assist in developing the TRPA plan, including experts in ecology, hydrology, geology, forestry, landscape, and recreational planning. Smith would also be able to utilize consultants from state and federal agencies and university scientists. But inventorying, analyzing, and publishing reports on the basin's resources and recommending policies would take time. The undermanned TRPA staff, overwhelmed by development proposals, had little opportunity to produce the required interim plan. The result was an interim plan that was an amalgamation of previously published county plans and maps. Local business leaders and developers were not sure what the plan meant for their interests, while one conservationist commented, "[The plan] can be looked upon either as a non-plan or as a blueprint for catastrophe."[7]

Prodevelopment forces and taxpayer groups, backed by a unanimous resolution by the El Dorado Board of Supervisors, sought and were granted a superior court restraining order, contending the preliminary plan would reduce property values, violating due process of law. Five weeks later, the judge lifted the injunction, and the interim plan was adopted.[8]

Even with the adoption, and summer population reaching an overwhelming 133,000, the agency did little to control projects inundating it. The TRPA Compact stated that development *may* threaten the environment. This meant the agency had to prove degradation in every separate action, and few proposals were rejected. The handful of rejected projects were denied without prejudice, so revised plans could be submitted. More often, the board ignored staff recommendations, approving projects likely to have adverse environmental effects. Smith commented that because "the staff is voted down 90% of the time," he had difficulty defending agency decisions.[9]

Even the agency's rare use of its power seemed an abuse of authority to some. The California counties met with the Nevada counties, calling for local entities to protect against "needlessly burdensome enactments." A major developer wrote to President Nixon, saying the developer might as well live in Cuba or Chile because of TRPA's "dictatorial power." The South Lake Tahoe Chamber of Commerce issued a resolution assailing the influence of "wild-eyed conservationists" and calling for year-round tourism to be the focal point of planning.[10]

At the end of January 1971, Nevada governor Mike O'Callaghan appointed seventy-three-year-old Tahoe champion and former state assemblyman Ray Knisley to the TRPA's governing board. For the next two years, Knisley was the leading spokesman for the Nevada delegation. He proved to be a stickler on following regulations and approving developments whether he agreed with them or not, saying, "I personally think that the whole basin should be publicly owned, but we got into the picture about 130 years too late."[11]

With profits growing rapidly, the expansion of existing casinos, as well as the construction of new ones, became an ongoing controversy. Large Nevada casinos consistently outperformed smaller ones in terms of net operating income, and the industry sought to increase the array of gaming activities as well as provide food and entertainment to attract a larger clientele.[12]

Harrah's brought a hotel project to the board first. In February 1970, the three-person Douglas County Commission, two businessmen and a long-time Carson Valley rancher, after hearing an hour of testimony "mostly in opposition," unanimously approved a Harrah's three-tower, thirty-one-story high-rise. In the face of protests that it would be setting a bad precedent, William Harrah had argued that his hotel would accommodate enough visitors to fill a mile-long strip of motels. He did not address the problem of attracting more vehicles that would create more pollution. TRPA chair Bray said Harrah's idea was to "cut all the trees down and let everybody drive right up to his casino."[13]

Smith argued that "the proposal does not meet the letter or spirit of the law," and Harrah finally reduced it to eighteen stories. Illustrating the relationship between local politicians and the casinos, the South Lake Tahoe representative commented, "It's not our prerogative to dictate to them as long as they say they're going to do the best job possible. We're dealing with an organization which is highly reputable."[14]

Smith's efforts were continually undermined by a lack of operating funds. In December 1970, Smith told reporters that based on cash on hand, "I have given the staff and myself notice as of Feb. 15." This caused Nevada senator Howard Cannon to pursue grants from the US Department of Housing and Urban Development and the Department of the Interior.

Political infighting hampered California's involvement. With the counties' refusal to pay their dues, Democrat Z'berg proposed that the state lend $150,000 to the agency. The *Sacramento Bee* commented, "[The bill] has languished because Gov. Ronald Reagan refuses to grant the necessary budgetary authority," adding, "Gov. Reagan, a strong advocate of local control, and Z'berg, a leader in the struggle for regional control, are in opposing political parties."[15]

At the end of 1970, California found $50,000 that had been appropriated two years earlier, before TRPA had a staff to spend it. HUD then awarded the nearly broke agency a matching planning grant, the first payment of an eventual $125,000. The moneys kept the agency afloat while Smith pushed for completion of the studies by government scientists and academics.

What came to be the most crucial issue in Smith's final plan was a land-capability system devised by a Forest Service planning team. Physical geologist Robert G. Bailey mapped it in its final form. Bailey had been enlisted by Forest Service team leader Andy Schmidt early in 1971. Schmidt, a thirty-year career forester who had served in three regions and the Chief's Office in Washington, DC, sought to have the Forest Service work closely with TRPA, realizing the new agency's limitations.[16]

Bailey had five years of Forest Service experience, doing watershed research and, shortly after arriving at Tahoe, received a PhD in geology from the University of California at Los Angeles (UCLA). He would go on to work forty-six years with the Forest Service, gaining acclaim, classifying and mapping ecoregions for the entire country. Bailey subscribed to the theory being used by the Forest Service in their Mountains West lands inventory: classifying lands into geomorphic units as systems with similar form and geology.[17]

At Tahoe Bailey would work with several consultants, in particular Robert H. Twiss, a University of California at Berkeley professor in environmental planning who also worked at the US Forest and Range Experiment Station in Berkeley. In 1968 Twiss had begun compiling information about Tahoe, including fifty-nine geologic variables, in a data storage and retrieval system. He and land-use planning graduate student Charles Schwartz, who compiled a bibliography of Tahoe environmental documents, utilized US Geological Survey maps. There was no comprehensive map, so they pasted together quad sheets of sections of the basin.

Bailey's synthesizing of data would provide a basin-wide land-use system, determining what the land might support without deterioration of the lake. But he did not begin until February 1971, with little time before the plan's mid-May deadline.[18]

Traditionally, planning for land-capability involved separating areas by use: agricultural, residential, commercial, and industrial. But Ian McHarg had just published his book *Design with Nature,* which emphasized decision making compatible with an area's geologic and social factors.

McHarg's approach involved understanding a place, its nature, and its patterns, realizing the threshold between ecological and human ecological planning. His work stressed processes and time, looking at a site's abiotic composition and its biotic and human uses—identifying the most fitting environments for users. McHarg utilized map overlays to display spatial data, including societal traits, with a transparency for each factor. His system gained national attention when he used overlays mapping human uses of land along with natural features to propose the best route for an important Staten Island roadway. All planning schools in that era adopted his theories, and he would serve on four different presidents' task forces. Both Twiss and Bailey agreed with his methodology, and each used similar map overlays.[19]

When Bailey arrived, Twiss and his coworkers were using stacks of reports to compile 1.6 million items of environmental information with which to encode maps. They used IBM punch cards to feed the information into the only existing Berkeley computer and created maps of some sixty environmental factors, including elevation, slope, aspect, soil, vegetation, and precipitation intensity. Stacks of overlays were then used to see combined effects. The results provided site data on 21,000 ten-acre "cells" covering all basin lands. This was one of the first applications of Geographic Information Systems, or GIS.[20]

Bailey focused on landforms as a clue to potential impacts if natural processes were interrupted. He broke the lands into thirteen geomorphic units based on their formation in geological times, context, setting, and soil properties as well as processes of hydrology and erosion.[21]

Twiss had earlier compiled a capability map, utilizing the key factors to rank areas as high, medium, or low in their capacity to sustain building. Another consultant, I. Michael Heyman, a professor of law and city planning at the University of California at Berkeley, who would assist in writing a code of ordinances for TRPA, pointed out that the map did not meet planning needs. Such a map required simplicity, so the public would understand use regulations, but also enough specifics so that administrators could work within its parameters. In utilizing only three categories for building, extremely bad and moderately bad areas would be lumped together and a governing board would have to decide which sections could be developed. So Twiss refined the system to incorporate a ranking scale with seven levels of buildability.

Bailey, emphasizing soil type and geomorphic setting, grouped and ranked levels of land tolerance. His work, a map showing each geologic area's capacity for use, would be revolutionary, if there was time to complete it.[22]

It was not just Bailey and the mapping team who were pressed for time. Smith's lack of staff became more apparent as the deadline approached. Daily work on development requests required three-quarters of the staff's time. Buried in administrative details, Smith had little opportunity to explain concepts or build support, even from the APC members or the board. Distrust was building. While acknowledging that Smith's staff was shorthanded, TRPA chair Bray dismissed their contributions. He believed any progress was due to Schmidt's Forest Service team.

Smith's take-charge attitude played a part in the evolving perception of him and his team. In shutting himself off from local politicians and pressure groups, he closed himself to the public as well.[23]

In mid-April, with the plan deadline a month away, the consultants' planning guides and reports were in various stages of completion. Glitches in the Berkeley computer delayed results. The staff was working overtime. Smith, with no clear idea of the plan's final configuration, held a series of meetings late into the night with environmental sciences expert Twiss; Antony Orme, a shorezone capability specialist from UCLA; and law professor Heyman. The three consultants would each go on to nationally and internationally distinguished careers. Twiss, a future professor emeritus at Berkeley, would act as a planning adviser to state and federal agencies, foreign governments, and the United Nations, consulting on Tahoe affairs for more than forty years. Orme went on to win several international awards for his geomorphology planning, and Heyman later served ten years as chancellor at Berkeley, worked as an attorney for the Justice Department, and became the first nonscientist to lead the Smithsonian Institution.[24]

Although Bailey's land-capability map did not take into account existing zoning or delineate specific uses, its importance was becoming apparent. At the eleventh hour, Smith proposed using it for the presentation. Twiss warned that a plan intended for public scrutiny needed to address social and economic issues as well as land capabilities. He pointed out that the lake highways were already cut through various lands. The airport at South Tahoe was being developed, and so was Tahoe Keys. Forest Service team leader Andrew Schmidt told Smith that the public would be expecting to see the uses that were to be allocated to each area. But with the deadline looming, Smith turned away from a McHarg societal-traits model. He used Bailey's capabilities map, affixing designations that resulted in 76 percent of basin lands being categorized as "high hazard," 10 percent "moderate hazard," and only the remaining 14 percent "low hazard."[25]

Time for the presentation grew short. The staff, needing to write the situation statement, goals, and policies, had no time for the news media, so there was no coverage of the planning efforts. Locals complained that their concerns were being ignored. Smith and his staff pressed on. Hoping to impress the public at the presentation utilizing "the magic of the computer," Smith decided to create the main map display by using computer printouts of the ten-acre cells. The sections were printed and colored just in time for the May 17 meeting.

A crowd of 450 spilled out of the conference center at South Shore's Sahara Tahoe Casino. Television and newspaper representatives came from Los Angeles, San Francisco, Sacramento, and Reno. Smith used the array of maps on the walls and spoke of the Berkeley computer's data processing. Bailey spoke, explaining the new land-capability system.[26]

The presentations stunned the audience. Bailey's map delineated undevelopable floodplains, meadows, and steep slopes, but the lands categorized as "very well suited for urbanization" totaled only 2 percent. The other two classifications that would allow for building, labeled "moderately well suited" or "well suited for urbanization," constituted another 12 percent of the land. These properties, in flat-lying areas, were already owned and generally built upon. Even in the limited areas yet to be developed, the recommended allowable percentage of cover by buildings, roads, and parking areas was 25 percent to 30 percent.[27]

The *San Francisco Examiner* called the plan "strong medicine against the forces of pollution." But in local circles, it fostered a frenzy of criticism: concerns were obscured by outside experts and planning jargon. Smith emphasized the role of the computer "working at lightning speed." Rather than impressing, this unsettled listeners. One referred to the Smith plan's scientific bent as "the mystification of knowledge."

The map was understood, though: virtually no land was zoned for building. Were those with properties on slopes going to lose the opportunity to profit from their investment? Were owners to be forbidden from building their small retirement cabins? The developments at Tahoe Keys—at the mouth of the Upper Truckee River—and Incline Village, with its steep slopes and streams, were catastrophic to the basin's environment. What was to be done with those developed lands? Smith had provided a matter-of-fact planning concept, proposing that science be adopted into ordinance form. He would pay the price for discounting the political aspects of the process.[28]

Three days after the presentation, Douglas County commissioners passed a resolution unanimously registering their disapproval. Other local groups followed. In early June, Smith met with trustees of the Incline Village General

Improvement District. The Smith plan showed Incline was greatly overdeveloped: an estimated four thousand people were residing in an area that should have eighteen hundred. The plan directed that a property owner who wished to build a three-thousand-square-foot house would now need three lots instead of one. Asked if that was fair, Smith gave a decidedly unpopular answer: "I've been looking for a stock broker to guarantee me a profit too."[29]

His statement and the negative reaction illuminate an interesting change in perspective by some Nevadans. It is often noted that Nevada was built on gambling—not just casino gambling. Prospectors, miners, and cattle and sheep ranchers in an arid state, whose precipitation comes largely in episodes, were all involved in forms of gambling. Every person was expected to fend for himself, creating a proudly proclaimed statewide ethos of individualism. As regarded Tahoe in the 1970s, despite the country's fifty-odd years of ad hoc regulatory takings jurisprudence and the advent of environmental protection laws, politicians abandoned the concept of purchasing land as a gamble. Some argued that developers and lot owners had the right to develop their properties without regard for the environment. Others demanded above-market-value settlements. The Nevadans were joined by landowning Californians.

Many of the hard-line environmentalists and traditionally liberal California politicians took the opposite tack, supporting Smith's contention that buying land carried the same risk of loss as any investment. Before Smith's poorly received presentations, there had been little TRPA Board support for him; now there was none. America's new regional agency appeared headed for failure.

"Absurd." "Unacceptably utopian." "A cruel hoax." The public attacked the Smith plan at public meetings held to discuss it. South Tahoe's city attorney recommended "a strong position against this plan." Former public utilities founder Mayor Les Nagy disparaged the entire TRPA, calling them "a bunch of carpetbaggers." The council ordered a resolution drawn that would oppose the plan. The South Tahoe Public Utility District Board, saying the plan would have a "disastrous direct financial effect," voted unanimously to oppose it.[1]

The APC held two public meetings in June 1971. Before the June 16 meeting, a citizen committee, headed by a developer whose thirty-three-hundred-unit proposal had already been delayed by the agency, placed large ads in the Tahoe newspapers. It urged every businessman, motel and hotel operator, and home owner to attend and stand up against the "most impractical proposal ever to face those of us who live, work and own our homes around the Lake." Developers, property owners, and their attorneys crowded the auditorium to deride the plan, said to be based on "alien philosophies." They overwhelmed voices advocating conservation and tough regulations. The *Sacramento Bee* termed the six-hour meeting "a verbal lashing."[2]

An APC member, Douglas County planner Raymond Smith, had commented, "The politicians want something to hide behind, but this plan gives them no place to hide." The contentious June 20 meeting of the TRPA Governing Board proved his assertion. The APC emphasized the fact that they had not seen the plan before its presentation and refused to recommend it to the board.[3]

The TRPA Board then rejected the plan and assigned Richard Heikka, the planner from Placer County and chief spokesman for the APC, to head a new planning team. The team, composed of the South Lake Tahoe and California county planners, was directed to develop a new direction for land use and zoning. Nevada's lone "expert" planner was Raymond Smith, who was not included on the committee because, according to Ray Knisley, he "had been

identified with too much private property sales." Further, the board forbade
J. K. Smith and his planning staff from appearances to discuss their plan in
public. Chairman Bray later commented: "[J. K. Smith] frequently spoke of his
own program, but made it seem he was speaking for the agency. [That] might
have been crosswise to the wishes of some members of the Board." The muz-
zling of Smith signaled the end of his directorship, and he left the agency in
September 1971.[4]

Shortly thereafter, the Forest Service urged HUD to take action regarding
sewage-disposal problems at Cinder Cone on the North Shore. The housing
agency had recently helped "bail out" TRPA with its $125,000 planning grant
that allowed the agency to stay in business. In July 1971, stating it would do
all within its power "to discourage development which may be contrary to
TRPA plans," HUD declared a moratorium on Federal Housing Administration
mortgage insurance programs in the basin. Something less than 15 percent of
construction received FHA financing, but the action shocked real estate agents,
who claimed it had an adverse effect on other loan sources. Local officials
were outraged. One APC member, a North Shore developer, blamed the Forest
Service for HUD's action. He wrote a letter to Nevada senator Alan Bible and
other federal officials, including President Nixon, accusing the Forest Service
of instigating "one of the most serious acts I have ever seen committed by a
government anywhere."[5]

That same month, the California Supreme Court heard the El Dorado and
Placer Counties' suit challenging the legality of TRPA. The justices disregarded
the dramatic rhetoric. The counties, contending the regional agency violated
"one man one vote" and "home rule" provisions of the Constitution, withheld
funding. The El Dorado County Superior Court had disagreed, ruling that the
agency was constitutional; the California Supreme Court upheld the decision.

The court said that the TRPA Compact was an innovative attempt to deal
with the fact that problems at the lake affected nonresident landowners and
visitors as well as residents. The court commented, "We find that the Agency
has been created to serve a regional purpose in preserving rapidly deteriorating
natural resources from imminent destruction. . . . [The agency] may accomplish that which it would be impossible for any one of the constituent munici-
pal or suburban units to perform." Finding that the compact did not violate the

California Constitution, the decision held that payment by the counties was "a clear duty" imposed by law.[6]

The fact that its status had been confirmed in California did not obviate the internal and external problems confronting TRPA. Heikka and the other planners, using much of the basic Smith Plan, had finished their work. The board scheduled the "Heikka Plan" for approval at their September 22, 1971, meeting. Although Heikka said at the time of his appointment that the committee would "coordinate completely with the TRPA staff," instead they had developed their plan in closed meetings, away from the staff. On one occasion, scientists Twiss and Bailey were summoned to answer questions, but otherwise only the county planners were involved.[7]

Smith had disregarded public relations and politics. Heikka was acutely aware of the failing. Bray called Heikka "a politician, a diplomat," and, when appointed, Heikka had commented that he and the planners "would put the people back in the plan." His approach was opposite Smith's. As planning progressed, Heikka was careful to hold public meetings revealing features of the proposal, many of which were what local jurisdictions wanted.[8]

The Heikka Plan proposed that the Bailey system be relegated to the background as a reference, while more conventional county land-use maps would be employed for decision making. It allowed intensive development on highly sensitive lands, and scientists and the Forest Service saw it as a disastrous proposal.

At a governing board meeting in September 1971, Forest Service Planning Team leader Schmidt argued that Heikka was not sufficiently concerned with two critical areas of development: population density and zoning regulations as related to the land-capability plan. He said that the objectivity of the Smith plan and the analytical manner in which "complicated physical, biological, and related factors were evaluated . . . should not be cast lightly aside." He brought up the point that Heikka's population figures were unrealistic, as they did not include a projected 100,000 or more daily visitors to public lands. He pointed out further that the new plan would allow sixty-eight hundred acres of land not previously developed to be built upon, including more than a thousand acres that were in extremely sensitive and fragile marshes, meadows, and floodplains.[9]

Although the Heikka Plan proposed the public acquisition of thirty-four thousand acres to remove the pressure of development from them, overall it was builder friendly. One of the major elements in the Smith Plan was limiting the percentage of impermeable surface coverage allowed on a parcel of build-able land to 30 percent. The total coverage included roofs, driveways, park-ing lots, and streets. The new plan increased the number of buildable lots by excluding streets and other easements from the calculations. In most cases, that increased a parcel's allowable coverage to 50 percent.

The Heikka map obfuscated the amount of urbanization in the basin by coloring thousands of acres green, signifying general forest, although in some of those areas subdivisions already existed. The new plan's population limit showed Heikka's ability to forge a compromise as well as another instance of shading the facts. A compilation of the existing local general plans revealed an eventual basin population of some 800,000. Whereas the Smith Plan would have held it to 136,000, the Heikka Plan allowed 280,000, not counting visitors using the national forests. When discussing the new plan, Heikka stressed the use of land capabilities as a reference and the restriction of population growth as major accomplishments of the committee.[10]

Although not as divisive as the Smith plan, there was extensive criticism of the new plan. Developers complained that Placer County's lower-density standards had been applied to the entire basin, limiting their projects. They threatened lawsuits based on inverse condemnation. Representatives of utility and sewer districts claimed the plan's limitations on population growth would restrict the tax base and cause bond defaults. Local government officials con-demned what they believed to be a usurpation of their authority.

Conversely, the Sierra Club, with a membership of 135,000, argued that the new plan's inclusion of provisions for several hotel-casino complexes was not compatible with the region's environment and did not address the Bailey map delineations. The *San Francisco Examiner* publicized the fact that Heikka was disregarding the Bailey system in an article headlined "Tahoe Basin Map Key to Environmental Fight."[11]

Nevada board members complained that land ordinances were unduly restrictive, having been incorporated from Forest Service recommendations in the Smith Plan. They also questioned whether the Bailey map, lacking public study and input, should be included even as a reference.[12]

At this time, Robert Twiss, noting the amount of subdivisions the governing board was approving—including multiple phases of some—thought to count the number of subdivided lots that had already been approved for building. Heikka, who was soon to be approved as the new executive officer, discouraged the effort, saying it was "bean counting" and they did not want to get into that. But Twiss went ahead, acquiring assessors' parcel maps as well as tax information from the counties without parcel maps. Then he and James Pepper, another planner, laid out the information on the living room floor of Twiss's Berkeley home and counted twenty-one thousand lots. Those properties needed only local building permits to construct homes.

Twiss and Pepper made a graphic map showing all the approved but unbuilt parcels. Heikka was furious. He first argued that the figures were wrong: there were perhaps a few hundred approved lots, he said; the others were paper subdivisions that did not really exist. Several years later, CTRPA did an official survey and found Twiss and Pepper's figures were within 2 percent of the actual figure.[13]

With the controversy raising a question about the constitutionality of their actions, in September 1971 the TRPA Board voted to install a ninety-day moratorium on construction other than single-family homes. Douglas County's Charles Meneley was the lone holdout in the eight-to-one vote. Already approved projects, like the next Tahoe Keys phase, were allowed to continue, but the agency had enacted its first moratorium.[14]

CTRPA, composed of the TRPA California Board members acting separately, voted to adopt the Heikka Plan but included the Bailey map and the land ordinances. Providing for both the general plan map and the capabilities map to be utilized was of utmost importance. As in the Ian McHarg–devised system, by overlaying the two, the areas of conflict, where developments would be allowed on sensitive lands, were readily apparent. If they incorporated both maps into the TRPA Plan, the governing board would be able to identify conflicting locales and reconcile socioeconomic and environmental needs.[15]

During the following three months, a committee heard objections to the

Heikka Plan from the public, and the Sierra Club presented lengthy arguments that the board, influenced by landowners and developers, was out of compliance with the law that created it. Regardless, the committee consistently granted increases in densities for the projects of developers who appeared before it. Of thirty-three approved changes, twenty-eight increased densities.[16]

On December 22, 1971, at a contentious meeting that necessitated Governor O'Callaghan directing the Nevada delegation by phone, the board adopted the Heikka Plan, with the Bailey map and land ordinances. The nation's first bistate agency had a compact by which to govern. A board member commented that the agency planning would now be "a continuous, dynamic process." Instead, having demonstrated the extent of its power with the building moratorium, the board significantly raised the stakes. Disputes and political machinations intensified, and the agency moved only by fits and starts.[17]

Once the governing board began acting in accordance with the compact, the new law's weaknesses became apparent. While restraining a few projects, the rules ensured passage of others, even those certain to create ongoing damage to the environment. In the early 1970s, the federal government's involvement would escalate dramatically, as US senators, the Nixon administration, and other agencies sought to intervene.

The Redstone Mining Company's massive development project called Lake Country Estates was the first major venture to become entangled in TRPA's new regulations. The company first sought board approval in July 1971, while the plan was still under consideration. The Redstone proposal contained 3,055 units, including a small shopping center and an elementary school, to be built on 956 acres dissected by the Upper Truckee River in Meyers, California. El Dorado County had approved the master plan. The TRPA planning staff opposed it, but the Advisory Planning Commission, as they were inclined at the time, ignored staff and recommended approval.[1]

When the matter came before the TRPA Board, APC member Raymond Smith spoke for the developer. He said the plan included 300 acres of open space, or 30.9 percent of the total development. Fellow APC member Steve Brandt, of the League to Save Lake Tahoe, challenged Smith's figure, pointing out that the 300 acres being counted as open space were actually undevelopable meadowlands and that unit densities and open space needed to be figured on an area's buildable lands. At the time, J. K. Smith was still TRPA executive director, and the governing board told the developer to reconsider the project. TRPA later proposed that the federal government acquire the land.[2]

The federal agencies made no move to purchase the land, and Redstone Mining began cutting trees on the land in violation of TRPA policies. In August 1971, El Dorado County cited the company for clear-cutting a large stand of lodgepole pine. In October the Sierra Club accused Redstone of illegally bulldozing 4 acres of sod and willows on a section of meadow within the

Truckee River's one-hundred-year floodplain. Draining the meadow into the river, their bulldozed ditch formed a delta that would wash into the lake when the river rose.[3]

That winter the company reintroduced the Lake Country Estates proposal for approval, but, because the TRPA's moratorium on major projects was in place, it was tabled. Redstone next brought the plan to the APC in the fall of 1972. Heikka had replaced Smith as executive director, and, in order to allow a "second look" at the Lake Country Estates development, he had the area on the general plan changed from general forest to a "development reserve." The latter category, described by the *Tahoe Daily Tribune* as "in direct conflict with TRPA's regional conservation plan," meant that the acreage could be built upon if it were proved construction would do no harm. When challenged by the league's Brandt, Heikka responded that "the developer must [still] come back and prove a program."[4]

In September 1972, the development company's attorney said that they were not interested in litigating, but threatened a claim in the millions of dollars if the project was denied. The following month, the company resubmitted their plan, proposing to modify the estate's environment through "'mechanical' drainage of the meadow": an elaborate system of underground rock-filled channels and perforated pipes that would lower the water table. The developers introduced a number of scientists who testified that little or no damage would result from the project.

TRPA consultants disagreed. The removal of trees would increase silt flows, and Charles Goldman said the system would increase the flow of nutrients into the Upper Truckee and then into the lake. Ray Knisley suggested denying the project but placing the entire site in the "reserve" category. He felt the board could not make a final decision until seeing a more detailed proposal with all the land in a common zone.[5]

When the APC again considered rezoning in April 1973, the vote deadlocked at nine to nine. Heikka, allowed to cast a ballot only in cases of ties, voted for the change. It was not enough. Lake Country's attorney said the action only put the development back where it had been three years earlier and that it would take another year before a new plan could get to the governing board. Instead, two weeks later, the company filed suit against the agency and the governing board members, claiming they were libel for inverse condemnation damages in the amount of $28.6 million.[6]

The US District Court dismissed the suit, finding that TRPA had no authority to condemn property and that the board members were immune from liability. The Ninth Circuit Court of Appeals upheld the condemnation ruling but reinstated the personal liability claim against the individual board members because the record did not disclose whether the board's conduct was legislative, which affords absolute immunity, or executive, which allows qualified immunity. In 1979 the US Supreme Court took up the case, determining that the TRPA Board was immune because its members were discharging legislative duties. Eleven years later, the developers again filed suit. In June 1984, California used money from the resolution of an unrelated offshore oil dispute to pay $5 million for the land appraised at $6.1 million in 1972.[7]

While the agency was in its formative stage, South Lake Tahoe had been busy issuing construction permits for apartments, motels, and single-family dwellings. In 1969–70 $5,510,383 in permits were issued, in 1970–71 $9,130,568, and in 1971–72 $20,396,652 in permits were allowed. With the construction industry unfettered, US senators began eyeing the national priority of Tahoe conservation.

As early as 1969, Nevada's Senator Bible had introduced the bill investigating the establishment of the lake as a national lakeshore. On the Senate floor, regarding Tahoe, Bible said, "We are in a race with the bulldozer of commercial development."[8]

California Democratic senator John V. Tunney, son of heavyweight boxing champion Gene Tunney, served in the House of Representatives from 1965 until 1971, followed by a term in the US Senate. Tunney had attended the University of Virginia Law School, where he was a roommate of Ted Kennedy, and served as a US Air Force judge advocate. Upon Tunney's election to the Senate in 1972, Democratic leader Edmund Muskie gave him a choice assignment on the air and water-pollution subcommittee of the Public Works Committee, gaining considerable leverage to deal with Lake Tahoe, in which he took special interest.[9]

In August 1971, the Bureau of Outdoor Recreation (BOR) leaked the confidential preliminary report on the feasibility of establishing a national lakeshore. The report concluded that only drastic governmental action would save the lake from environmental disaster. Its recommendations included revising TRPA to give the federal government control rather than local interests; broadening and strengthening land-use controls, perhaps including the national lakeshore designation; and spending up to $110 million to purchase sensitive lands. At the same time, Tunney introduced the "Lake Tahoe Environmental Quality Act," legislation that proposed enlisting the Environmental Protection Agency to oversee TRPA.[10]

TRPA officials and local government representatives denounced the BOR findings and the Tunney proposal, saying they would "destroy the careful balance in inter-government relations." California assemblyman Eugene Chappie feared lands being removed from tax rolls and the idea of owners paying property taxes without being able to develop the land. He said Tunney "should take care of the Salton Sea where 500,000 gallons of raw sewage are pumped daily from Mexicali, and leave Tahoe alone."[11]

Nationally, Nixon's White House also attacked the measure. On the environment, advisers like Undersecretary of the Interior Russell E. Train, who later led the EPA, strongly influenced Nixon. The administration first proposed the EPA and backed numerous initiatives including the Clean Water Act and the Endangered Species Preservation Act. But the water-pollution control legislation was sponsored by Muskie, a Democratic presidential prospect, and, for Nixon, politics trumped environmental policy. When Governor Reagan sent a telegram urging California lawmakers to oppose Tunney, the senator told a news conference it demonstrated that "the Nixon Administration asked the governor to help gut the water quality bill." In the end, a joint House-Senate conference committee scrapped the Tunney proposal, agreeing instead to a one-year $500,000 study by the EPA on the adequacy of Tahoe's various government agencies and their land-use controls.[12]

Displeased that the BOR report had been suppressed, Tunney publicly called for its release. It was long overdue, and he had heard that "substantial revisions were being made." Instead of publishing it, in April 1972 Secretary of the Interior Rogers Morton sent two staff members to Tahoe to assess the situation.[13]

In January 1973, eighteen months late, Morton released the official Interior Department report. The new findings were opposite the original draft.

The study claimed a Tahoe national lakeshore would "endanger Tahoe's fragile resources" by increasing recreational visitations. Morton said TRPA was the most appropriate agency to handle land-use decisions, promising priority consideration for grants to help with land purchases. Senator Bible approved Morton's determination but added, "This pledge will mean little if the dollars aren't there."[14]

Taking a different view, Tunney blasted the report as "bland, uninformative, noncommittal, and virtually useless in formulating federal policy." Because it was titled *Lake Tahoe—a Special Place,* Tunney commented that the report "ought to be relegated to a special place." The *Sacramento Bee* added, "Such timid approaches would never have saved for posterity some of the great national treasures as the Grand Canyon, Yosemite, Glacier National Park and others." Morton wrote back to the *Bee,* saying he was "vitally interested" in preserving Tahoe, but arguing that TRPA would be most effective in overseeing it.

Two weeks later, Tunney wrote directly to Morton, commenting on the forthcoming EPA report: "I can only hope that the EPA study is courageous enough to deal with those crucial questions of policy which your department's report sought so assiduously to avoid." Tunney would not have that information for a long time. Due to be completed within months, the EPA report was not released until June 1975, more than two years late.[15]

Still, the report was valuable. Advanced by its principal author, John Wise, who would serve in the agency thirty-one years, it supported Tunney's contentions, concluding that sediment and nutrients, derived from careless land development, were decreasing the lake's clarity to such an extent that it could become irreversible. Although not advocating federal intervention, the study recommended modifying the TRPA voting procedure that favored development and produced an important recommendation that a "threshold carrying capacity" system be formulated for management of Tahoe's environment.

The threshold system would describe limits of Tahoe's capacity to provide for the needs of a given human population and establish points, or thresholds, beyond which ecological damage occurs. The thresholds, including capacities for water, air, soil, vegetation, wildlife, fisheries, noise, recreation, and scenic resources, would take a number of years to create.[16]

In the interim, when Nixon was forced to resign, President Gerald Ford moved Morton out of his position at Interior, ultimately appointing him "special counselor to the president." Senator Bible had opted not to run for reelection in 1974 and in 1976 Tunney lost his reelection bid, so none of the key players were in a position to continue the dispute. Others would take up each side of the cause.

Unsurprisingly, gambling had proved to have significant influence on Nevada's TRPA contingent. Analysis of the industry's growth revealed that expansion and clustering of establishments had not led to market saturation but rather had strong spillover effects. The Harrah's high-rise expansion, originally approved in 1971, had created fears that it would set a precedent. In 1973 those fears were realized. The two other major casino operators on the South Shore, Harvey's and the Del Webb Corporation, operating the Sahara Tahoe, built in 1964, looked to expand by creating high-rise hotels. Harvey's intended to add 500 rooms that would raise its hotel to eighteen stories. Del Webb proposed building a new high-rise across the highway from its Sahara Tahoe on land owned since 1897 by the Park family and the Park Cattle Company.[17]

In November 1972, after first agreeing to wait until TRPA completed a master plan for the casino core area, the Park Company instead presented its plan to the Douglas County Planning Commission. With Park heirs pursuing the plan, Douglas County approved the fourteen-story, 494-room project, to be called the Park Tahoe Hotel and Casino. The commission issued grading permits to allow construction to start immediately. TRPA was forced to get an injunction against the county to delay the project. Douglas County had two more major basin hotel-casinos on the drawing board, Tahoe Palace and Hotel Oliver. The new developments, to be built outside the casino core area, were projected to mean annual increases of $12.5 million in taxes for Nevada and $850,000 in room taxes for the county.[18]

Stateline hotel-casinos had 1,337 rooms at that time; the new developments called for an additional 4,500. An estimated eight thousand more casino employees would need housing on the South Shore, where housing was already inadequate.

South Shore roads posed a similar problem. TRPA executive director Heikka called overloaded Highway 50 through Stateline on weekends a "parking lot." A recent study of traffic had reported maximum development would require widening the four-lane Highway to eight lanes, with a bypass of six lanes and several four-lane collector arterials. TRPA's Knisley said, "The uncontrolled expansion of that area is the worst thing that can happen to the image of this state."[19]

It was commonly acknowledged that TRPA, under its original bylaws, could not stop the development. With environmentalists and influential officials, including Governor Mike O'Callaghan, questioning the feasibility of the projects, Nevada's legislature reinstituted the Nevada TRPA. Its purpose was to review the Douglas County–approved projects. The revived agency was approved over the objection of several representatives, including Douglas County's assemblyman Jacobsen, who argued that the Douglas County Commission was doing a good job.[20]

The five Nevada TRPA members constituted the NTRPA Board, and a nine-person planning commission was appointed to advise them. Within a month, the advisory commission recommended that if traffic congestion was relieved by new road construction, the agency should approve the Park Tahoe and the two other hotel developments. The two new projects were in the development stage, but the Park Tahoe was said to be shovel ready.[21]

The traffic plan that seemed most possible in alleviating the problem called for construction of loop roads circling Stateline, diverting through-traffic around the casino core. But neither the City of South Lake Tahoe nor the California Department of Highways was financially able to build its portion of the bypass.[22]

Regardless of the traffic plan, two weeks later, on June 27, 1973, TRPA's compact flaws allowed construction of the Park Tahoe to begin. Four of the five TRPA Board members from Nevada, arguing that it was well conceived, voted to approve it. The fifth Nevada representative, Walter MacKenzie of Washoe County, joined the entire California contingent in voting against it. Doug Leisz, the nonvoting presidential appointee to TRPA, had discussed the air-quality aspect of the impact study with scientists. Finding it defective in several areas, Leisz expressed "great reservations" to the board about the approval. But the vote, six to four against, was not enough.

In order to reject a proposal, the majority of *both* states had to vote to deny it. If it was not rejected after sixty days, it was deemed approved. Because the majority of Nevada's representatives voted for it and sixty days had passed, the development could go forward. It was the first time a major project had received "approval by default." In mid-July, three weeks after the "nonapproval," grading operations began at the Park Tahoe high-rise hotel-casino that later became Caesar's Tahoe and then Mont Bleu.[23]

At the same TRPA meeting, June 28, the board members approved a Raley's shopping center that appeared headed for rejection. It passed six to four, mixing votes of representatives from each state. The agency's staff had recommended against allowing the twenty-six-acre, 234,500-square-foot project, which would be the largest in the basin—two and a half times larger than a center recently completed at South Shore.

Asked about the decisions, Steve Brandt, president of the League to Save Lake Tahoe, said, "It means the TRPA is a failure." In a letter to the *Nevada State Journal,* Brandt let it be known that he was stepping aside from the league. He called the government officials, politicians, and appointees "spineless," saying they did nothing but assist developers. "For three years I have urged people that the TRPA could work, would work," he said. "I was wrong." The *Journal* editorialized that thousands of people would share Brandt's disillusionment, saying, "Perhaps it was just too much to believe that local officials could be tough enough to accomplish the League's objectives. . . . Probably against these pressures no place of great beauty in the nation can be saved under local government."[24]

As if to emphasize the agency's dysfunction, TRPA repeated its nonaction decision. The board granted Harvey's hotel its expansion to eighteen stories, the same height as Harrah's, and enlargement of its casino to make it the biggest at the lake. The states again split their decision on the expansion, with Californians against approval and the Nevada board members, except MacKenzie, for it. At the TRPA meeting of August 22, 1973, the sixty-day rule allowed the expansion to be deemed approved. In this case, apparently knowing the stalemate would not be broken, the application was not even discussed.[25]

The meeting was notable also because J. Allen Bray, the first chair of the board, sent a letter of resignation. Bray later said that since being appointed, he had spent 80 percent of his time on agency business. His service gave him ulcers. He said, "I got sued for something like $270 million and had to pay my attorney out of my own pocket." He also explained why, although the TRPA Compact "desperately needed" modifying, he had never entertained such an effort. "Once it started through Congress," he said, "it would open up the whole gamut of the agency in general. . . . The Compact in general could have been obliterated."[26]

Environmentalists now took action. In September 1973, the League to Save Lake Tahoe joined the Sierra Club, filing a sixty-page suit challenging the Raley's mall and the high-rise casino projects. A year earlier, the league had set up a committee of four lawyers and offered to assist TRPA in fighting lawsuits by property owners; the group's attorneys would now be employed in attacking the agency. It was in this context that board member Knisley, in attempting to gain state financial aid in Nevada, commented, "I've even tried to panhandle some private legal firms to help us, but I found that most of them were suing us."[27]

The environmentalists' suit contended TRPA was not meeting its legal responsibility of providing development controls and asked for a temporary moratorium on building. Two Sacramento federal court judges disqualified themselves because they were members of the league, and the case was heard by a district court judge from Montana. A battery of eleven lawyers representing the defendants, including those of the projects as well as TRPA, contended that the federal court should have no jurisdiction: if it took jurisdiction, "it could easily become the planning review agency for the entire Tahoe Basin."

The judge decided that a federal question might not be involved and rejected the suit. All parties had agreed to an expedited appeal to the US Circuit Court in San Francisco. The "expedited" case would take a year to be decided. In its November 1974 ruling, it overturned the lower court, finding that ratification by Congress made the bistate compact federal law.[28]

In the meantime, the maelstrom of lawsuits intensified in October 1973, as TRPA obtained a writ from the Nevada Supreme Court to temporarily prohibit Douglas County from issuing construction permits for the second new casino, Tahoe Palace. The previous week, the county commission, with one commissioner calling TRPA "illegitimate," issued a grading permit for the $40 million project. In seeking Nevada Supreme Court intervention, TRPA also demanded

Douglas County pay the $23,325 in dues it owed the agency, which the county did grudgingly.[29]

With the intervention, the owner of the Tahoe Palace land, a South Dakota cattleman, Ted Jennings, began following through on a threat he had made, putting up poles and plastic sheeting to construct hog sheds for a feeding lot. Douglas County Commission chair and local furniture-store owner Harold Dayton said that zoning permitted a hog feedlot. "[Jennings] thought if he can't go on with the other project that he would put animals on the land. Jennings is in the pig and cattle business in the Midwest and he probably wants to use the land in connection with his business." A Jennings spokesman said that 150 young Fallon hogs were expected in two weeks, and the plan was to fatten up 50,000 hogs a year for slaughter in West Coast meatpacking plants. A casino representative said the joke had gone far enough, and TRPA officials corrected the local commissioner, issuing a statement that a commercial livestock operation at that location violated agency ordinances. Ray Knisley added that there would never be hogs there, because if the county district attorney did not stop the building, he would be disciplined by the state attorney general.[30]

A week later, in yet another surprising move, the Douglas County Commission again approved a grading permit for the Tahoe Palace. Commissioner Dayton said they took the action to avoid a legal fight over the hog feedlot, saying as long as the project did not exceed forty feet in height, approval by TRPA was unnecessary. Dayton, who believed "California do-gooders" were trying to control Nevada gambling, said the Jennings hotel, designed to be ten stories, could be spread over more land. He also said the Oliver Kahle seven-story hotel would be similarly approved if its owner reapplied.[31]

The TRPA Board was facing other substantial problems as well. By July 1973, claims totaling $260 million and $35 million in lawsuits had been filed against the agency.[32]

Two local members of Nevada's contingent, including Washoe County environmentalist MacKenzie, were replaced in the spring of 1974. It was alleged that the replacements were individuals "more responsive to casino interests." When the Tahoe Palace and Kahle's Hotel Oliver projects came before TRPA in 1974, the proposals passed three to two, with the new members joining the other local representative in voting for approval. Knisley later said that although the state representatives and O'Callaghan opposed them, the county representatives "entered into a cabal against us." He contended it was more than just the casino issue alone. "Carson City," he said, "thought it had to play ball with Douglas County to get water out of Douglas County."[33]

Although the TRPA Board now voted seven to three against the two new projects, because the majority of Nevada members had voted to approve them, after sixty days they were approved by default. The compact's favorable bias toward casino development ensured ongoing environmental destruction. When the State of California attempted to secure a temporary injunction against the two new casino hotels, US district judge Bruce R. Thompson, in Reno, said the court could not overrule the unequivocal language of the agency's compact. Although forced to reject the California bid, Judge Thompson, who served on the US District Court for more than thirty years and for whom the US courthouse and federal building in Reno is named, added a personal remark that the proliferation of casinos at Tahoe was an "abomination."[34]

NINE ■ INFLUENCES

osing critical day-to-day battles, environmentalists looked for new ways to obviate the TRPA Compact's deficient language. Assemblyman Z'berg had held hearings at Tahoe in 1972 to find ways the government could acquire and protect private lands designated too fragile for building, and in the summer of 1973 he introduced a bill proposing to reconstitute CTRPA. With the lake's local officials calling for the abolishment of the "cumbersome and useless" agency, Z'berg argued that if the public needed to fund land acquisition, it should have a bigger voice in making policy.[1]

The National Science Foundation (NSF) funded a study that issued a scathing indictment of TRPA, finding that only the nonlocal California board members were voting to protect the environment most of the time. If expectations of the Z'berg bill were realized, the study concluded, CTRPA would be able to protect the environment on the California side of the lake. In the fall of 1973, Z'berg pushed the bill through the California Legislature. It added a second state representative; the governor would now appoint one from Northern California and one from the South, and the six members would choose a seventh as chairperson. This configuration meant state representatives would outnumber local members, shifting the balance of power. The bill provided funds for the CTRPA directly from the state legislature, avoiding the county finance battles, and assigned the agency wide-ranging jurisdiction over state public works and transportation in the basin. Governor Reagan was slow to appoint the new representative, but once staffed in the spring of 1974 the new CTRPA immediately joined the development melee.[2]

CTRPA proposed limiting building on the California side of the lake to single-family houses until they could develop a master plan. Local businessmen and builders claimed outsiders were using a moratorium on construction to shut down the tourist trade, and they formed an organization to promote development, a short-lived group called the "Council for Logic."

Plainclothes officers attended CTRPA's public meeting at a Tahoe high school in June 1974. The chairman of CTRPA, local West Shore real estate agent Gordon Hooper, contended that the agency had an obligation to citizens of the state and the United States as well as local property owners, but the message went unheard, as an unruly crowd of several hundred shouted him down.[3]

The lead federal government agency in the basin, the Forest Service, was consistent in balancing public lands for a combination of uses. Regional forester Doug Leisz had a substantial history of protecting the lake basin's watershed values. He had previously served as forest supervisor of the El Dorado National Forest, one of three forests with public lands jurisdiction at Tahoe in the 1960s. As supervisor he had denied California's Department of Fish and Game a permit to raise the water level of Grass Lake, on the south rim of the basin, to create a fishery. Grass Lake was California's largest sphagnum bog, and adding water to it would have destroyed several endangered bog plant species. He had also shielded Pope Beach from incursion by the Tahoe Keys development, resisted the proposed West Shore freeway, and protected the Desolation Wilderness from the construction of unwarranted power-company roads. In the same post, he got the Sierra Club and the Four Wheel Drive Association to endorse trail boundaries for off-road wilderness travel and oversaw the expansion of Heavenly Valley and Sierra Ski Ranch.[4]

Leisz was also active in acquiring land for public use in the Tahoe Basin without condemnation actions. In May 1971, the *Tahoe Daily Tribune* asked: "Who owns Meeks Bay Resort?" Before Americans arrived, the Washoe Indians had used the idyllic West Shore bay for home sites, fishing in the lake and Meeks Creek, gathering food and medicinal plants in the meadow behind the bay, and hunting in the timber stands leading into the Desolation Wilderness. Americans originally used the area for grazing and timberland. Beginning in 1921, as the forest grew back, a private owner developed the land as a resort, offering camping and cabins. In 1968 the Macco Corporation, a subsidiary of the Penn Central Railroad, bought the property, planning to build a seventeen-hundred-unit condominium complex on its 645 acres. In 1970 Penn Central ran into financial difficulties, and the Forest Service's Andy Schmidt became aware that the company would be receptive to an offer for the property's purchase.[5]

At the time, the Forest Service had no money available for acquisitions.

In a discussion with League to Save Lake Tahoe executives, Schmidt let it be known that the land was for sale and that, if saved from development, the Forest Service would surely buy it when funding became available. In March 1971, regional forester Leisz wrote to the league, formally promising to work to acquire the necessary funds. Two months later, an undisclosed buyer purchased Meeks Bay Resort.[6]

In the midst of the Nixon administration's policy of cutting federal spending so it could cut taxes, it was an uphill battle for Leisz to obtain the necessary moneys. At the time, as the president's representative to TRPA, Leisz would meet bimonthly with Office of Management and Budget director Caspar Weinberger, known as "Cap the Knife" for his cost-cutting skill. When Leisz first met with Weinberger and his aides, Weinberger told him that Tahoe spending on land purchases had to be brought under control. Leisz explained the Forest Service land-acquisition plan and what they had spent so far, and Weinberger exploded, "Don't you understand you're hemorrhaging the budget!" Leisz responded that fortunately, they were already a third of the way through the purchases. Exasperated, Weinberger stomped out of the meeting. It was not until Weinberger had moved to the Office of Health, Education, and Welfare, two and a half years later, that Leisz procured the money for Meeks Bay.[7]

In December 1974, the Forest Service bought the property for $3.1 million, the same price for which the league's private buyer, William R. Hewlett, had acquired it. Hewlett, winner of the National Medal of Science, the nation's highest scientific honor, owned a home on the West Shore. He and David Packard were cofounders of Hewlett-Packard, the technology company that sparked California's Silicon Valley movement.

Leisz had told Hewlett before the Meeks Bay purchase that he would only cover Hewlett's costs and might pay less if the value went down. This was not Forest Service policy, but Hewlett liked the fact that Leisz was concerned about government spending, and he agreed to assume the risk. Rather than resenting that the property's value had risen $500,000 by the time of the resale and he did not receive its current value, Hewlett told Leisz to let him know if he could help again.

That his role in acquiring Meeks Bay for the public was kept secret typified the unassuming engineer's manner of engaging in philanthropy. Stanford

University president John Hennessy, in praising the hundreds of millions of dollars Hewlett gave to the university as well as other endowments, said the inventor never sought the spotlight but worked quietly, believing simply that "those who have had the good fortune to succeed should devote themselves to the betterment of society."[8]

When Leisz became the president's representative to TRPA, in October 1972, his first action was to assign Andy Schmidt as the single administrator for all Forest Service activities at Tahoe. To further unify the approach to public lands, in April 1973 Leisz combined the parts of the three national forests that reached into the basin, Toiyabe, El Dorado, and Tahoe, into one entity: the Lake Tahoe Basin Management Unit (LTBMU). The management unit functioned as a unique national forest, allowing it to be an effective administrator of the basin's public lands.[9]

In that era, limnologist Charles Goldman was well on his way to being designated the "father" of ecological research at Lake Tahoe. When he began his experiments in the 1960s, he was surprised that aquatic scientists had paid so little attention to the lake. In its history, only three scientific observations had been undertaken, the last in 1937. Goldman speculated that the paucity of investigations was due in large part to the fact that there had never been a research station at the lake. The studies begun by Goldman and his former student Bob Richards continue to this day, providing one of the longest and best limnological data sets in the western United States.[10]

Goldman's Secchi dish experiment, first used in 1968, is arguably the most important study in the history of the lake. Although sophisticated equipment can now divide the white light into the various colors, taking thousands of measurements per profile at various depths, the single measurement of the Secchi dish simplifies the findings. In doing so, it allows the public as well as the politicians and institutes that control funding to understand the loss-of-clarity trend and appreciate that Tahoe needs protection.[11]

Goldman's initial Secchi dish study reproduced John LeConte's experiment of August 1873, in which LeConte viewed a white plate at 108 feet below the surface. LeConte spent six weeks at Lake Tahoe conducting various experiments to dispel sensational assertions, such as that the lake had no bottom, and to explain why a number of drowned bodies had never been recovered.

For much of his work, LeConte used a self-registering thermometer attached at varying positions to a sounding line. The physical results of the sounding line disproved the rumor that the lake was fathomless. Instead, it indicated that a subaqueous channel traversed the lake south to north. He measured depths at stations along the way ranging from 900 feet to 1,645 feet, deeper, he noted, than Switzerland's Lake Geneva or Italy's Lake Como. The thermometer provided an answer for why the bodies of drowned persons were never found. With temperatures of 41 degrees at 772 feet and 39.2 at 1,506 feet, when the bodies sank the cold kept gasses from forming in the intestines. Unlike in warmer waters, because they did not inflate, the bodies did not rise.[12]

Beginning in 1959, Goldman did eight years of primary productivity research, pioneering studies of lake eutrophication, focusing on Tahoe's algal growth and water clarity. Because science is temporal and dynamic, based on accumulated knowledge, Goldman knew the study of the lake needed to be long term. While continuing to teach at the University of California at Davis, in order to consolidate data and focus Tahoe research, in 1967 he founded the Tahoe Research Group.

In 1969 he hired Bob Richards to captain the TRG research vessel, a position that included collecting samples, taking the Secchi dish readings, designing and engineering the physical aspects of visiting scientists' experiments, managing the day-to-day field operations, and, in storm conditions, working in the lab running water chemistry or building equipment and laying out anchor lines. Richards had worked for Goldman collecting data at Castle Lake, the lake used as a comparison to Tahoe, while Richards was conducting his own studies to earn a master's degree. Richards took the temporary Tahoe job, continuing in the position for three and a half decades.

The TRG's first boats were entirely inappropriate as research vessels, small inboards and outboards and then a donated mahogany-and-teak yacht that, while docked on the West Shore during a major winter storm, capsized and pounded itself to pieces on the bottom of the harbor.

Goldman and Richards replaced the yacht with a 1942 horseshoe-stern salmon trawler from Fisherman's Wharf in San Francisco. It was a classic fishing boat featuring a two-cylinder diesel engine that allowed a top speed of about three knots. Named the *San Giuseppe*, it had hydraulic winching capabilities and would be used for a number of years until railroad iron and concrete weights, used as anchors in experiments, pulled the planks of the stern apart. Richards ran experiments, collecting a suite of physical, chemical, and biological measurements out on the lake every ten days at an "Index Station." The station, about a quarter mile off Homewood, California, was selected as representative of the entire lake based on synoptic comparisons.

To determine the amount of near-shore influence, sampling profiles were also collected on average of every thirty days at a midlake station, in Tahoe's deepest waters. After a number of years, the scientists stopped collecting midlake data, as the differences were insubstantial. The information from the stations was used as background data for other experiments and was gathered year-round. Onshore, Richards and Goldman utilized working spaces in garages and borrowed buildings.

By 1974 Goldman reported that the lake had lost 25 percent of its clarity over the fourteen years of his studies. Aerial photographs revealed spectacular increases in murky deposits of sediment coming from damaged watersheds.

In 1975 Goldman secured a laboratory: the state Fish and Game Department's old North Shore Fish Hatchery. Built in 1920, just east of Tahoe City, the large, drafty building was in disrepair, lacking insulation and featuring scissor beams supporting a high, leaky roof. The building was known mostly for the fact that John Steinbeck lived and worked at the hatchery one summer while he worked on his first novel. Goldman furnished the space with desks, cabinets, and other furniture from condemned buildings on the Davis campus. Goldman's studies attracted other faculty, doctoral associates, and students; then members of other California universities came to run experiments on the lake and evaluate their data in the unheated building.

Goldman used the National Science Foundation as a primary funding source for his Tahoe projects. An NSF grant of eighty-six thousand dollars in 1976 was intended for construction of a new field station and laboratory. Although the McClatchy family, who owned the *Sacramento Bee* and other newspapers, offered to donate land for the lab, the proposal was vetoed by the TRPA Board, whose local members were never pleased with the publicity generated by Goldman's findings. Ironically, the board cited environmental restrictions for rejecting the project.

With money allocated, but unable to build, Goldman returned to Washington, DC, and successfully pleaded with the NSF to allow him to redirect the funds to the acquisition of a custom boat. Richards searched the West Coast, finding a small company in Oregon building fishing trawlers that could build a workboat and incorporate the needed limnological research features. The *John LeConte* then replaced the *San Giuseppe*.

The new vessel was thirty-seven feet long, with an aluminum hull and an oversize cabin to house research electronics. It had extra bench space for filtrations and water-sample processing and was powered by a 180-horsepower diesel engine. The boat featured depth sounders, a global positioning system (GPS), computers, and twenty-mile-range radar. The aft workspace had hinged doors to provide access to the water. Three winches held three-thousand-foot wire rope to reach the lake bottom. At times, if there was little wind and Richards was careful, three different experiments might be conducted off the *John LeConte* concurrently: for example, running profiles for chemistry or temperature and light off one side, collecting zooplankton for a biology experiment from the other, and taking a bottom core sample off the stern.

With the old hatchery as a workspace and the new lake craft, studies of Tahoe water's physics, chemistry, and biology accelerated. Along with Goldman's research and the collection of invaluable long-term data sets on clarity and algal growth rates, scientists from around the world visited to run experiments. Richards had to invent the physical procedures for many of the sample-collection processes. For experiments that were left underwater for long periods, from six months to a year, Richards set subsurface buoys ten feet down so they would not be a navigation hazard. Without GPS, they had to be relocated utilizing land sights or sextant angles. There were times when Richards returned to where the experiments had been set to find them gone. Inevitably, winds had pushed the samples, floats, and anchors toward midlake, and he had to retrieve them. Finding them was especially difficult if waves or snow were causing poor visibility. After several incidents of chasing experiments across the lake, he came up with a solution, using a radar reflector on the buoys when they were set out.[13]

In 1973 and 1974, TRPA itself had been awarded two NSF grants, totaling $74,300, for research coordination. Doug Leisz acted as chairman, and a board, a coordination staff, and an eight-person science advisory panel, including Goldman, developed research needs in the areas of air, water, land and vegetation, fish and wildlife, social sciences, and resource systems. The research findings emphasized the basin's significant problems owing to the intense interaction of people with the natural environment. Among other findings, the final report suggested the need for the provision introduced in the EPA's "Lake Tahoe Study," defining the basin's human carrying capacity to establish thresholds for environmental factors.[14]

The scientists' recommendations conflicted with pressure to continue economic growth, stemming from gambling, real estate, and recreation. This emphasized the fact that the State of California, as represented by the restructured CTRPA, tended to back the scientists, while local governments and the State of Nevada generally supported the economic interests.

An exception was Nevada governor Mike O'Callaghan, who throughout the 1970s advocated for the protection and preservation of the lake's environment. In his "Message to the Legislature" in 1975, he noted "certain deficiencies" in the TRPA Compact that needed to be corrected or supplemented and requested that the lawmakers work with California to initiate necessary changes. Nevada's director of conservation and natural resources, Elmo J. DeRicco, who was the state's representative on the TRPA Governing Board, lobbied the legislators, pointing out that the state had invested more than $11 million in the past decade to preserve Tahoe's environment and the federal government had invested $86 million. He argued that, with the counties as a majority on the board, minority interests controlled each vote.[15] O'Callaghan's and DeRicco's arguments fell on deaf ears.

The Nevada Legislature, the third smallest of all the states, with sixty-three members, is one of the handful that meet only every two years. When it convened in 1977, the governor again addressed the issue, pointing out the irony that neither state could act alone, but that either was capable of the lake's destruction. "We are dealing with a priceless natural resource and we cannot hesitate," he said. "I urge this legislature to take bold, decisive action." Although revision was taken up, once again the legislators failed to act.[16]

The primary concern of Nevada lawmakers was that they would lose sole authority over their gaming industry. Under the TRPA agreement, casinos were exempt from agency control, and the state was able to veto any regulation that might affect them. Gambling was the lifeblood of Nevada's economy, the keystone in its budgetary planning. Without a personal income tax or corporate income tax, throughout the 1970s gambling taxes constituted nearly 50 percent of yearly general revenue. After Las Vegas and Reno-Sparks, South Lake Tahoe had the greatest gross gaming revenues in the state, generating more than $110 million in 1974.[17]

In 1966 Paul Laxalt had won the governorship in part by portraying himself as able to legitimize the gambling industry, which had long been associated with Mob interests. Taking the lead from William Harrah and Baron and Conrad Hilton, the new governor encouraged passage of the Corporate Gaming Act of 1969, allowing corporations to own casinos. The previous governor, Grant Sawyer, had fought against such a measure because it might be too easy for undesirables to hold interest in public companies' stock. Although the 1969 act did in fact create difficulties in finding the corporations' hidden interests, the gaming industry's public image improved as the Hiltons, MGM, Hyatt, and Holiday Inn entered the field. By 1980 publicly owned operations generated 50 percent of Nevada's gross gambling revenue, and soon thereafter all the major casinos at Tahoe were owned by corporations.[18]

In the late 1970s, Nevada university economists Thomas Cargill and William Eadington compiled time-varying characteristics of quarterly gaming revenues from 1960 to the mid-1970s, showing that neither the industry's capacity nor market saturation in Nevada was being approached. From 1960 to 1967, gross gaming revenues grew at Tahoe by 120 percent and from 1967 to 1974 by 100 percent. The professors noted that even more substantial increases in revenues would have been realized at the lake if legal maneuvers by environmentalists and TRPA actions had not slowed its expansion of tourist and casino facilities.[19]

Between 1970 and 1978, the number of basin residents grew from 33,600 to 73,200, and visitation grew from 11.2 million to 20.8 million visitor days. Gaming accounted for 43 percent of the total and 48 percent of the increase. By comparison, outdoor recreation accounted for 26 percent of the total and only 3 percent of the increase. By 1978 gaming, which is a year-round, seven-days-a-week, twenty-four-hours-a-day attraction, directly constituted 33 percent of all employment. When jobs created in secondary industries, such as retail, schools, and health services to support casino employees, were included, gaming accounted for 67 percent of basin jobs.

Employment created demand for housing, transportation systems, water and sewage, police and fire protection, and other infrastructure. Whereas the casino expansion had taken place in Nevada, the major housing and support network had been built in California. Between 1970 and 1978, an average of 1,970 new housing units were built per year. Consequently, the land-capability system had been met with widespread noncompliance, and urban land use increased by 78 percent, to 28,300 acres. Vegetation was removed entirely from some 9,000 acres. Some 4,000 acres of land classified as "high hazard" for erosion had been covered with impervious material or had its vegetation removed. Urban development had taken place on more than 3,000 acres of meadows, marshes, and land surrounding streams, with another 6,000 acres of stream environments similarly zoned. By the end of the century, 50 percent of the basin's meadows and fully 75 percent of its marshland would be destroyed.[20]

Actions mitigated on an individual-case basis had led to the environmental losses, and there seemed no possibility of a holistic solution. Instead, bitter differences played out in the court of public opinion. When the loop road, proposed to ease traffic at the state line on South Shore, was tied up in the courts, a casino spokesman used the *Sacramento Bee* to accuse CTRPA and other agencies of refusing to work to solve the Tahoe Basin's problems. Jim Burns, assistant to California's resources secretary, countered in the same paper that the casino spokesman represented the very ones causing the degradation. "The casinos are slowly destroying the very things that people go to Tahoe for."[21]

A side issue besmirched TRPA in 1976 when it was discovered that executive director Heikka had taken a free fishing trip to Harrah's Middle Fork Lodge in Idaho in June 1973. Although Heikka insisted that "there was absolutely no connection" between his being hosted at the upscale lodge and agency action on casino expansion projects, the mini scandal further damaged confidence in the board as it was composed.[22]

The stalemate between the states led California's new secretary of resources, Huey Johnson, to call for federal intervention. He began promoting the establishment of a National Recreation Area (NRA) in the Tahoe Basin. Such a designation would place management under the secretary of agriculture and would, at least temporarily, invalidate locally or state-issued permits, licenses, and variances. The Forest Service would administer such a program. Neither LTBMU supervisor William "Bill" Morgan, who had begun a ten-year stint as the lake's forest supervisor in 1975, nor regional forester Leisz felt the Forest Service was equipped to manage the basin's private lands. Morgan, referring to the agency's long-standing support of TRPA, said, "We believe that it represents the best solution to control activities on private lands from a regional standpoint."

Realizing what a large impediment to cooperation between the states the TRPA-approved casino projects were and what damage they would incur, at a press conference in 1977 Morgan suggested that perhaps some entity should step forward to buy the yet-to-be-built-upon sites. Over time the idea gained traction. During the same period, arguments between California and Nevada over their partnership intensified.[23]

Glenbrook Bay, the hub of logging operations for the Carson Tahoe Lumber and Fluming Company on Lake Tahoe's East Shore in 1876. Note the sawmills operating on the shore. (Courtesy Special Collections, University of Nevada, Reno, Library)

A similar view of Glenbrook some years later. (Courtesy Special Collections, University of Nevada, Reno, Library)

A nineteenth-century steamer pulling a boom of logs to the shoreline sawmills. (Courtesy Special Collections, University of Nevada, Reno, Library)

After Americans appropriated the land, in order to continue a semblance of their traditional way of life at Lake Tahoe, Washoe Indians had to adapt. Washoe Billy Merrill, in the middle, acted as a fishing guide in the early twentieth century. (Courtesy Special Collections, University of Nevada, Reno, Library)

A log chute on the Truckee River in 1886. (Courtesy Special Collections, University of Nevada, Reno, Library)

Throughout the twentieth century, businesses and government entities fought over the dam at Lake Tahoe's only outlet at the Truckee River. (Courtesy Special Collections, University of Nevada, Reno, Library)

The Tallac Marsh, the natural filter for the lake's largest tributary, the Upper Truckee River, before it was dredged to create fingers of land for the large Tahoe Keys subdivision. (Courtesy Special Collections, University of Nevada, Reno, Library)

Incline Creek, one of two important Incline Village tributaries, carrying silt into the lake when the area was being developed in the late 1960s. (Courtesy Special Collections, University of Nevada, Reno, Library)

Road construction above Ward Creek in 1967. The silt from the project would be carried in the stream at the bottom left of the photo to the lake. (Courtesy Special Collections, University of Nevada, Reno, Library)

In 1969 Bob Richards uses a nine-meter Van Dorn water sampler to collect lake water. When a "cast" is made to the correct depth, the sampler's rubber end covers snap closed, collecting the water to be studied. (Courtesy Bob Richards)

A February 19, 1971, newspaper photo of Robert Twiss explaining the use of map overlays to develop Tahoe's land-capability system. (Courtesy *Tahoe Daily Tribune*)

A gully at Heavenly Valley Ski Resort, circa the 1970s, caused by erosion after the removal of vegetation. (Courtesy Bill Johnson)

The results of a Forest Service revegetation project at Heavenly Valley.
(Courtesy Bill Johnson)

Top: Cement foundations built at the Jennings casino site when it was acquired by the US Forest Service. A stream that had meandered through the property had been rerouted to run down the street to the lake. (Courtesy Bill Johnson)
Bottom: A work crew planting vegetation on the former casino site.
(Courtesy Bill Johnson)

The casino site after Forest Service restoration. (Courtesy Bill Johnson)

The new research vessel, the *John LeConte,* alongside the about-to-be-retired *San Giuseppe* in 1976. Note the improvement in deck gear from old to new. (Courtesy Bob Richards)

Two key players in battles over TRPA in the 1970s and 1980s: California state senator John Garamendi and the League to Save Lake Tahoe's Jim Bruner. (Courtesy League to Save Lake Tahoe)

CTC executive director Dennis Machida and League to Save Lake Tahoe executive director Rochelle Nason conferring at a panel discussion regarding environmental restoration at the lake. (Courtesy League to Save Lake Tahoe)

US Forest Service hydrologist Bill Johnson, in the parka standing to the right, explaining the installation of a fish ladder in Blackwood Canyon to government agency representatives. (Courtesy Bill Johnson)

Oily sludge coming from a drainage pipe that runs from the highway to the lake in the middle of South Lake Tahoe. (Courtesy League to Save Lake Tahoe)

A Russian researcher joins Professor Charles Goldman, in the middle, and Bob Richards, in the foreground, to do light readings on the lake in 1993. (Courtesy Bob Richards)

Senator Harry Reid (*right*), one of the organizers of the original Lake Tahoe Presidential Summit, with "the father of Lake Tahoe ecology," Dr. Charles Goldman, at one of the annual Tahoe gatherings. (Courtesy League to Save Lake Tahoe)

The importance of gambling to Nevada cannot be gainsaid. Its interests dominated the 1970s TRPA. The weak bistate partnership allowed the state to maintain control over gaming decisions. Still, Nevada's perception of the Tahoe casino issue was evolving, with owners at the lake seeing the benefits of reducing competition by curbing new casinos.

The federal government approved the idea as well. Although a deal would not be consummated for another year and a half, in September 1978 US House-Senate conferees set the stage for an eventual deal by approving $12.5 million in federal funds for casino land acquisition.

That same month, negotiators finished secret bargaining addressing differences between California and Nevada. A federal official, Charles Warren, the chair of President Carter's Council on Environmental Quality, had spent six months leading talks on the issues. From 1963 to 1977, Warren had been a member of the California Assembly, where he was one of the principal authors of the California Coastal Protection Act. TRPA federal government representative Leisz knew the assemblyman and had convinced him to mediate between the two states.[1]

The main points of contention were strengthening the TRPA Compact and limiting casinos at the lake. California wanted a red line around the establishments already there, and Nevada did not want to bargain away the state's gaming options.[2]

The final document, negotiated mostly in secret, arrested casino building in the basin and incorporated a long list of measures to strengthen the compact: changing the board's makeup to shift power from local entities to the states, doing away with the "dual majority," and including utilization of the threshold approach, establishing standards to regulate land use. The agreement was endorsed by both governors, but needed the approval of the two state legislatures.[3]

The *San Francisco Chronicle*'s Charles McCabe, a curmudgeonly essayist

whose daily column had run since the mid-1950s, filled his space with a pes-
simistic evaluation of the chances for the proposal's ratification. Calling Tahoe
"one of this country's greatest natural treasures," he wrote that without immediate federal intervention, "the rape of the lake" would be impossible to undo.
McCabe said the compromise was doomed to fail because gaming ran Nevada
politics, and "these chaps are unlikely to relinquish any one inch of the power
they possess over their own industry."[4]

A survey conducted by a San Francisco firm in 1978 found that 83 percent of
Nevadans wanted environmental controls at the lake strengthened. Although
nearly all respondents felt tourism and casino gaming were extremely important to the state, only 7 percent thought there should be more casinos at Tahoe.
But as the Nevada Legislature prepared to gather for their 1979 session, members began speaking out against the negotiated proposal.[5]

Las Vegas Democratic state senator Joe Neal, chair of the Natural Resources
Committee, was seen by many as a maverick in the legislature. He was a proponent of protecting the lake and said that, despite the public's view, legislation tightening environmental controls would be difficult to pass. He alluded
to intense lobbying by the casino interests and described an organized effort to
kill the Warren compromise, saying, "I've found the Legislature doesn't always
do what the people want."[6]

For their part, the casino representatives said they simply could not accept
California tampering with their industry. One of their representatives made a
statement reflecting the degree of threat the gaming operators felt. Although
no one was proposing eliminating established casinos, he said, "We're never
going to leave this lake. Gaming is here, it is going to be here, and we're going
to stay here."[7]

On the eve of the legislative session, Democrat Joe Dini, a Yerington,
Nevada, casino owner who would serve as Speaker of the assembly longer than
anyone in Nevada history, said the proposal would have to be amended, or "it
wouldn't see the light of day."[8]

Although sanctioned by Nevada's outgoing governor, Mike O'Callaghan,
Robert List, who took office on January 1, 1979, flatly rejected the compromise.
While saying there was a "moral mandate to protect and preserve the lake," List
said he also wanted to protect the rights of property owners.

List's political career was continually entangled with Nevada's casino interests. While serving as Nevada attorney general, he had returned a three-thousand-dollar donation from the Las Vegas Stardust hotel-casino after denying that the money had influenced his findings in a state probe of the club. Russell Elliott, in his *History of Nevada,* reported that List's actions "suggested the governor's office politicized the Gaming Control Board and the Gaming Commission." Elliot attributed List's loss in his bid for a second term to the public perceiving as much. When List replaced two TRPA Board members, a conservationist observed, "The mix of appointees in Nevada is clearly not on the side of reversing Tahoe's degradation."[9]

In December 1978, as the Warren compromise was being considered, TRPA approved two immense casino parking garages. California representatives protested that the projects encouraged car use, and the agency had a policy in place withholding consideration of traffic-generating projects until an air-quality plan was completed in January.

The first project, enabling Harrah's to construct a 3,572-car structure, passed under dubious circumstances. During one and a half days of discussion, although projecting that on peak days the garage might cause 1,012 new vehicle trips, Harrah's consultants presented a Nevada Highway Department statement that overall the garage would generate no new vehicle trips. Environmentalists, CTRPA, the California attorney general, the Department of Transportation, and the Air Resources Board all challenged Harrah's figures, saying the facility would dramatically worsen traffic-congestion air pollution.

When it came time for the board to consider the plan, local California representatives voted to exempt the project from the interim air-quality delay so it could be discussed. After a Nevada member huddled with the Harrah's attorney, a majority of the Nevadans unexpectedly voted not to exempt the project. This failure to reach bistate agreement invoked the dual-majority rule, allowing default approval without discussion.[10]

Three weeks later, the board approved Sahara hotel-casino's six-story, 2,100-car parking garage, seven to three. That project had been exempted from the interim air-quality policy when first proposed eight months earlier. In the interim, the plan changed, adding some 750 vehicle spaces. TRPA staff recommended denial, and counsel advised that approval was procedurally and substantively illegal. He suggested the project be denied without prejudice and reconsidered with changes the following month. Instead, after seven hours of opposing testimony by California and federal agencies, the board reduced the project by 350 spaces and gave its approval. California filed suit in federal court to block the construction.[11]

California state senator John Garamendi had introduced the Warren proposal in the California Legislature, calling it "a very delicate agreement." Garamendi, a rancher from the Central Valley, began a long career in government service in 1974. His jobs included stints as state assemblyman, two terms as state insurance commissioner, fourteen years as a state senator, deputy secretary of the interior under President Clinton, and, beginning in 2009, US representative—a post he holds at this writing. The California Legislature was amenable to the plan. But when Nevada balked, Garamendi said he was willing to reopen negotiations. This was despite California secretary of resources Huey Johnson's declaration that the reformed compact proposal was a bottom line.

Garamendi, Nevada's lead negotiator, Assemblyman Thomas "Spike" Wilson, Dini, and a few others from each state met several times to discuss possible amendments. Included in the Nevada delegation was the procompromise Senator Neal, whom "some people with influence," presumably gaming lobbyists, tried to exclude. Neal had walked out of a Nevada legislators' session several weeks before when "it became apparent the panel was following every recommendation contained in a casino industry analysis" of the proposed compact bill. Twenty-five to thirty issues divided the two sides, with the makeup of the TRPA Board and the dual-majority rule the primary stumbling blocks.[12]

As the deadlock remained unbroken, the current TRPA chair, Jim Henry, the prodevelopment representative from Placer County, commented that the agency was like Disneyland's Haunted House, comparing the media to the Mickey Mouse Club and the League to Save Lake Tahoe to pirates. The TRPA staff, he said, was in Fantasyland. On the opposite side of the issue, an assistant to California resources secretary Johnson called TRPA's performance "appalling" and said that "it would be foolish for California to support the bi-state compact."[13]

For their part, Nevada legislators, declaring the Warren agreement incompatible with the Nevada Constitution, introduced a bill to withdraw the state from TRPA. Mediator Warren now predicted that "the entire effort to preserve Lake Tahoe will be disbanded, and either the lake will be overwhelmed by gambling and development interests, or the federal government will intrude and establish the area as a National Recreation Area."[14]

In the spring of 1979, Nevada officials, looking past the withdrawal proposal, began deliberations to alter the Warren plan. In all likelihood, their change in direction had to do with Warren's threat of the establishment of an NRA. The idea of nationalizing the basin had been broached periodically since 1969, and just weeks earlier California senator Alan Cranston and California representative Vic Fazio had reintroduced the idea. Cranston and Fazio were powerful national politicians: Cranston was the Democratic whip who had served ten years in the Senate; Fazio was recently elected but would serve nine terms in succeeding Congresses as a strong voice for environmental causes. If an NRA was formed, decision making would shift from the states to the federal government, which would limit building and certainly stop further development of casinos. Such an action was even more threatening to Nevada's gaming interests than California's interference.

As the Nevada Legislature considered revisions in the Warren proposal, representatives of the two states continued to negotiate. Finally, on May 22, after two hours of discordant discussions, Garamendi and California's negotiators walked out. Garamendi declared that the state was going to secede from TRPA and indeed pursue the creation of the NRA. He said the talks collapsed because Nevada casino attorneys "hovered around the negotiating table as vultures might around a carcass." Three days later, Nevada governor List went to Sacramento and secretly met with California governor Jerry Brown, reopening communications on the states' options.[15]

In Carson City, with its legislative session days from ending, on May 29 the Nevada Legislature produced its "best response" to the months of negotiations over Warren's plan. The proposal had been composed by an ad hoc committee during four nights of meetings in an otherwise deserted legislative building. It allowed a limited moratorium on building until environmental thresholds could be developed and adopted. It also prohibited construction of new gaming establishments, but it grandfathered in the building of the Park Tahoe and the other two default-approved casinos. Further, it watered down the changes to the TRPA Board, ensuring the continuation of local control, and placed limits on TRPA's enforcement powers: making parties suing over regulations post a bond equal to the damages a delay might cause the developer. California's Garamendi later pointed out that that amendment would force government agencies to post a bond to enforce their own laws.[16]

The bill exempted various subdivisions from new restrictions that Californians speculated could lead to as many as seventy-five hundred new housing units. The bill also directed that the controversial loop road be completed and CTRPA be incorporated into TRPA. All of the actions, including remarks to be used in support of the provisions, issued from an anonymous "analysis." The *Sacramento Bee* learned that the document had been authored by Gordon DePaoli, the Park Tahoe hotel-casino attorney. DePaoli said his involvement was no secret. "It was never intended that it not be revealed," he said.[17]

Governor List signed the Nevada measure. He told reporters that casino operators' influence had "never been a bad one, to my knowledge in state government," that he would oppose any effort to create a federal recreation area at Tahoe, and that the new law "serves notice on the State of California . . . that we in Nevada are not shirking our duty." Jim Bruner, of the League to Save Lake Tahoe, expressed the widely held view that the Nevada Legislature had "just let the gaming industry write its own bill."[18]

While plans to revise the TRPA pact were being contemplated and argued, California had been enforcing higher regulatory standards than TRPA through CTRPA. Decisions by the California agency were frequently the result of four-to-three votes, with local representatives in the minority. The narrow margin of their majority did not dissuade the environmental faction in their pursuance of strict regulations. The agency devised a land-use ordinance that prohibited approval of any new subdivision until 85 percent of existing lots were built upon and called for the purchase of all existing undeveloped lots in land deemed environmentally sensitive. CTRPA required a review of developments of an acre or more, and it would not approve building where a significant environmental impact would occur. Although its actions had triggered panic building beginning in 1976 when residential construction doubled from the annual rate of about six hundred units to twelve hundred, the agency remained undeterred.

To combat low air quality, CTRPA required developments that would attract additional vehicles to Tahoe Basin, such as new highways, parking lots, or shopping centers, to offset anticipated pollution levels by constructing bike-trail connections, bus-turnout areas, or other mitigation projects.

In transportation the CTRPA rejected TRPA's bistate approach. Specifically, it opposed the loop-road system around the South Shore casinos. Nevada and South Lake Tahoe City officials insisted the system would reduce Stateline traffic congestion, but CTRPA, believing it would merely stimulate more vehicular use, fought the proposal in the courts.[19]

In a major defeat for California and environmental groups, in February 1979 the TRPA-approved hotel-casino projects on the South Shore, Harvey's expansion and the Park Tahoe construction, were found to be legal by the Ninth Circuit Court of Appeals. The other two proposed casino projects remained in limbo.[20]

In March 1979, at the South Shore in California, because of sewage limitations and building restrictions, officials held a lottery to allocate permits for single-family dwellings. The drawing, conducted by a blindfolded parish priest to ensure fairness, gave 250 lot owners the right to build during that construction season. More than 5,000 property owners had paid a nonrefundable twenty-dollar fee to participate in what was comparable to a high-stakes game at the nearby casinos. Lots that were selected realized an immediate increase in value of ten to fifteen thousand dollars.[21]

On May 4, an already angry crowd of 350 persons in Tahoe City disrupted a meeting of the CTRPA Board after a public hearing session was postponed. The local crowd of builders, real estate agents, and lot owners had organized to protest rumored further land restrictions. Boos and insults drowned out Gordon Hooper, the North Shore real estate agent who, as chair of the agency, lived with threats of physical violence and the loss of business. He was attempting to explain that California state senator Garamendi requested the delay of public input because of "delicate circumstances" in negotiations with Nevada. As armed sheriff deputies watched, the three local government board representatives urged on the crowd.

South Tahoe city councilman Terry Trupp said the right of the people to speak superseded the "arrogance and ego of Senator Garamendi." A builder yelled that the agency board was picking his pocket. "It's called stealing," he shouted. Finally, Placer County's CTRPA representative, Jim Henry, announced he would not participate in "tyrannical government" and, with Trupp and the other local government board member, walked out. The cheering crowd sang a chorus of "America the Beautiful," and a large group of them joined the local officials across the street.

Trupp said he was "darn tired of transient politicians determining the lake's future." Supervisor Henry told the crowd to "fight for their lives against CTRPA" and urged them to picket Hooper's nearby real estate office. Placer County sheriff Don Nunes played to the unruly crowd, saying that even though the jail was overcrowded, "it has been suggested I save one cell for Mr. Hooper." He won more cheers by announcing that the $350 in police protection for the meeting would be charged to CTRPA.[22]

In mid-May the City of South Lake Tahoe abandoned CTRPA. Citing the agency's air-pollution ordinance, the city withdrew its representative from the CTRPA Board and declared it would no longer enforce the agency's ordinances. At the end of the month, city councilman Trupp led sixty-five Tahoe businessmen to the county seats in El Dorado's Placerville and Placer County's Auburn, urging support for the CTRPA boycott. Some grievances, including that private enterprise was hampered by the agency's regulations, were real; others were imagined, such as the claim that the agency was considering weekend closures of casinos. Within two weeks, the counties joined the city in withdrawing from the agency. CTRPA continued to do business with a board composed of only the four state-appointed members.[23]

Bob Pershing, a mason from South Lake Tahoe, was one of the speakers who had accompanied Trupp to the county seats. Trupp later termed Pershing "a symbol of guts." To environmental protectionists, he represented those with a mindless disregard for ecosystem damage. At the time, Pershing was engaged in a personal war with CTRPA. He had moved from Southern California in the mid-1970s and took it upon himself to confront CTRPA by making no effort to secure permits before building a house.

Pershing bought a lot on the Upper Truckee River near South Lake Tahoe. Supported by South Tahoe contractors, who came out on successive weekends to help with construction, and several businesses that donated building materials, Pershing built a forty-two-hundred-square-foot, five-bedroom house on the lot. Saying, "No one has a right to dictate to a man what he can put on his property," Pershing built a deck out into the stream environment zone behind the house and brought in some twenty pickup loads of dirt fill so he could landscape the area with turf. Calling CTRPA "a Gestapo-type agency," Pershing returned building-violation notices smeared with his excrement.

While building the house, and over the course of several years, he petitioned El Dorado County, requesting that they issue him a building permit without forcing him to go through CTRPA. The best the supervisors offered was the issuance of a county permit with the statement: "This permit does not authorize permittee to violate the rules and regulations of any other governmental body."

Years later, after his death at age sixty in 1990, his widow said, "Telling him not to do something on his property was where the problem started." In the end, Pershing served two jail sentences for his civil disobedience. Regarding the antiregulatory movement, his widow said that Pershing and the others thought they could run CTRPA out of town. "But Bob was the only one," she added. "When he went to jail, he went alone."[24]

For twenty years, the house remained livable but unfinished, without siding on the outside or paneling inside and with a temporary, minimal electrical connection. In 1997 Mrs. Pershing, in failing health, finally reached agreement with TRPA, which had never pursued removing the building. The resolution allowed her to connect to utilities and sell the house so she could move to a more healthful climate. A provision of the settlement was that structures in the backyard and river riprapping they had put in be removed, restoring the natural floodplain.[25]

A few years after Pershing's incarcerations, his enthusiastic supporter and property-rights leader Trupp served his own jail time. After riding the wave of antiregulatory sentiment to be elected mayor of South Lake Tahoe in the mid-1980s, he was caught in one of Tahoe's most infamous incidents. A sting operation by the Federal Bureau of Investigation broke up a major cocaine ring with the arrest of nineteen individuals. Trupp had attempted to launder $650,000 in purported cocaine revenues supplied him by undercover agents. After a year of loudly proclaiming his innocence, he pleaded guilty in 1990 and was sentenced to nine years in prison.[26]

Throughout the summer of 1979, California courts repudiated the local governments' positions regarding CTRPA. On June 19, 1979, the superior court enjoined Placer County from issuing building permits without the approval of CTRPA. In August the California Third District Court of Appeals ordered El Dorado County to prevent the release of building permits without a CTRPA review. The appeals court also invalidated any permits previously released without CTRPA approval.

Additional pressure was brought to bear on the local governments when it was revealed that although they had refused to submit private projects for CTRPA approval, they had protected themselves by continuing to present public works for CTRPA review. By early 1980, all three local governments ended their boycotts, returning their representatives to the CTRPA Board.[27]

While California had established their version of overarching governance at Tahoe, Nevada was taking on a new fight with the federal government. Its representatives were leading the "Sagebrush Rebellion."

On June 4, 1979, Nevada governor Robert List signed a bill declaring state sovereignty over almost fifty million acres of federal land. Years of ranchers' and mining companies' complaints over Bureau of Land Management (BLM) red tape and environmental restrictions came to a head with the federal government's 1976 Congressional Organic Act. The act declared that the federal lands would be held in the public domain in perpetuity. Nevada legislators, led by representatives from ranching districts, drafted the "Sagebrush" Bill, hoping to induce other western states to join the rebellion.

Sagebrush rebels pointed out that the federal government had taken control of hundreds of millions of acres of land as conditions of statehood for the twelve western states, controlling 52.6 percent of their land. Because similar requirements had not been imposed on the other states, where the federal government controlled only 4.3 percent of the land, Nevada argued that the constitutional requirement that all states enter the Union "on an equal footing" had been violated.[1]

Although Nevada provided their attorney general a $250,000 war chest to pursue a lawsuit against the US Interior Department, List stipulated that all existing uses, licenses, and leases were still to be recognized. The state's constitutional arguments were not taken seriously by the Interior Department. Its top lawyer said it was a congressional issue, but that if it did get to the courts, he "wouldn't give a plugged nickel" for Nevada's chances.[2]

Environmental groups and sportsmen later claimed the real motive behind the action was a land grab by ranchers and real estate agents. Still, other western states followed Nevada's lead, joining the "rebellion." In Alaska, where a lawsuit similar to Nevada's had been filed, a National Park Service airplane was set afire. Legislatures in Washington, Wyoming, Utah, Arizona, and New Mexico also passed similar laws, claiming millions of acres. The rebellion was a concept even California's resources director, Huey Johnson, could agree with.

"We've been robbed blind for 100 years by mismanagement of federal lands," Johnson commented.[3]

One of the rebellion's champions was Ronald Reagan. Nevada's senator Paul Laxalt, leading Reagan's second campaign for the presidency, provided access to the candidate for Sagebrush leaders. The senator affixed a "Sagebrush Rebellion" bumper sticker to his office door in Washington and, as the 1980 election neared, promised a push to give western states control of seven hundred million acres of federal land. In an August 1980 campaign speech, Reagan declared, "Count me in as a rebel."[4]

After Reagan was elected, his actions, and those of the now Republican-led US Senate, actually helped quell the rebellion. In adherence to his philosophy, Reagan refused to approve new wilderness designations, and his administration began a program to privatize thirty-five million acres of federal land. But in time, Reagan also let it be known he had no intention of giving up control of the rest of those seven hundred million acres. Led in the House by Nevada's James Santini, Congress passed the Western Lands Act, by which federal lands could be conveyed to the states. But suspicions arose over whether the transfer would merely allow profiteers to gain from the conversion of public lands.

Privatization was soon opposed by the traditional rebels, cattlemen, and mine owners, as well as environmentalists. Even Representative Santini changed his mind, commenting, "I will not stand idly by and see Nevada or the West put on the auction block." On the other hand, if the states gained control, how could they finance their management? Once conveyance was at hand, it no longer seemed to be the rebellion's goal.

James G. Watt, Reagan's secretary of the interior, previously affiliated with the Mountain States Legal Foundation, which provides legal representation to fight constraints on public lands, led the administration's early attacks on environmental protections. Watt endorsed dismantling regulations in areas where surface mining and use of off-road vehicles might be pursued. He also promoted mining, coal and oil, logging, and other commercial interests' exploitation of federal lands. Although slowing the environmental movement's momentum, Watt's plans of action were never fully implemented. He had a combative nature and a penchant for insulting remarks, and in a speech to the US Chamber of Commerce he made a statement demeaning minorities, women, and the disabled. In a short time, the comment, publicized across the country, led to his resignation from the cabinet. His departure further weakened the Sagebrush Rebellion movement.

By Reagan's second term, List would be defeated as Nevada's governor by Democrat Richard Bryan. Bryan, although serving as the Nevada attorney general and filing the Sagebrush lawsuit, was a moderate who would not pursue the issue as governor. Eventually, Senator Laxalt also let the issue drop, as he was busy advocating cuts in domestic spending and serving as the general chairman of the Republican Party. Other states' fervor over the Sagebrush Rebellion would be tempered, and, for a number of years, the movement lost its impetus.[5]

Although resources director Huey Johnson condemned the federal government's control of other California lands, he and Governor Jerry Brown began planning to withdraw from the bistate TRPA in order to induce federal intervention at the lake. By October 1979, Brown was allotting funds to CTRPA that might have been used for TRPA. Charging that "extremist environmentalists" were bleeding TRPA to death, combative agency chair Jim Henry advocated scrapping the bistate enterprise once and for all. "When you have an animal that's wounded," he said, "you do it the favor of destroying it."[6]

Early in his term, List had rejected the Charles Warren–brokered agreement reached by his predecessor, Governor O'Callaghan. He now called Brown's refusal to accept the Nevada proposal for amending TRPA "obstinate, arbitrary, emotional, and damned unfortunate."[7]

California's Johnson cast blame on Nevada, saying its special interests had stymied efforts to allow the agency to halt environmental damage at the lake. Mediator Warren was more direct. He said that once the negotiated package went to the legislature, "we began to feel the deadening and clammy hand of the gambling industry in Nevada."[8]

While relations between the states deteriorated, Charles Goldman used a new means of pursuing scientific research, supported financially by the *San Jose (CA) Mercury News*. Its publisher, Tony Ridder, joined Goldman on five days of underwater explorations of the lake's depths. The project employed the *Pioneer I*, a seventeen-foot, three-person submersible unit that went down more than a thousand feet. The lake's remarkable clarity and powerful floodlights allowed the group to observe firsthand things previously studied only from the surface.[9]

The submarine used a mechanical arm to collect water samples as well as rock and large bundles of algae. As expected, severe erosion had caused sediment deposits to accumulate on steplike shelves off South Shore, while off Incline Village an "enormous blanket of sediment extended like a vast desert" down the Crystal Bay canyon. The explorers made another disturbing find as well: algae attached to rock at depths over five hundred feet.

The submarine, traversing the bottom at one thousand feet, triggered the rise of "billowing brown clouds," but its chief pilot said Tahoe's clear water was unlike anything he had ever seen. The submarine was usually used for inspecting underwater oil pipelines in the Gulf of Mexico, and the pilot, comparing those voyages to this one, commented that "there was very little of anything" to mar the lake's "beautiful blue color." Still, Goldman, mentioning nine-inch "mats of grass-like macro green algae," concluded that Tahoe needed to find less harmful methods of developing property on its shores.[10]

At the time of the *Pioneer I* explorations, the hostility of earlier TRPA discussions between the states had quieted. California state senator Garamendi and assemblyman Victor Calvo and Nevada state senator Dini and assemblyman Spike Wilson quietly resumed meeting about the TRPA Compact. Concurrently, federal legislators started becoming more directly involved. California's US representative Vic Fazio prepared a National Recreation Area bill, while Nevada's Santini began touting an alternative he called the "sagebrush strategy."

Originally suggested by the League to Save Lake Tahoe, the Santini proposal might ameliorate the Tahoe situation while addressing a problem of an arrested Las Vegas and Nevada tax base. The plan was to sell public Las Vegas land to private interests, hence its "sagebrush" label, and use the money to buy environmentally sensitive Tahoe lands.[11]

The idea that the Sagebrush Rebellion was continuing a tradition in Las Vegas or Nevada or the West in general of being fiercely self-reliant was a fiction. As early as 1934, historian Bernard DeVoto had commented that westerners' attitude toward government was "Get out and give us more money." In Las Vegas, although the casinos were privately financed, US taxpayers subsidized its infrastructure, from the dam that generated the city's power and water to its highways and airport and its nuclear test site and defense jobs.[12]

Santini enlisted support for his plan from California's Phillip Burton, chairman of the House National Parks Subcommittee. Burton, first elected in 1964, would serve eleven terms. He was a powerful legislator, known for steering a Redwood National Park expansion measure through Congress, authoring the bill that created the Golden Gate NRA , and creating legislation and funding for AIDS research. The Point Reyes National Seashore includes the Phillip Burton Wilderness.

The two congressmen disagreed about how to proceed with the Santini strategy. The Nevada congressman envisioned emphasizing the sagebrush concept, expanding it so that public lands could be sold throughout the West. Burton was strongly opposed to a sell-off of other federal lands, wanting Congress to consider only the limited Las Vegas venture. Another dispute developed because Burton feared that as private Tahoe land was purchased, development on the remaining parcels would intensify. He believed a bill without stringent land-use controls would be untenable. Santini balked at writing land-use controls into the bill. This brought the plan full circle, as the most logical scenario that would satisfy Burton would be for California and Nevada to strengthen TRPA.[13]

Early in 1980, scientists made an alarming announcement: some sixty-one thousand metric tons of sediment were entering the lake each year, compared to the natural level of about thirty-one hundred metric tons. The California Water Resources Control Board determined that "only a major reduction in erosion will stop the decline [of clarity]." State senator Garamendi went to work immediately to introduce a one-hundred-million-dollar bond act that, if approved by voters, would provide funds for purchase of sensitive lots.[14]

Although the bond act was reduced to eighty-five million dollars, voters rejected it in November 1980. At five public meetings in various Northern California locations, landowners, builders, and businessmen had assailed the proposed condemnation of parcels, labeling it "illegal" and "unconstitutional." At the meeting held at Tahoe City, most of the crowd of one hundred supported Larry Hoffman, a Tahoe Vista attorney representing the recently formed Tahoe-Sierra Preservation Council, which was supplanting the Council for

Logic. The new group, organized to oppose the Fazio NRA bill and the water board's plan, would eventually be composed of hundreds of lot owners and real estate and construction interests. Hoffman spoke for more than an hour, charging that the water board's plan had manipulated data and was written by people who "want to close Tahoe down."

At South Tahoe, the following day, the arguments were much the same. The audience accused the water board of, among other things, being environmental fanatics and promoting "un-Americanism," saying land-use controls were "similar to actions in Nazi Germany."[15]

In San Francisco, three weeks later, a similar public meeting ran seven hours long, not adjourning until two thirty in the morning. As with the other meetings, the preservation council led the opposition. They had rallied property owners with newspaper ads saying that California was plotting to take private property without compensation. At the meeting, the group's technical consultant challenged scientific findings. "To assume the lake is changing is a basic error," he argued. More algae plants were being seen, he said, because "[people] look for more algae."[16]

Had limnologist Goldman been at the meeting, he would have vigorously disagreed. At a symposium in Tahoe City three months later, he told a crowd of 250 that there had been "an explosion" of algae in the twenty years he had been studying the lake. Describing his submarine deep-water explorations and other experiments, he said, "Recent data indicated algae growth has increased 110% in the past two decades." Over the same time period, the remote control lake, Castle Lake, had no increase in algal growth.[17]

The Forest Service gave cause for optimism in the spring of 1980, purchasing the Jennings casino site. In early April, after several glitches that made it appear it would not occur, Congress again approved $12.5 million. Even then the sale appeared in jeopardy. The Forest Service had appraised the property at $13.5 million, and the Washington office wanted $1 million for its work in securing the money. The Forest Service's Bill Morgan was left with $11.5 million for the purchase. As a public official, he could not offer to buy the land for less than fair market value. At a meeting with Jennings's attorneys, Morgan explained the situation; they left the room to contact Jennings.

Interest rates were so high at that time that $11.5 million might earn some

$5,000 a day. That consideration may have secured the deal. The attorneys returned and offered to sell the land for $11.5 million and receive credit for donating the $2 million. Two years later, the State of Nevada and Douglas County bought the other pending casino site and turned it into a recreation complex.[18]

Morgan charged watershed staff officer Bill Johnson, a hydrologist from Colorado, with rehabilitating the Jennings site. Jennings had stripped and sold the topsoil from the eighteen-acre parcel and left forty concrete foundation casings sticking out of the ground. They were especially difficult to remove, as blowtorches, heavy equipment, and dynamite were all used with varying levels of success. Johnson began the three-year restoration project in the summer of 1980 by trying to determine where the area's stream had originally run. Jennings had diverted the stream into a cement ditch along the street so that all debris and silt from the disturbed land ran directly into the lake.

The Forest Service project included planting one thousand native trees and shrubs to help restore the soil. Within a year, Johnson's crew had built a pond to collect silt and rerouted the stream in a meandering pattern that attracted killdeer and American plovers to nesting grounds along its banks. The level of nitrogen and nutrients carried into the lake was 10 percent of previous amounts. But part of the property's past could not be restored. Based on scattered arrowheads, archaeologists presumed the site had archaeological significance that was destroyed when the casings were put in.[19]

In August 1980, talks to reform the TRPA Compact were far enough along that the governors were conferring. The new pact included many of the Warren proposal components: a revised board of seven members from each state, four state representatives and three from local jurisdictions; doing away with the dual-majority voting rule; and a ban on any new casino development at the South Shore unless already approved. It required the creation of threshold standards and included a thirty-month moratorium on subdivisions or other large-scale developments while the thresholds were prepared. Garamendi, calling it "the best and perhaps the last opportunity we have to protect the environment of the Lake Tahoe Basin," ushered the bill through the legislature, and in early September Governor Brown signed it.[20]

California's US representative Vic Fazio had been promoting the NRA at

Tahoe for well over a year. By the time he introduced a bill in January 1980, he had changed it, proposing a National Scenic Area. The difference was that an NSA would not simply be a stalemate to development, but allow the area to be managed to improve the basin for visitors—meaning cleaner air and water and more open space. When introduced the bill attracted some fifty cosponsors. The mayor of San Jose, California, Janet Gray Hayes, had been an active proponent of Tahoe's nationalization for a number of months, convincing the executive board of the US Conference of Mayors and the National League of Cities to endorse it. The *Los Angeles Times, Sacramento Bee, San Francisco Chronicle,* and *Las Vegas Valley Times,* run by former governor O'Callaghan, all supported the need for federal action, but by August it was clear that the representative himself was going still another direction.

Coming to realize that owing to the Nevada senators' opposition, passing an NSA bill would be an uphill battle, Fazio now preferred that his proposal serve as a catalyst. In a speech to the League to Save Lake Tahoe, he urged members to pressure US senators to support the Burton-Santini bill that could raise $150 million for Tahoe land acquisition. Allowing his legislation to serve as a threat of federal intervention, he said that he was keeping it "on the back burner."[21]

The Nevada Legislature was called into special session for the first time in twelve years to consider the new compromise compact. At a presession meeting, casino representative DePaoli declared that, although the group he represented could not endorse the compromises, with federal intervention as the alternative, they backed the bill. The organized property owners, who now would be compensated for unusable lots, also joined environmentalists and most local politicians in supporting it, and the measure passed overwhelmingly.

Fazio's legislation had been emphasized time and again in Nevada's deliberations as reason to accept the compromises and approve the new compact. Governor List said that although the legislators should not be intimidated, if they failed to strengthen the agency the federal government was likely to become involved. Representative Santini pointed out the number of prominent cosponsors Fazio's bill had attracted, and Senator Laxalt said, "I suspect we are going to have enough trouble fighting off federal intervention without opening the door for it."[22]

The White House approved the compact, calling it "entirely consistent with the President's previous statements and program concerning the protection of Lake Tahoe." Congress passed the twenty-page act, and it became law in December 1980.

Article V, item g, buried in the middle of the document, said that the agency needed to adopt ordinances prescribing findings prior to approving any project. This was required, in part, so that proposed projects "will not cause the adopted environmental threshold carrying capacities of the region to be exceeded." This seemingly minor item would soon wreak havoc as TRPA officials attempted to implement the new pact.[23]

Another consequential term of the act limited the future of CTRPA. Incorporating its rules into TRPA for use on the California side of the lake, the bill provided that when the new compact and threshold limits were adopted, there would be no further state funds expended for that agency's support.

Environmentalists worried that the agreement would reduce the role of CTRPA in the interim, but the agency was now chaired by Robert Twiss, the UC Berkeley land-use planner who had been active as a consultant in Forest Service and agency planning for the basin since working with Robert Bailey on the land-capability system ten years earlier. The Tahoe-Sierra Preservation Council's Larry Hoffman proposed that CTRPA coordinate its plans with the reconfigured bistate agency; instead, the CTRPA Board adopted stiff new guidelines to control building in fragile areas, proposed a regional public transportation system, and introduced tougher environmental standards.[24]

On September 8, 1980, the US House of Representatives unanimously passed the Burton-Santini Bill. It authorized $150 million to purchase environmentally sensitive lands at Tahoe. The money would be generated by selling up to nineteen thousand acres of federal lands in Clark County, Nevada, including several hundred on the Las Vegas Strip. The sales would put that land on the tax rolls and directly return 10 percent of the revenue generated to Clark County, as well as provide 5 percent to Nevada's public education. The Carter administration, the Office of Management and Budget, and the Department of Agriculture all endorsed the bill. But with the Senate session coming to a close, Nevada's Laxalt threatened to block it. The senator had several demands: an exemption for new development at Incline Village, TRPA veto power over any condemnation action, and the elimination of air and visual qualities as a basis for acquiring such land.[25]

Once, describing President Reagan, Laxalt might have been talking about himself: "He had a great sense of timing, coming right down to the moment of truth. And then cut the deal, make the bargain. Part of a reasonably good bargain is better than none." With only weeks left in the legislative year, Laxalt insisted on a public meeting at Incline Village to discuss his proposed changes. Representative Fazio urged Nevada and California citizens to contact their senators, saying developers wanted the bill to fail. "It's the same old wolves in sheep's clothing," said Fazio. For his part, California representative Burton said if the support of Laxalt was not forthcoming, some pet Nevada bills might get stuck in the House.[26]

Still, the Incline meeting was held on October 13, 1980, and Laxalt's witnesses pressed his points. The bill, with his changes, passed the Senate in the waning moments of the year-end session. By the time it got to the House, Burton conceded that there was no choice but to accept Laxalt's changes. On December 23, President Carter signed the new compact into law.

In the midst of his reelection campaign, Carter also issued an executive order establishing an interagency committee to develop the environmental thresholds for the lake basin. The action was taken "in order to ensure that Federal Agency actions protect the extraordinary natural, scenic, recreational, and ecological resources in the Lake Tahoe Region." Because federal agencies had at times been working at cross-purposes, the coordinating council would also be charged with scrutinizing federal projects, denying those that might accelerate environmental decline.[27]

The federal government's all-out support of tightening protections did not last long. Within two months of taking office, new president Ronald Reagan rescinded Carter's order.

In the early 1980s, President Reagan, four governors—two each from California and Nevada—and the federal courts all involved themselves in efforts
to affect TRPA's course. Reagan's actions were the result of his antipathy toward
regulations and his position that the cost of protecting the environment must
be reduced.

Senator Laxalt's office first released the news that the new president was
giving "very serious thought" to killing the Carter executive order. It was no
surprise that Laxalt, who had become the most prominent national politician
in modern Nevada history, was leading the charge against federal regulation
at Tahoe. He had a history of challenging federal agencies. In 1978 he had
attempted to head off an EPA lawsuit against two Tahoe sewer districts, charging that environmentalists had been allowed "untoward involvement, unfair
input, and undue impact" on the EPA. The following year, he claimed the Interior Department was trying to "blackjack" Nevada and California into adjusting their agreement regarding bistate river waters to ensure enough water for
the Paiutes' Pyramid Lake. In the dispute, he commented that the federal government wanted "its nose inserted into Western water matters in perpetuity."[1]

Laxalt's announcement regarding Carter's executive order induced Representative Fazio to send a letter, cosigned by twenty-nine California Democratic
congressmen, urging the new president to reject the idea. Fazio said rescinding Carter's order would signal that "Tahoe's environment can be sacrificed for
urban growth," promoted by Nevada's gaming interests. The letter pointed out
that there was no coordination between federal agencies: while the Forest Service spent $50 million to stop growth by purchasing land, other agencies spent
$50 million on growth-inducing projects.

The new administration had made clear it was looking for cuts in federal
spending, and decreased funding for environmental programs was a top priority. Reagan's appointments of Watt as secretary of the interior and Anne M.
Gorsuch as director of the EPA were blatant assaults on environmentalism.

Gorsuch relaxed clean air and pesticides regulations and was cited for contempt of Congress for refusing to release records that might show she mishandled the $1.6 billion toxic waste Superfund. Watt lasted less than three years, Gorsuch less than two. But early on, Watt and Gorsuch were leading the way in reducing funding, and it was easy to speculate that eliminating Tahoe moneys was on their agenda.

Regional forester for California Zane Smith offered $300,000 from a Forest Service planning fund to TRPA for their environmental threshold study. "I believe we should move rather quickly," Smith said. "It is no secret that Reagan is looking at [possible cutbacks] in the Basin."[2]

California newspapers responded to the threat to Carter's executive order with editorials expressing doubts and making accusations. The *Sacramento Bee* asked if, without the federal council, the new TRPA would be able to stand up to developers and casino owners. The *Los Angeles Times* followed a similar theme but personalized it, speculating that Laxalt's motivation in calling for the council's elimination had to do with the influence of Nevada gambling interests.[3]

A few days after its editorial, the *Bee* published an inflammatory article. Its headline read: "Hotel-Casinos Could Benefit from Laxalt Move to Kill New Tahoe Federal Council." The piece reported that Laxalt's brother Peter, an attorney, represented Harvey's Casino, which was trying to push through its parking garage. Peter Laxalt was also a member of a partnership that recently purchased the North Shore Club at Crystal Bay whose six-story addition was tied up in litigation by California's attorney general. Because Carter's order directed the council to deny pollution-creating developments, its elimination would limit the federal government's ability to block such projects. A Laxalt spokesperson said Peter Laxalt's activities had nothing to do with Senator Laxalt's philosophy regarding Lake Tahoe.[4]

In mid-March 1981, Reagan issued his one-sentence executive order abolishing Carter's order. When it was announced, California's assembly Speaker pro tem, Leo T. McCarthy, who with California state senator Garamendi had promoted the idea of a coordinating council, charged that Reagan had "knuckled under to Nevada's gambling and commercial interests." Laxalt reacted by saying the council would have only complicated and confused things. "I believe, and the president seems to agree," he said, "that the TRPA is entirely capable of making the hard decisions that need to be made."[5]

Laxalt also felt compelled to respond to the editorial in the *Los Angeles Times*. He sent a lengthy letter, arguing that "substantial progress" had already been made in addressing Tahoe's land, air, and water problems and that blaming Tahoe's troubles on the "ever-present whipping boys," the casino owners, was "nothing less than pure demagoguery."[6]

Early in 1982, the Tahoe-Sierra Preservation Council announced it would fight the agency's threshold study. At the same time, it became apparent that Laxalt's and Reagan's confidence in the reconfigured TRPA as a safeguard for the lake was misplaced.

Nevada's governor, Robert List, replaced a Nevada TRPA Board member who generally voted "on the environmental side" of issues with a developer in January and in March replaced the agency chair, Nevada's director of conservation and natural resources, Roland Westergard. His replacement was state parks director John Meder, who had previously served eight years on the board and was described by League to Save Lake Tahoe director Jim Bruner as having been "in the majority on most pro-development votes." Bruner charged that the board members had been replaced because "development interests could not get either of them in their back pocket."

Mike Van Wagenen, executive director of the preservation council, responded that Meder was not in anybody's pocket. "Obviously he will chat with Governor List and ask 'What are my marching orders, sir?'" said Van Wagenen. "But remember, he is only one person on that Board."[7]

David Roberti, California's senate president, and Willie Brown, Speaker of the assembly, reacted with a letter to the Nevada governor. Saying that Westergard was highly regarded by California's TRPA contingent, they commented that the change was especially disturbing because the environmental thresholds were due to be adopted shortly.

List responded with a note a week later. He said that the action "should not be considered a signal of change affecting Nevada's commitment to the Tahoe Compact" and that he looked forward to the states' continued good working relationship.[8]

Three months later, when another Nevada member resigned because of time demands, List appointed former TRPA executive director Richard Heikka. Heikka was part owner of a company developing a six-thousand-home community in Fernley, Nevada. While List said that Heikka would be "a mediating influence," Bruner pointed out that most of the decline in Tahoe's health occurred when Heikka was the agency director. California governor Jerry Brown's TRPA appointee Dwight Steele, an acclaimed environmental activist, commented, "It's like having a recurring dream. The same voices wanting to go back to business as usual."[9]

Other agencies were suffering other setbacks. The Forest Service had begun evaluating properties that might be part of the initial buyout program, but delays had plagued the process. Its 1982 allocation had been set at $10 million but was cut to $6.7 million in last-minute budget negotiations. The Reagan administration appeared ready to cut its 1983 allocation entirely. The estimated total cost of acquisitions was between $52 million and $208 million. It had been hoped the Las Vegas land sales would raise $150 million, but in its first year it made only one sale, for $37,000.[10]

After months of public hearings and debate, by June 1982 planners had devised thresholds for ten environmental components. The TRPA Board did not adopt any of them. There was a lack of scientific data for some, and the reconfigured Nevada group feared that adoption of any standards might lead to a building prohibition. The new delegation makeup resulted in six-to-one votes against staff proposals, creating deadlock.[11]

The Nevada contingent's negative votes prompted Roberti and Willie Brown to send another letter to List. They said fear that property rights might be affected was being addressed by their appointees, who would include in the adoptive document that the agency was not permitted to "take or damage private property for public use without payment of just compensation." They asked List to urge his representatives to approve the environmental standards and ended by advising the governor that if they did not cooperate, "California will act without Nevada to do whatever is necessary to protect one of our nation's greatest scenic and recreational assets."

Two days later, on August 26, 1982, with the California delegation agreeing to a case-by-case program that allowed some Nevada owners of environmentally sensitive land to apply for permits, the board passed the new environmental standards.[12]

Those seeking to protect the lake received several pieces of good news in the last quarter of 1982. The Forest Service began its buyout program, California voters approved state senator Garamendi's long-pursued $85 million bond for buying sensitive lands, and, against Reagan policy, the US House Appropriations Subcommittee approved $10 million for purchases. At the same time, despite a recession throughout the country, Burton-Santini sales suddenly boomed. By November 1982, the government had netted $14 million in Las Vegas land sales.[13]

The Forest Service, charged with implementing the Burton-Santini plan in the basin, dramatically expanded its staff to meet demands. A team of hydrologists, wildlife and fishery biologists, and technicians was brought in to assist watershed officer Bill Johnson in identifying environmentally sensitive lots. The team studied parcel maps and aerial photographs, verified by field studies, to ascertain which parcels needed protection or restoration.[14]

In 1983 the dynamic between Nevada and California underwent a dramatic reversal, as Nevada's conservative governor, List, and California's liberal governor, Brown, were each replaced. Nevada elected Richard Bryan, a moderate Democrat, as governor, while California elected George Deukmejian, a conservative Republican. Bryan immediately reappointed the conservation-minded Roland Westergard to the TRPA Board, although he left Heikka as a member. Deukmejian replaced two environmentalists with prodevelopment individuals, a former Placer County official and a Beverly Hills developer whose father was a major Deukmejian campaign contributor. The developer, Alexander Haagen III, later gained notoriety by submitting vouchers for expenditures double those of any other member, causing the Senate Finance Committee to restrict expenses allowed board members.[15]

The preservation council's Hoffman, whose group had contributed to the new governor's campaign, took credit for the personnel changes. He proclaimed that there was now greater likelihood the two states could find areas of agreement.[16]

With the new TRPA plan, based on environmental thresholds, due midyear, planners introduced a twenty-year growth-control proposal in March 1983.

The plan would permit up to sixteen thousand new homes and cost more than $500 million. Hearings were held at various locations to gather public reactions. As usual, no one was satisfied. Deliberations and board debates followed without agreement as the year wound down.[17]

Having failed to meet its mandate, TRPA was unsure it had authority to approve projects, so it suspended further project approvals for ninety days. Its fourteen-member board argued possible plans, parts of which were revised by planners three or four times. In November, toward the end of the building suspension, the board appeared ready to reach accord on a plan that would allow the consideration of 100 environmentally sensitive lots a year for development. Prodevelopment members, holding an eight-to-six majority, backed the plan. At the eleventh hour, Nevada's governor, Bryan, replaced Heikka with a more preservation-minded individual who voted against the proposal. The board was again deadlocked, and the moratorium on building remained in place.[18]

Along with building on environmentally sensitive lands, the main disagreement was the amount of surface coverage that should be allowed on each lot. Whereas proponents of development argued that the Bailey geomorphic unit mapping, in place for more than a decade, was outdated and there should be flexibility in deciding how much surface could be covered, environmentalists countered that watering down the system would be sabotaging it. The environmentalists' opinions were punctuated by periodic news releases by limnologist Goldman and his associates, who said the clouds of algae and clumps of "brown, decaying scum" that were appearing on beaches were symptomatic of the "environmental tragedy" that was occurring. In the spring of 1984, in one particularly graphic Sacramento Bee news photo, biologist Stanford L. Loeb stood waist-deep in the lake in a wet suit and snorkeling gear holding up a slimy rock and a beaker of brackish water. The article's headline read: "Lake Tahoe's Algae Woes Ooze into Tourist Season."[19]

After four more months of dispute, on April 27, 1984, the TRPA Board unanimously passed a compromise twenty-year plan. It would allow 12,600 new homes, as well as lesser amounts of commercial developments, tourist units, and multiple-family units. CTRPA would be officially closed. As part of the agreement, an amendment allowing 100 homes a year on sensitive parcels would be postponed until 1986.

Conservationists complained that the plan lacked timetables for achieving the adopted environmental standards. Bruner, of the League to Save Lake Tahoe, said it was unacceptable. "We're being asked now to accept a great deal of new development at the front end of the plan and being promised that in later years the protective measures will go into place." California's attorney general, John Van de Kamp, agreed and, before TRPA's meeting adjourned, filed suit in US District Court on behalf of the people of California. The next day, as the eight-month moratorium on building was lifted and lot owners and builders lined up at 8:00 A.M. to secure permits, the league joined the California suit. At 2:30 P.M. TRPA director Gary Midkiff called from Sacramento, telling staff to shut down the permitting process. Judge Edward Garcia, a recent Reagan appointee, had issued a restraining order, extending the building moratorium another thirty days.[20]

Van de Kamp's suit was unique in that it was filed representing "the people." Ordinarily, the attorney general represents state agencies in court, and in other states that is all the office is allowed to do. But California's attorney general is charged with representing the populace, and when no agency in Deukmejian's administration expressed interest in joining the suit, the attorney general filed for the people. The basic contention in the suit was that TRPA's actions would seriously harm the lake while contravening its compact.[21]

Protests by frustrated lot owners and the development-rights faction resounded from the lake basin and the affected counties. Local TRPA members, led by South Tahoe builder and mayor Norm Woods, said the agency was not working. "We're being run by a pipsqueak attorney out of the attorney general's office," Woods said. "They've stopped every project of any size up here on technicalities."[22]

On June 6, 1984, Judge Garcia began hearing California's and the league's case against TRPA. He took arguments for two days. Robert Twiss, the environmental scientist and former chair of the recently disbanded CTRPA, presented slides chronicling environmental damage caused by development. One photo showed soil running down the street away from a house under construction, another depicted road cuts causing hillsides to slide, and a third indicated a muddy stream running toward the lake. Charles Goldman testified, reporting on algal growth in the lake that would lead to loss of the lake's clarity within forty years.

TRPA's chief of long-range planning, David Ziegler, testified for the defense. He said that the moratorium caused the loss of development fees, community support, and public confidence. He was forced to admit under cross-examination, though, that water, air, and transportation projects were unfunded, dependent on hoped-for government contributions.

On June 15, Garcia announced his decision in a ten-page ruling: he granted the preliminary injunction. In his explanation, he noted that TRPA's plan would exempt some two hundred homes that violated Article V, item g, of the new compact. That section clearly mandated that "no project can be approved without written findings that will show how such project will not cause the [environmental] thresholds to be exceeded." Of those exempted, eighty-seven, if built, would cause the adopted threshold for impervious cover to be exceeded. Finding that TRPA would be acting contrary to the clear directive of the compact, Garcia left his injunction and the building moratorium in place.[23]

The ruling generated reactionary responses at the lake. The *Tahoe Daily Tribune* editor said that going back to the bargaining table could well break the agency and declared, "Frankly, we hope this does break TRPA's back. It would serve the state and those who don't want to give this plan a chance to work right." Prodevelopment board members indicated they would fight rather than attempt to amend the plan, even if it cost another building season. The preservation council's Hoffman spoke of lobbying the Nevada Legislature and Deukmejian in California to defund the agency.[24]

Ten days after the ruling, the preservation council engaged in an additional strategy, attacking TRPA by filing a $26 million lawsuit in US District Courts in Reno and Sacramento. The suits specifically attacked the limitation on building on environmentally sensitive lots, claiming those lots had decreased in value some 65 to 70 percent because of the limits. Hoffman said the case was "pure ma and pa property rights," in that TRPA was violating the Fifth and Fourteenth Amendments to the Constitution. In mid-July 1984, TRPA took its own legal action, appealing Judge Garcia's ruling. Those board members pushing for the filing acknowledged the chances of winning an appeal were remote, but argued it gave them leverage in negotiations with California and the league.[25]

In June Vic Fazio announced the House Appropriations Subcommittee had approved $12 million to continue action protecting Lake Tahoe. The amount was $9.5 million more than the Reagan administration had proposed. The appropriation pegged $2 million for erosion control and $10 million for acquisition of lots on erodible slopes.[26]

Another important measure to facilitate the lake's environmental protection finally got under way in June 1984. A year and a half after voters approved the $85 million bond sale to buy Tahoe lands, the California Assembly reactivated the Tahoe Conservancy to manage the fund. The conservancy was originally proposed as a bistate agency in 1973, intended to purchase private properties at fair market value. California had ratified the compact, but, in an early demonstration of its reluctance to partner further with the larger state, the Nevada Legislature refused to approve it. Now renamed the California Tahoe Conservancy, the agency was charged with offering to purchase California properties that, if developed, would adversely affect stream environment zones or contribute to the further degradation of the region's waters.[27]

Dennis Machida, an attorney for the Coastal Conservancy, was hired as the CTC's executive officer. As well as creating a land-purchasing program, Machida, meticulous in his attention to detail, began haunting the halls of the state capitol. Listening to the legislators and government officials, he learned who the power brokers were and how and when to approach them to bring attention to the needs of the basin.[28]

At the same time, the Forest Service, managing federal lands that now constituted some 70 percent of the basin, was involved in an intense program of reconstructing and rehabilitating meadows and stream zones. Bill Johnson and his watershed team were undertaking major restorations on highly visible lands like the former Jennings casino site and Heavenly Valley Ski Area, which required establishing drains, gully control, and revegetating stripped ski runs. Projects also included closing off-road vehicle trails through meadows and along streams and rehabilitating tributaries and lands adjacent to steep, developed areas like Rubicon Point.

A developer had drained South Shore's Osgood Swamp fifteen years earlier.

When Johnson's crew built a coffer dam, which reflooded the area, it allowed dormant plant life to come back naturally, so the swamp again collected silt and nutrients previously carried by a stream to the lake. At Blackwood Creek on the West Shore, Johnson's crew rerouted a stream to follow its original course. They repaired the Meyers landfill, South Tahoe's former garbage dump, capping it, planting trees, and diverting a stream that transported highly toxic pollutants as it ran through it.[29]

In January 1985, the Nevada Legislature followed a path similar to that of its last three sessions in the 1970s, seeking to withdraw from TRPA. Many Nevada legislators saw themselves as underdogs, fighting for individual property rights, and used terms such as *demagoguery* and *despotism* to describe the agency. Nevada TRPA representative Jim King exemplified the protesters' attitude, asserting, "I'm a Nevada resident. I do not want to be governed by the attorney general of California."[30]

On February 28, the bill passed the assembly, twenty-eight to fourteen, with all Republicans and three Democrats supporting it. Governor Bryan vowed to veto the bill should it reach his desk, but the Republicans threatened to hold the state budget hostage unless Bryan acquiesced to the pullout.[31]

During March and April, splintered negotiations were pursued in numerous venues. Spike Wilson, president pro tem of the Nevada Senate, met with California's Van de Kamp, attempting to get the attorney general to shelve the California lawsuit. Van de Kamp's deputy was meeting with a TRPA negotiating committee in hopes of finding an out-of-court settlement. The committee was led by Nevada's Jim King, whom another TRPA Board member accused of being more interested in shutting down the agency than finding common ground. In Carson City, Governor Bryan met with legislators and discussed a new bill that, rather than having Nevada withdraw from TRPA, would restructure the makeup of the agency. The bill, which passed both houses of the legislature unanimously, would amend the master plan to allow more building and give the legislature, rather than the governor, the right to appoint two board members. The latter change was certain to create a prodevelopment majority. California and the US Congress were required to approve the Nevada changes, and California's senate leader, Garamendi, vowed not to let that happen.[32]

On April 1, 1985, in the fifteenth year of the bistate regional experiment, Bill

Morgan, the Forest Service's Lake Tahoe supervisor, was named TRPA's seventh executive director. The agency faced myriad problems. Unable to follow its own compact, it was facing lawsuits from both sides of the political continuum. The court injunction and building moratorium meant people granted permits in 1983 were still waiting, and the construction industry was disappearing. Nevada was poised either to radically change the makeup of the TRPA Board or to pull out of the agency. The economy was in decline, and the TRPA Governing Board was utterly divided. Morgan was faced with frustration and disillusionment. His first public action made things worse.

Bill Morgan stepped into a situation later characterized by analysts evaluating the agency as a "war zone." The unique government entity was failing because of the battles. At a large TRPA public meeting in April 1985, having begun his tenure as executive director only days before, Morgan's job was to present a draft of a proposed settlement to relieve the Tahoe building injunction. TRPA staff lawyers and the California attorney general and the League to Save Lake Tahoe had spent a year negotiating before reaching the tentative agreement. The TRPA Board was poised to vote to approve or reject the long-awaited settlement. The crowd, which filled an oversized meeting room at Harvey's Casino, was largely hostile, wanting an end to the moratorium but against the agreement because of its severe building restrictions.

Morgan agreed with California and the league that TRPA's plan from the year before had not met terms of the compact, but he believed the settlement went too far in siding with them. He read the proposed resolution aloud and sat down. A board member pointed out that normally, the director gave his opinion of such a proposal, saying the board would like to hear what Morgan thought. Morgan said, "Frankly, I don't like it. I would not recommend your approval of it." When the board went along with Morgan and voted down the proposed settlement, the disputing parties had reached a dead end. The process had completely broken down. The injunction and building moratorium would remain in place. There seemed no way forward.[1]

At a time when others were calling for disbanding the agency, Morgan proposed an idea. Before officially taking the position of executive director, and during the first month of his tenure, Morgan met with members of the Nevada Legislature, lobbying them to give TRPA a last chance. In order to maintain their role in the partnership, he offered them veto power over any eventual agreement. His statement at the Harvey's meeting seemed to gain him credibility with the Nevadans as an honest broker, and on May 1 sponsors of the bill to pull out of the agency withdrew it.

Morgan then introduced what, to many, seemed a far-fetched plan. The skeptical TRPA Board gave him ninety days to test the proposal. In separate meetings, he spoke to the league board, California attorney general Van de Camp and his assistant Rick Skinner, representatives of the Forest Service, the Tahoe-Sierra Preservation Council, the Gaming Alliance, the Tahoe Basin Association of Governments, the water-quality agencies, and other interested parties. He was proposing a process of collaboration among all entities, whereby they might reach consensus on an agreement.

More than thirty interest groups agreed to meet. TRPA Board members were not invited to participate. Morgan chaired the meetings, introducing issues for discussion from the lawsuits or those raised in the settlement talks. Morgan brought in an outsider, Geoff Ball, to facilitate and make sure everyone was allowed an opportunity to be heard. Ball also had to ensure disagreements did not get out of hand, as two hostile and deeply entrenched positions had been clearly delineated throughout the years. Skinner of the California Attorney General's Office, league president Tom Martens, and its attorney E. Clement Shute, who in the yearlong settlement talks had proved to be a canny negotiator, led the environmental protectionists. Preservation council spokesperson Larry Hoffman led the growth-and-property-rights element. Mike Van Wagenen, previously executive director of the preservation council, represented the casinos.[2]

At the time of Morgan's meetings, social scientists had found the conflict over Tahoe's evolving policy to be a fertile research field. One study used questionnaire data over seventeen years to conclude that whereas stakeholders in favor of environmental protection were more likely to trust the findings of scientists, university researchers, and consultants, those favoring development tended to distrust scientific findings. Years later one of the leaders of the development community commented, "They claimed it was all based in science. To me it always seemed more like political science."[3]

In fact, as well as scientists, the intensity of the conflict attracted the attention of political scientists studying policy systems. Paul Sabatier developed one of the three or four major theories of policy making in the world by generalizing his study of the condition of Tahoe affairs. Sabatier and his associates tested a major hypothesis concerning stakeholders' perceptions called "the devil shift." The term referred to how actors in policy subsystems perceive their opponents: in particular, the perception that opponents seem to be stronger and more "evil" than they actually are. The political scientists found that "actors will impugn the motives and/or reasonableness of their opponents while perceiving themselves to be reasonable people acting out of concern for the public welfare." The scientists also found that Tahoe stakeholders evaluated their opponents' behavior in harsher terms than did most members of the community.

The researchers elicited invectives from individuals active in the Tahoe disputes that illustrated the intensity of feeling held by each side. Negative comments about the league included "[They want to] make Tahoe once again a rich man's lake—their principal support comes from 'fatcats' with lake front homes, some of them [on highly erodible land]," "[They are] overzealous environmentalists who wish to stop growth, reduce the economy to a shambles, keep Tahoe pristine at all costs," and "[Their goal is] to destroy the rights of property owners and residents through the taking of property by regional zoning rather than just compensation." Negative characterizations of the preservation council included "[Their] basic goals are simple—build, build, and build more. Preservation should be deleted from their title" and "[Their interests] ostensibly are the small lot owner, but, in reality, [they are] the real estate, construction, and legal business interests who profit off continued fear and controversy involving those lot owners."[4]

When Morgan began his meetings, he needed to overcome the distrust of each side toward the other, including those who thought of the opposing side as "devils." Morgan was counting on two factors: that the stakeholders were exhausted from the never-ending settlement talks and that they would rather meet in workshops than continue to fight in court. His plan was to begin with items that would be easy to agree to and take them to the TRPA Board for approval, beginning to forge a new comprehensive agreement, taking up the more difficult issues as prejudices and mistrust broke down. "If you can narrow the scope you can solve any problem," Morgan said at the time. "You have to get the problems down to manageable scale."

He told the newspapers that the process might allow the groups to reach the equivalent of an out-of-court settlement. This became more important to the

TRPA Board when in mid-July a federal appeals court upheld the lower-court injunction against their long-range plan. The appeals court concurred with the original decision that TRPA's proposed plan would contribute to the deterioration of the microcosm of the region and likely do irreparable harm to Lake Tahoe's waters.[5]

California governor Deukmejian's visit to Tahoe in August 1985 was a good sign. His political platform had previously included protecting landowners' and developers' rights, and he had dragged his feet in getting the bond money of eighty-five million dollars for protecting sensitive land allocated. "I haven't been in the forefront of some of the environmental organizations," he admitted; as he toured the lake, though, he now declared his support for the land-acquisition and erosion-control programs. He was struck by the extent of erosion occurring on one of the steep parcels considered for purchase, declaring himself supportive of whatever was needed to deal with the problem.[6]

By the beginning of 1986, the TRPA Board had extended indefinitely Morgan's consensus program. The parties involved were forging delicately balanced pacts and conditional agreements. As had been planned, facilitator Ball was intervening less at each session. The negotiators, meeting for two days at a time, two or three times a month, were making substantial progress. They agreed to modest growth in commercial developments, no more than a 7 percent increase over the next decade; rehabilitation of existing facilities; and construction of three hundred homes yearly, rather than the eighteen hundred that would have been allowed by the 1984 plan targeted by the lawsuit.

With that part of the compact gaining consensus, Judge Garcia's approval would allow the economically depressed Tahoe Basin to have its first building season in three years. At the insistence of plaintiff attorneys Shute and Skinner, these compromises excluded properties identified as environmentally sensitive under the Bailey system. But Morgan had introduced a proviso that there be an individual lot-evaluation system, making all parcels potentially buildable, which allowed them to maintain their market value.[7]

Other positive news came from the California Tahoe Conservancy in January. In the CTC's initial efforts, 350 of the 400 landowners with environmentally sensitive lots they approached expressed interest in selling their sites at the price quoted by agency appraisers. The preservation council's Hoffman attributed the high acceptance rate to people being frustrated and simply wanting to get out, but conservancy director Machida, encouraged by the responses, said owners' motivations varied, including tax benefits, the poor health of owners, or in a number of cases a "genuine interest in preserving Tahoe's beauty." He was optimistic at that time because of Deukmejian's new-found support, as the governor was assisting in seeking additional funding for the conservancy's programs.[8]

Nevada entities were not satisfied. They did not approve of private property rights being restricted even in stream environment zones or on environmentally sensitive lands. Nevada state leaders called Morgan to a meeting at the Nevada governor's mansion. Attorney Hoffman, who was closely associated with a number of Nevada legislators, also attended.

Morgan presented his idea for an individual parcel-evaluation system, whereby criteria were used to evaluate and give points to every vacant lot in the basin. Ratings would include characteristics such as erosion hazard, run-off potential, and ability to revegetate. Owners of the highest-rated lots, upon receiving a local building permit, would be allowed to build right away, while the Forest Service or the California Tahoe Conservancy would target for purchase the lowest-rated parcels, in particular those in stream environment zones receiving a score of zero.

His plan was designed so that over time, as more parcels were removed from the market, the level of ratings that might be buildable would drop so that those lots with lower ratings could retain value. The idea was that after a number of years, there would be so few lots on sensitive lands remaining that, even if they were built upon, the effect would be minimal. The Nevada leaders gave the plan their approval, as would California officials and the consensus group. Once its details were developed, the TRPA Board incorporated the plan, called the Individual Parcel Evaluation System, into the TRPA General Plan. By 1988 all seventeen thousand undeveloped residential parcels in the basin had received an IPES score.[9]

One of the property-rights advocates' major objections through the years was that land-coverage restraints affected small lot owners and those who wished to build oversize structures whether on sensitive lands or not. The percentage of land that could be covered was strictly mandated, and a small parcel might not accommodate a house and driveway. Likewise, a large multiroom house might be too big for a single lot. Morgan, Machida, and a small working group created an ordinance allowing transferable development rights (TDRS) so landowners might transfer coverage from parcel to parcel. The system included establishing a land-coverage bank that could coordinate the purchase of additional coverage by owners of nonsensitive parcels. Machida agreed to have the conservancy serve as a land-coverage bank for California, and the Nevada Legislature took on limited responsibility for their state. The mitigation fees generated could be used to buy lots and conduct restoration and water-quality improvement projects on sensitive lands. The land bank became an integral part of the TRPA plan, relieving some landowners' grievances while advancing the agency's top priorities.[10]

By June 1986, a year after consensus meetings began, the group had met more than thirty times and resolved all outstanding issues. Of the twenty-four members who had consistently attended the meetings, only two balked at the final proposals, one feeling the results were economically unfeasible, the other, involved in a lawsuit over inverse condemnation of properties in stream environment zones, vehemently opposed to such a prohibition. All other members supported all parts of the plan. Local TRPA Board members, under immense pressure from their constituents, were anxious to approve almost any building schedule. A Douglas County commissioner told consensus committee member Skinner, "If we can get going with this building season, I will conform with anything you want."[11]

Criteria for building had been established, numbers had been agreed upon, and the process to be followed had been created, so the plaintiffs in the lawsuit agreed to recommend that Judge Garcia relax the terms of the injunction. Judge Garcia modified the decision to allow building to resume on an interim basis, including three hundred homes and three commercial projects.

The actions were the first steps in untangling the suit's complex legal problems. It allowed TRPA to begin dealing with other problems to which the plaintiffs, California and the league, objected. It would take another year for the resolution of all objections, and property-rights advocates' opposition continued to roil under the surface. Nevada TRPA member King, who had qualms about "several basic ingredients" of the plan, suggested the state might initiate another pullout effort.[12]

Hoffman was another individual who expressed skepticism over the agreements, and he was continuing to pursue a remedy for his preservation council constituency in the courts. In June 1986, Judge Edward C. Reed of the US District Court in Reno rejected Hoffman's sixteen-million-dollar suit on behalf of 364 property owners on the Nevada side of the lake. In doing so, Judge Reed was affirming the legitimacy of TRPA's zoning capabilities. Hoffman appealed the decision.[13]

Other Nevadans differed with Hoffman's approach. A group of professors and activists associated with the University of Nevada in Reno aligned itself with larger national environmental trends in seeking to protect the lake. The university group advocated for passage of a thirty-one-million-dollar Nevada land-acquisition bond, and, supported by basin property owners, in November 1986 it was approved by Nevada voters.[14]

In April 1987, Judge Garcia heard another suit attacking the TRPA zoning regulations. The preservation council and Hoffman again filed the claim, this time representing 415 California landowners. The case, similar to the one thrown out the previous June in Reno, occasioned the same result. Judge Garcia found that curtailing development on high-hazard lands constituted a "legitimate governmental interest in preserving Lake Tahoe's water quality."[15]

On May 27, 1987, the TRPA Governing Board adopted the master plan shepherded through by Bill Morgan. Even with agreement over the plan, Judge Garcia's injunction would remain in place until the lawsuit was settled. That meant California's Attorney General's Office and the League to Save Lake Tahoe had to approve it. Negotiations between those entities and Morgan's chief of long-range planning, David Ziegler, began immediately. In the meantime, the Nevada Senate passed another bill that would repeal the TRPA Compact and related statutory provisions. Its sponsor, Douglas County's Lawrence Jacobsen, who had been fighting TRPA since its inception, pushed it through, saying, "We can't let [the League to] Save Lake Tahoe and the California attorney general's office dictate policy."[16]

On June 25, two weeks after the Nevada Senate approved revoking the compact, it withdrew the bill, as all contending parties approved settlement of the lawsuit that brought the injunction and moratorium. The TRPA Board vote was twelve to one. Although supporting it when the master plan was proposed, California contractor Alex Haagen had said if it were not tied to the suit's dismissal, he would not have even considered voting for it. After a month thinking about it, he changed his mind and cast the lone dissenting vote. During the meeting, Nevada's first female secretary of state, Frankie Sue del Pappa, chastised Haagen for browbeating the staff, noisy obstructionism, and acting like a spoiled child. Early the next year, Haagen quit the TRPA Board, storming out of a meeting shouting, "Come visit our non-environmentally sensitive Southern California." On the settlement vote, South Lake Tahoe mayor and contractor Norm Woods broke from his ally Haagen, saying that after fifteen years of battling regional government, he was ready to concede.[17]

Revisions to the plan included limiting allocations for single- and multiple-family houses built in the basin to 350 per year for a six-year period, a ban on all new subdivisions, requiring new developments to offset water-quality impacts by 150 percent with improvement projects such as erosion control, and Morgan's items, ranking all residential lots in the basin and transferable development rights.

The compact included the environmental threshold carrying capacities that would serve as its guiding principles. Unlike the original 1984 proposal, with its innumerable exemptions, TRPA assessment was required for all plans to "ensure that the project under review will not adversely affect implementation of the Regional Plan and will not cause the adopted environmental threshold carrying capacity to be exceeded."[18]

Completion of the master plan enabled TRPA to again begin planning and managing environmental impacts in the basin. It gave the staff and governing board a framework to determine the fragility of lands and a more equitable process in procuring them. At the same time, the agency's previous decisions were under attack in the courts, including two that would be resolved in the US Supreme Court.

As the public evaluates the appropriateness of mandates and the efficacy of decisions, experiments in governance are bound to encounter opposition. Because TRPA was restricting private use of valuable lands, personal involvement was unusually intense.

Three main Tahoe property court challenges confronted TRPA in the last part of the twentieth century: *William Cody Kelly v. TRPA, Suitum v. TRPA,* and *Tahoe-Sierra Preservation Council v. TRPA*. Kelly's case was ultimately decided in the Nevada Supreme Court; the others ended in US Supreme Court decisions.

The *William Cody Kelly v. TRPA* case was the first frontal attack on the science behind TRPA regulations and land capability. The decision would be the culmination of a twenty-year battle over forty-five acres on a mountain above Glenbrook. Kelly owned the old Fleishman Estate, and he had subdivided it into thirty-nine lots.

Kelly was a wealthy attorney who bought the property in 1966. In the early 1970s, he subdivided it to create "Uppaway Estates," home sites for thirty-nine of the "finest and most exclusive" residences in the world. His project gained TRPA approval through the dual-majority system. All five California board members had voted against it. The Nevadans split two to two, with the local Nevada county representatives voting yes and one member absent. Because the two states had not agreed to reject it, no action could be taken, and after sixty days it was deemed approved. Many of the lots were on extremely steep slopes rated Class I, or "high hazard." The Kelly attorneys claimed that the development project would not cause any significant environmental damage, but that, "in fact, it would cure existing environmental problems of natural erosion."

Douglas County had already issued an administrative permit to allow land coverage in excess of that permitted by the regional agency when TRPA filed suit to stop the project in federal court in 1975. Judge Bruce Thompson rejected the

TRPA action, saying in a memorandum and order that agency policy had been followed, and, in filing the suit, the agency was attempting to act arbitrarily.[1]

Changes to the TRPA Compact in the 1980s resulted in the subdivision's not-yet-developed Phase III, or Hilltop Lots, being adjudged "in need of further consideration." The agency's building moratoriums during that same period prevented consideration of approval of the Hilltop Lots. Once a road was built, and with TRPA's 1987 plan implementing IPES, or Individual Parcel Evaluation System, the agency immediately found one of the six Hilltop Lots eligible to receive a building permit. On July 24, 1987, while appealing the remaining scores, Kelly filed suit, asking for monetary relief and punitive damages. Prior to the commencement of the trial, his appeal resulted in another lot being rated buildable. That left four lots that were not immediately eligible.

The defendants, TRPA and the two states, made motions for summary judgment, and the district court granted in part and denied in part. In February 1990, Kelly proceeded to trial on the two remaining issues: temporary taking of lots without compensation and deprivation of economic use of property without due process. In presenting the case, Kelly argued that the science on which TRPA's regulations were founded was flawed.

Robert Twiss testified as one of the expert witnesses regarding the scientific foundation of TRPA regulations. In his tenure of more than forty years dealing with Tahoe issues, Twiss had served the California attorneys general in trials in three ways. Because he was a consultant who could defend the science of TRPA's regional plan or because he was CTRPA chairman, he was at times a percipient witness—that is, a party to issues on trial. He also served as a consultant, sitting in on depositions to advise the state attorney on lines of questions that might be pursued. At still other times, he served as an expert witness on environmental land use. It was in this last role that he served in the *William Cody Kelly* suit.

The trial was held before District Judge Charles McGee in Gardnerville, a small town outside the basin, in Douglas County. Much of Judge McGee's experience had been in family law; this would be an entirely different kind of case. The jurist proved to be a quick study.

Twiss and Charles Goldman were two of the TRPA's leading witnesses with others acting as advisers, among whom was National Wildlife Federation Hall of Fame member Luna Leopold, called the "intellectual father of geomorphology." The experts discussed stream environment zones, high-hazard lands, how impervious surfaces increase lake nutrient loading, and the decreasing lake clarity. Every evening the defense attorneys and witnesses would meet at a riverfront cabin at Sorensen's Resort in nearby Alpine County to prepare for returning to court. In his testimony, Twiss illustrated the nexus between public purpose and any imposed prohibitions, refuting Kelly's contention that the agency had used a shotgun approach.

The court agreed with Twiss, rejecting Kelly's claims. The 128-page decision found that the IPES system was based on solid scientific principles and was evenly applied. The trial had revealed that the 1987 TRPA plan had not deprived Kelly of his property without compensation. He had bought the estate for $500,000, earned some $5.6 million selling lots, and sold the main house, in which he lived for nearly twenty years, for another $1.1 million. The court also determined that TRPA's actions benefited Kelly as well as the public, for if the lake were despoiled, the Uppaway lots would diminish in value.

Kelly appealed to the Nevada Supreme Court, and again lost. It concluded that TRPA could postpone building in critical areas for a reasonable time, if the "benefit received by the property from the ordinances is direct and substantial and the burden imposed is proportional."[2]

The *Suitum* case against the TRPA involved the Tahoe-Sierra Preservation Council's Larry Hoffman representing Bernadine Suitum, whom Hoffman dubbed the "perfect client." Hoffman joked to bar-association members that the plaintiff was perfect in that she was an eighty-two-year-old widow in a wheelchair simply hoping to build on her lot. Mrs. Suitum became a legal cause célèbre in the 1990s. She and her late husband had bought an 18,300-square-foot lot at Incline Village for $28,000, in 1972. They intended to build a home when they retired. Her husband's poor health kept them from building while he was alive, but, in the meantime, the neighbors on three sides did construct houses. Finally, in 1989, after the 1987 regional plan was adopted, she obtained a building permit from the county and applied to construct her house. Her property, 2,000 feet from the lake, bordered Mill Creek, which runs directly into Tahoe. Described by a reporter as "a boggy tangle of willows and ponderosa pines," it was entirely in a stream environment zone. Because the regional plan prohibited "permanent land disturbance" in stream zones, the parcel's IPES score was zero, and TRPA turned down her request. An appeal to the governing board was also denied.[3]

TRPA allowed Suitum TDRs (transferable development rights) that would enable her to sell her lot. She chose not to attempt to do so and instead brought legal action against the agency. She claimed the restrictions deprived her of "all reasonable and economically viable use" of her land, which, as a taking of her property without just compensation, violated the Fifth Amendment. TRPA argued the lawsuit was not "ripe," or ready for consideration: because she had not attempted to sell the development rights, the value of her compensation had not been determined. The federal district court and circuit court found for TRPA, saying Mrs. Suitum must attempt to sell her development rights to determine if a taking without fair reparation had occurred.[4]

The US Supreme Court agreed to hear the *Suitum* appeal, and the arguments were presented in 1996. The Pacific Legal Foundation took over as lead counsel for Mrs. Suitum before the High Court. The PLF is a nonprofit, conservative litigation organization that has been involved in nearly all property-takings cases before the Court in the past thirty-five years. The *Suitum* case attracted the PLF because it presented an opportunity to broaden property rights against government regulation. Several of the justices were interested, because it gave them the chance to examine the same issue.

Before the trial, Mrs. Suitum had said that on his deathbed her husband had urged her to go ahead and build their dream home at the lake. The PLF issued a press release, quoting her: "When her husband, now deceased, became ill, Mrs. Suitum said her husband told her, 'Hon, keep on going. Build the house, and I'll be with you.' And that's what I tried to do."[5]

Mrs. Suitum argued that TRPA had made no "individualized determination" that construction on her lot would have adverse effects on Lake Tahoe and pointed out that building had been allowed on the three adjoining parcels. The PLF attorneys contended that the fact that she would be able to sell her "land coverage" was irrelevant; the question was whether her land had been taken. They argued that the TDR program was an arbitrary "administrative contrivance," and because Mrs. Suitum could not exercise "her personal autonomy and dominion by realizing her longtime dream of owning a retirement home on her own land," it had been taken.

TRPA attorneys had presented all the relevant facts about Tahoe's geologic history and the damage done to its fragile ecosystem. They explained that the TDR program was not arbitrary but the product of years of consensus building among the government, environmentalists, and property-rights advocates. They said that without the kind of restrictions TRPA had implemented, the lake's clarity would decline to the point of ecological collapse and everyone at Tahoe would lose. They pointed out that the TDR market could allow her as much as $56,000, and the market value of her lot to her neighbors, wishing to expand their lots, was as high as $16,750. At some $72,750, her parcel was likely worth far more than her original purchase price.

Initially, the issue appealed from the lower courts had been the "ripeness" of the case, if all other avenues for determining it—such as Mrs. Suitum's attempting to transfer development rights—had been exhausted. The PLF had expanded the case by saying it was a demonstration of how lower courts were misapplying a previous Supreme Court ruling. PLF attorneys asserted that TDRs, being used in a number of locales across the country, were a ruse, preventing landowners from essential uses of their property, such as building a home. In what would dramatically expand property owners' Fifth Amendment rights, they asked the Court to invalidate overreaching by the state such as "fabricated" TDRs. If the Court agreed, landowners would be far more likely to succeed in future regulatory takings claims against land-use regulators.

Supreme Court decisions are rendered only on lower courts' records without allowance for new arguments, and this worked against the PLF. Their attorneys were attempting to collapse aggressive libertarian theories into the narrow argument regarding the ripeness of the landowner's case.

Briefs in support of TRPA reflected the importance of the issue across the country. Among others, including the League to Save Lake Tahoe, the US solicitor general, California and Nevada joined by six other states, the National League of Cities, and the US Conference of Mayors filed briefs.

In its decision, the Court found unanimously that the Ninth Circuit Court had erred. It ruled Mrs. Suitum's takings challenge was ripe; courts routinely value property rights based on appraisal evidence. But the opinion addressed only the ripeness issue. It specifically omitted the larger matter regarding the significance of TDRs. In a separate concurring opinion, Justice Antonin Scalia, joined by Justices Thomas and O'Connor, would have had the Court agree with the broader claim that TDRs are wholly irrelevant to the basic question of whether a regulation amounts to a taking. That opinion suggested that TRPA stream environment zone regulations may, in fact, effect a categorical taking. Because Scalia's minority opinion did not set precedent, the ruling allowed similar regulations around the country to be imposed, while remanding the *Suitum* case to Nevada's federal district court in Reno.

In May 1999, the parties reached a settlement averting a "takings" trial. TRPA, while conceding no liability, paid Mrs. Suitum $515,000 for the property and her legal fees and $85,000 to the PLF. But the TDR program had been left intact. The case had taken a decade to decide. Because no legal precedents had been set and Mrs. Suitum had not received a financial windfall, the settlement did not encourage similar lawsuits.[6]

Tahoe-Sierra Preservation Council v. TRPA was the most anticipated of the court decisions regarding the agency. It was appealed to the Supreme Court in 2002. The case began in 1984 when the preservation council sued the agency, seeking compensation under the Takings Clause of the US Constitution. Constitutional law develops incrementally. The phrase "nor shall private property be taken for public use, without just compensation," in the Fifth Amendment is a prime example.

In 1986 US District Court judge Reed had rejected a version of the complaint in Reno, affirming TRPA's zoning capabilities. At that time, a 1978 decision, *Penn Central Transportation Co. v. New York City,* identified three factors as being particularly important in takings claims: the economic impact of the regulation, the extent of interference in investment-backed expectations, and the character of the government action—for example, whether it amounts to a physical invasion or affects properties while promoting the public good. The preservation council appealed Reed's decision, and, in the meantime, a 1992 Supreme Court finding, *Lucas v. S. Carolina Coastal Commission,* reevaluated compensatory requirements. The Court found that property, deprived of economically viable use—unless such use was already prohibited—required automatic compensation to the owner. In *Lucas* the fact that the coastal

commission was protecting against erosion had no bearing: unless conflicting with "the State's law of property and nuisance," compensation was required
without regard to the purposes of the regulation.

In its amended pleadings, the preservation council sought compensation for
landowners and former landowners for three time periods: the 1981–84 moratorium, Judge Garcia's injunction from 1984 to 1987, and post-1987, a period in
which the plaintiffs were challenging the TRPA restrictions. Years of litigation
produced three procedural decisions by the Ninth Circuit, including the issue's
ripeness for adjudication, so that the liability phase of the trial did not take
place until 1998. Now senior judge Edward Reed again presided.

The preservation council mounted a "facial" challenge, arguing that their
assertion that TRPA's enactment of regulations constituted a taking was valid
on its face: that it was apparent. Because of this, they chose not to present evidence of plaintiff-specific economic impacts, which would have been a difficult
task because of the hundreds of plaintiffs.

The preservation council's allegations included that the building moratorium had been too long and that the TRPA Board members had been dragging
their feet. The defense answered that the agency's actions showed that it had
listened to all parties. In waiting to decide, TRPA had deliberated, ensuring that
it accommodated the complex forces at work. It had been a democratic process, defense attorneys argued; the alternative would have been for the agency
to issue fiats.

Robert Twiss and Charles Goldman again testified for the defense, making
presentations similar to those in the *William Cody Kelly* case in state court.
Twiss explained how the Bailey system's land-capability map had been developed and why it came out the way it did. He described TRPA's administrative
process, how the science got implemented, why the ordinances had been put
in place, the chronology of the entire process, why building in stream environment zones was prohibited, and why there was a subdivision building ban.
Goldman presented evidence of the increased nutrient loading in the lake due
to development. Twiss's slides illustrated the damage to the environment.

The preservation council presented a theory that TRPA had passed an inadequate plan in 1984 because it secretly wanted an injunction against all construction in the basin. They argued further that a lawsuit and Judge Garcia's

injunction had been foreseeable consequences of the plan. As per its amended complaint in 1991, it also alleged that the 1987 development restrictions constituted a taking that required compensation.

The last claim was dismissed, barred by the statute of limitations. Constitutional challenges need to be filed within one year in California and within two in Nevada. The preservation council had waited four years to pursue its claim and had difficulty explaining the delay, as it had been an active participant in the consensus process that established the 1987 regulations. As to the injunction, Judge Reed disagreed that TRPA was somehow responsible. It had been enacted not by the agency but by the courts. Judge Reed found that the agency had acted in good faith in attempting to comply with the compact and that there was absolutely no evidence that they had tried to pass a deficient regional plan that would force an injunction.

But Judge Reed found in favor of the preservation council regarding the 1981–84 moratorium, although writing a lengthy analysis agreeing with the TRPA witnesses' arguments. "Unless the process is stopped," he said, "the lake will lose its clarity and its trademark blue color, becoming green and opaque for eternity." He also supported the agency's actions, noting that the process had been messy but illustrated democracy in action. Given the complexity of the task of defining threshold carrying capacities and the division of opinion within the governing board, it was unsurprising to the court that consensus took a long time. Judge Reed concluded that the character of TRPA's action strongly suggested finding against compensation because the moratorium was a reasonable measure in attempting to protect the lake. Nevertheless, because of the substantial economic impact on lot owners from 1981 to 1984, the judge determined that a temporary taking had occurred. Reed believed this part of the decision was supported by the Supreme Court's *Lucas* ruling and a 1987 finding, *First English Evangelical Lutheran Church v. County of Los Angeles*, which held that government cannot avoid compensation for a temporary taking by repealing the regulation.[7]

The sides cross-appealed. TRPA sought to reverse the finding regarding its compensatory liability for the moratorium; the preservation council sought to reverse the holding that TRPA was not liable for the injunction and the 1987 plan. In June 2000, the Ninth Circuit Court of Appeals gave an outright victory to TRPA. The preservation council's appeals were denied on causation and statute-of-limitation grounds. The Ninth Circuit distinguished *Lucas* from the temporary moratorium because *Lucas* required that all use of the land be denied for the foreseeable future. The court concluded that *First English* did not apply because that ruling dealt with the *remedy* for a taking, not guidance regarding *when* such a taking occurred. It concluded that the entire time frame must be considered in analyzing a regulatory taking.[8]

A preservation council petition for an en banc rehearing, before all the judges of the circuit court, was denied. But the petition revealed a deep split in the court, as four circuit judges dissented from the denial. They believed that *First English* determined that moratoriums are takings requiring compensation. They felt strongly that the Supreme Court would concur if presented with the issue.

The Supreme Court granted a preservation council writ of certiorari, limiting it to the Ninth Circuit's decision that the temporary moratorium did not constitute a taking. Illustrating the importance of the case across America, a dozen amicus briefs were filed. Among others, briefs supporting TRPA came from the United States; the State of Vermont, on behalf of twenty other states; the National League of Cities; and the National Audubon Society. Briefs supporting the Preservation Council included the Pacific Legal Foundation, the National Association of Home Builders, and the American Farm Bureau.

John G. Roberts, the future chief justice of the Supreme Court, argued the case for TRPA, and Solicitor General Ted Olsen used ten minutes of the thirty minutes allowed for oral arguments. Olsen contended that government moratoriums should be treated no differently from other permit delays.

In an audacious display, the preservation council brief ignored the limit placed on the appeal, saying, "[TRPA] regulations plainly took the property's use and potential for whatever period of time the Court cares to examine between 1981 through the present." During arguments the Court emphasized that it was considering only the 1981–84 moratorium.

On April 23, 2002, the Court announced its decision. A six-person majority held that TRPA did not need to compensate the property owners for the thirty-two-month moratorium. It found that *Penn Central*, not *Lucas*, was the proper tool for evaluating the constitutionality of planning moratoriums and confirmed the Ninth Circuit's finding that *First English* bears only on the remedy once a taking is determined. The opinion pleased government entities around the country, endorsing moratoriums as tools in comprehensive planning efforts.[9]

It was an overwhelming victory for TRPA. The Court had accepted their witnesses' testimony regarding the threats to Tahoe's delicate ecosystems as well as the need for agency controls.

Three other significant Tahoe court cases were argued in the latter part of the twentieth century. They did not involve TRPA or constitutional issues. The first two related cases, *Hewlett v. Cushing* and *People of the State of California v. Squaw Valley Ski Corporation,* had ecological importance in the basin. The other case concerned Cave Rock, *The Access Fund v. U.S. Department of Agriculture,* and had national importance for Native American rights. In each case, Tahoe's heritage was given precedence over unrestricted use of its resources.

Alex Cushing was a Harvard-educated attorney recruited as an investor by ski-industry visionary Wayne Poulsen to help develop Squaw Valley into a ski resort in the 1950s. Shortly before the area opened for business, a bitter dispute broke up the partnership. Cushing owned 52 percent of the stock, and he called a stockholders' meeting while Poulsen, the president, was out of town. Cushing ousted Poulsen, taking control of the area that comprised a small lodge, one rope tow, and a long double chair lift. Intent on gaining publicity, in 1954 Cushing submitted a bid to host the 1960 Winter Olympics. When, against all odds, Cushing's dogged lobbying resulted in the US nomination, Avery Brundage, the president of the International Olympic Committee, commented that the US committee "obviously has taken leave of their senses." A similar effort by Cushing at the international level created one of the biggest coups in sports history, bringing the Games to the resort that one Olympic committee member called "a glorified picnic ground."

Cushing earned his way to the Ski Industry and U.S. National Ski Halls of Fame by putting on hugely successful Games. Infrastructure built for the event included the Reno Tahoe International Airport in Reno and improvements to the highways from Sacramento and Carson City to the lake. An estimated 240,000 people attended, and the televised coverage, revealing Tahoe's scenic wonders, was a primary factor in making it a worldwide destination resort.

After the Olympics, Cushing spent large amounts of time on the East Coast, and throughout the 1960s and 1970s the lifts and facilities deteriorated. The collapse of the Olympic ice rink's roof symbolized the resort's plight. In 1975 Cushing decided to revitalize the resort. As evinced by his procurement of the Olympics, Cushing would charge headlong into projects. He also believed that dealing with state and federal politics "was chaos," following the maxim "Build first, then get permission."[1]

Owing to those attitudes, Cushing became the poster boy for bad environmental stewardship. The resort was fined year after year for emitting pollutants into Squaw Creek, which runs into the Truckee River. The water-quality board identified Squaw Valley's management as repeat violators "who disputed almost every regulatory or enforcement action." In 1983 Cushing was fined $350,000 after being found guilty of trying to hide a two-thousand-gallon diesel-oil spill in the snow.[2]

Cushing acquired the part of Shirley Canyon that had been a state park adjoining Squaw Valley in the early 1970s, as Governor Ronald Reagan did not want the state in the ski business. When Cushing sought to improve his resort, Placer County approved the removal of 90 trees in Shirley Canyon for a "through-the-trees" expert run. But, noting that the area had "sensitive geologic, soil, slope, and vegetative characteristics," the county included severe restrictions in the approval: the county permit specified no other trees would be removed and no roads developed "now or in the future."

Throughout the 1980s, the resort's plans evolved, until in 1988 its management sought, and the county board of supervisors approved, the removal of 1,858 trees to enlarge the Shirley Canyon ski trails. Nearby property owners and the Sierra Club filed suit to block the clear-cutting of the canyon slope. In January 1989, before the court could hear the case, Cushing met with his mountain manager. Another employee overheard Cushing say, "We have a very short time frame here. We have the legal documents to proceed on this. Let's get these things cut. What are they going to do, make us replant them?"[3]

A plan to sell the timber had been in the works but had not received approval from the California Department of Forestry. When informed that the cutting was to take place the following weekend, the resort's professional forester had "pointed discussions" with Cushing's manager, attempting to get him to wait. But on January 28–30, 1989, the resort cut more than 1,800 trees, a number of which were three to six hundred years old. Immediately thereafter, the Sierra Club obtained a temporary restraining order, prohibiting further cutting. Several weeks later, in violation of the order, 18 more trees were cut.

The neighboring property owners dropped out of the lawsuit, which the Sierra Club wished to pursue. When he read of the violations in the newspaper, William Hewlett, who owned a home nearby and hiked the canyon with his father in the 1930s, joined the lawsuit. Hewlett had provided the money to protect Meeks Bay from development in the early 1970s until the Forest Service was able to buy it for the public. Now in his eighties, and one of the forty richest men in America, Hewlett became involved, saying he wanted to make sure Cushing, also an octogenarian millionaire, could not "outgun" the plaintiffs. Although Placer County also joined the suit against the resort, because of Hewlett's ownership of Hewlett-Packard, the *Los Angeles Times* dubbed the case "Silicone Valley versus Squaw Valley." Cushing told the paper the plaintiffs were attempting to crush him. "I'm the biggest employer in Placer County, and they treat me as if I'm running a crack house."[4]

Two skiers had died at the resort after running into trees, and Cushing contended that he logged the canyon as a safety precaution. "We took those trees out for a good reason," he said, "and we would take them out again." The court saw the actions differently, noting that when developing the area, the resort had described it as an expert ski run and that profits were the motive rather than safety for removing "the very trees which previously would have provided the unique skiing experience."[5]

Despite the fact that the cutting had occurred in January and again in March, resort attorneys tried to portray it as one act. The judge and attorneys visited the site to view the cutting themselves. All parties were surprised to find felled trees with fresh saw marks and branches with needles intact, evidence that they had been cut down since the last injunction.

The suit sought prohibitory injunctive relief and civil penalties, citing unlawful business practices, violation of the Forest Practice Act, violation of conditions of a use permit, and violation of the terms of a temporary restraining order. Cushing's lawyers disputed all issues, and lost on them all.

The court imposed penalties totaling $223,000, as well as attorney fees to

Hewlett of $480,000 and to the Sierra Club of $192,000. As to the injunctive relief, it noted that Cushing would like to develop additional trails in the area and ordered that "the area covered by the preliminary injunction issued herein shall constitute a zone free from further development in any manner." The finding was upheld on appeal. Calling Squaw Valley's attitude "cavalier," the Third Appellate District Court commented that the monetary penalties were "modest in light of Squaw Valley's egregious behavior." As to the injunctive relief ordered by the trial court, the appeals court said it represented an appropriate response to "the disdainful attitude exhibited."[6]

Cushing's attorney had commented that Cushing liked to do things his own way. "[Cushing] realizes he scarred the mountain in years past, and now he's trying to make up for that," the attorney said. "But he hates to slow down just because someone wants him to wait and go through the bureaucratic process."

In fact, Cushing's disdain for the environment carried the battles into the twenty-first century. The resort's activities substantially harmed Squaw Creek, and it and the Truckee River were listed among the nation's most polluted waterways due to excess sediment loads. In 1998 Squaw Valley was charged by the Lahontan Regional Water Quality Control Board with engaging in a series of violations of the Clean Water Act and the Rivers and Harbors Act. The resort in obtaining permission to construct a new gondola described the project to county and state officials as involving minimal excavation. Instead, dynamite blasting resulted in the excavating of thousands of cubic yards of material and the reshaping of a ridge. The debris, which was supposed to be removed, was instead cast off the ridge toward Squaw Creek, where it was allowed to wash into the stream.

In June 2000, EPA agents seized more than two hundred items at the Squaw Valley offices, including documents, computers, hard drives, and files, looking for information on the creek pollution as well as a charge that the ski area destroyed a wetland and failed to restore it in a timely fashion.[7]

In January 2002, the California attorney general filed a complaint identifying fourteen causes of action against Squaw Valley. Specific offenses included constructing projects without permits, using dynamite in direct violation of a permanent injunction, removing trees, removing or burying vegetation, illegally modifying stream channels, misrepresenting the number of chairlifts to be in place after construction, removing wetlands, significantly expanding ski trails without authorization, failure to report a waste discharge, and misrepresenting a project that obliterated a natural drainage.[8]

Numerous meetings between the enforcing agencies, representatives of Placer County and the state, and the defendants resulted in an out-of-court settlement involving Squaw Valley's payment of $900,000 and millions of dollars in mitigation work. The 217-page consent agreement for final judgment listed in detail the required projects, including rebuilding wetlands; soil, stream, channel, and culvert restoration; revegetation and riparian vegetation work; and audits to evaluate monitoring data. Automatic fines from $25,000 to $125,000 would be assessed for future disturbances or work done without a permit.[9]

Over the next several years, Squaw Valley met the terms of the settlement directives. At Cushing's death in 2006, his third wife, Nancy, an attorney who worked alongside him in modernizing the resort, succeeded him as president. She reversed the resort's course, and, devoting considerable resources to the effort, Squaw Valley was recognized three straight years by the Ski Area Citizens' Coalition as the nation's number-one resort for environmental practices.[10]

As for William Hewlett, at his death in January 2001, owing to his "tireless contributions to the public good," he was eulogized as having offered "the best of what philanthropy is."[11] His efforts to preserve Meeks Bay for public use gained an added historical benefit in 1998 when the Washoe Indian Tribe became reestablished there. The Forest Service, influenced by two President Clinton executive orders directing federal agencies to partner with Native American tribes to enhance historic preservation programs and traditional Native sites, awarded the Washoe a twenty-year lease to operate Meeks Bay Resort and restore Meeks Bay meadow to utilize its plants.

At the same time, the tribe was involved in litigation involving a site directly across the lake from Meeks Bay, "De' ek wadapush," or Cave Rock. It is the most dominant feature on the lake's shoreline and has been the most important source of power for Washoe shamans from before written history. In the fall of 1992, Washoe tribal chair Brian Wallace made a startling discovery: climbers had used metal anchors drilled into the rock in building routes up the sheer cliff face below and above the main cave. Wallace notified authorities that the climbers were damaging the site, saying, "We believe the most recent destruction of Cave Rock . . . adds insult to injury in the disturbing recent history of this very religious place." Seventeen years of bitter dispute followed, until the Ninth Circuit Court of Appeals finally decided the case for the Washoe.[12]

In the pre-American Washoe world, Wegeléyu, or "Power," permeated the universe. Power's essence animated all living things and could be used for good or evil. A select few Washoe, the dreamers and shamans, most of whom were healers, could tap into Wegeléyu's constant flow at Cave Rock. Misuse of the site threatened the individual and Washoe and non-Washoe communities alike. So traditionally, with the exception of shamans, Washoe avoided going near the cave. A highway tunnel blasted below the main cave in 1931 and another in 1957 did nothing to change the feelings of traditional Washoe regarding the site's power. Many believe it so sacrosanct that to get to nearby destinations, they will follow the winding mostly two-lane highway seventy-two miles around the lake rather than drive through the tunnels.[13]

Sport rock climbers discovered Cave Rock sometime around 1988, setting the first of an eventual 325 anchors in the granite. The complexities presented by the site's steep walls and its aesthetic qualities made it the apex of the 112 climbing areas in the Tahoe area. A number of climbers did not want to give it up even after finding it was a traditional sacred site.

Concerned about the dispute, in 1996 US Forest Service supervisor Robert Harris inquired and found that because of its long association with the Washoe Tribe, the site was eligible for the National Register of Historic Places as a "Traditional Cultural Property." In February 1997, Harris, whose retirement was imminent, issued a closure order for climbing so that the issue could be studied further.[14]

Three months later, Juan Palma replaced Harris as forest supervisor. He stepped into a hornet's nest. A national climbers' advocacy group, the Access Fund, had notified the Forest Service Regional Office that they were preparing to take the issue to court, and climbers bombarded the agency with protest letters. Palma lifted the ban, although he urged climbers to continue to avoid the site out of respect for the Washoe people. That did not happen. Five days after the ruling, the *Tahoe Daily Tribune* reported a seventeen-year-old climber saying, "We went out there yesterday, and some of the best climbers in Tahoe were there. We're really happy just to be climbing back there again."[15]

The Forest Service strategy for resolving the dispute began with five public meetings intended to find areas of compromise. A Forest Service official revealed at one meeting that climbing had been determined to be an ongoing adverse effect on what was now considered a national historic site. He pointed out, though, that that finding could be mitigated or even ignored by the supervisor, who would make the final decision.

The Tahoe meetings were doomed from the start. By the third meeting, climbers were proposing eleven things they would do differently if allowed to continue climbing at the site. These ranged from signs in the area describing the significance of the place to Washoe to camouflaging the slings dangling from anchors. Their suggestions included asking those who had named the routes to change offensive names (a sample of which were "Bat Out of Hell," "Cave Man," "Super Monkey," and "Shut the Fuck Up and Climb").[16]

Regarding criticism that only the climbers were attempting to compromise, the tribe's Wallace said, "Washoes would respond that we've been forced to compromise for the last 177 years."[17]

On January 13, 1999, two years after the original closure, Palma announced his finding in a draft environmental impact statement. He explained that he had attempted to strike a balance. The proposal stated, "Public Access, including rock climbing, is allowed . . . and will be managed to minimize conflicts."[18]

There was a major flaw in Palma's decision. It did not follow the guidelines of LTBMU's Forest Plan. The plan included a prioritized list of resources to be used in resolving conflicts. Protection of cultural resources is third on the list and recreation four places below. The ranking obviously had not been used when Palma came up with his solution.

Letters to the supervisor included Wallace's calling attention to the fact that to disregard the rankings deviated from the agency's own plan. Former forest supervisor Harris stated that it was "of utmost importance" that the public be told why the forest plan was not followed. Palma would not answer these objections. He had announced he had taken a job as a BLM ranger in Oregon. So a final decision remained pending.[19]

When she arrived at Lake Tahoe in July 2000, the new forest supervisor, Maribeth Gustafson, began personally interviewing key participants and reviewing all that had been done previously: reviewing the draft impact statement and public comments and watching videotape of the collaboration meetings. Gustafson was struck by the vehemence of the opposing sides.[20]

In October 2002, Gustafson issued the final environmental impact statement, which had been delayed for two years. It turned Palma's draft judgment upside down. According to the Gustafson determination, Cave Rock would be managed as a Traditional Cultural Property, and anything adversely affecting it was prohibited. That meant climbing would be banned. Appeals were filed immediately by climbers and the Access Fund.[21]

The Forest Service itself first considered the appeal. The agency looked into climbers' complaints and the supervisor's responses.

Climbers claimed that the democratic process had been denied. Gustafson replied that there had been extensive public participation, but that agency decisions were made by its managers, not by popular vote. She pointed out that it was not until participation failed that the decision was made by the supervisor following the forest management plan.

In responding to the contention that the agency's decision unfairly restricted the rights of users, Gustafson responded that the Forest Service had a duty to ensure fair use on federal land. But it does not require the agency to allow every activity everywhere, and she listed examples: prohibiting grazing in areas to protect water quality and restricting fires.[22]

On November 5, 2003, the agency affirmed Gustafson's decision, saying that all laws, policies, and regulations had been followed. The Access Fund now appealed to the courts.

The Washoe had reason to be leery about a court case. The judicial system has consistently found for state interests over Native American land rights. Moreover, the Access Fund was asserting that a ban on climbing promoted Washoe religion. Gustafson had said the decision was not made to accommodate religious practices, stating, "This is not a choice between religious use and recreation use; it is a decision to reduce impacts of recreation on an historic resource." The Access Fund did not accept her contention for a reason: if ever Native property rights were tied up with religious values in court cases, the Natives lost.

There are religious sites that are national monuments. The National Cathedral, the Touro Synagogue, and the Sixteenth Street Baptist Church in Birmingham are examples, but entering the twenty-first century none were Native American sites. Court cases regarding sacred Indian places have always been based on the First Amendment, which states: "Congress shall make no law respecting an establishment of religion, or prohibiting the free exercise thereof." Commonly referred to as the "Establishment Clause," the first part of the pronouncement prohibits the government from promoting one religion over another. Anytime a sacred site was considered by the courts, the Establishment Clause trumped all other issues.

A 1988 Supreme Court case ended once and for all the First Amendment venue as a possible safeguard for Indian sacred sites. The Rehnquist Court heard the case *Lyng v. Northwest Indian Cemetery Association.* The case came after the Forest Service approved a paved road through an Indian cemetery and allowed timber harvesting near a religious site in Six Rivers National Forest. The lower courts had found for the Indians, saying the site was indispensable to their religion. The Rehnquist Court overturned the finding. The only limitations on the government, the Court said, were that it not coerce any group into violating its religious beliefs or penalize it for practicing them.

Sandra Day O'Connor delivered the decision, commenting, "Even assuming that the Government's actions here will virtually destroy the Indians' ability to practice their religion, the Constitution simply does not provide a principle that could justify upholding their legal claims."[23]

It was not until a year later that district court judge Howard McKibben heard the Cave Rock case in Reno. It was difficult to speculate how Judge McKibben might view the issue. He had previously accepted federal authority in a case against Indians, allowing the government sale of Shoshone cattle confiscated on land claimed by both the BLM and the tribe. In another instance, he did not seem overly protective of Native antiquities, giving two men relatively short sentences, two months and four months, for stealing large petroglyph-covered boulders. As regarded a federal agency protecting an Indian site, how he might decide was anybody's guess.[24]

A team of attorneys for the Access Fund presented an argument similar to the earlier appeal: the Establishment Clause of the First Amendment had been violated. Following their contention that Gustafson had unjustifiably reversed Palma's decision, they now added the complaint that the Forest Service had acted arbitrarily and capriciously.

Although he stated that he would not necessarily have made the same decision as the forest supervisor, Judge McKibben rejected the Access Fund's contentions. Because the supervisor had observed all applicable laws and followed her agency's policies, he found no reason to annul her decision.[25]

The appeal then was taken to the Ninth Circuit Court, which heard the case on February 15, 2007, in San Francisco. Each side was allowed a short oral argument, and the judges questioned the attorneys regarding the Establishment Clause and why the agency's action might be arbitrary or capricious.

The Access Fund insisted the decision promoted religion, with Washoe themselves consistently referring to Cave Rock as sacred. Limiting free access, it was argued, coerced the public to support Washoe religion.

The decision was not released until a number of months later. The court disagreed with the Access Fund. It said that there was no hint that the Forest Service favored the Washoe religion over other religions. It wrote, "The facts reflect only that climbers, whatever their religious beliefs, would prefer climbing on the rock, and the government's policy prevents them from doing so." It noted that the Forest Service presented thorough documentation that although Cave Rock may at times be discussed in religious terms, its significance was based on the Washoe historic and ethnographic record.

The Access Fund's last hope to overthrow the decision lay with the claim that forest supervisor Gustafson had been arbitrary or capricious. The court concluded that her action was neither, saying, "The ban was adopted after deliberate and thoughtful analysis and based on nonarbitrary historical considerations."[26]

With the last decision, the climbing group gave up their legal challenge.

In August 2007, the Forest Service put into effect the ban on climbing, and in the spring of 2009, seventeen years after the dispute began, the anchors were removed from the rock.[27]

Along with the contentious court cases, a movement in a diametric direction began in the last years of the twentieth century. Environmentalists and business representatives began working together in support of the lake's ecological health. The effort, which lasted nearly twenty years, created what key players came to call the "era of collaboration."

The opposing Tahoe political groups' differences regarding the natural and man-made environments caused their associations to be confrontational. TRPA director Bill Morgan had broken through the mistrust between the groups at a time when the sides were tired of fighting in the courts. He had convinced them to come together to forge agreements once differences were reduced to a manageable size. Environmentalist Dwight Steele used the same strategy a few years later.

In 2000 *Sierra* magazine named Steele one of the San Francisco Bay Area's environmental "urban legends." He was an attorney who in the 1960s largely abandoned his career as a leading labor lawyer to become the legal adviser to the "Save the Bay" movement, fighting development that threatened to fill San Francisco Bay. From the 1970s until his death in 2002, he served on dozens of commissions and foundations and won prestigious awards for his conservation work, but he was not a stereotypical environmentalist. He did tai chi and enjoyed cigars; he belonged to the Sierra Club but also to California's exclusive Bohemian Club. This last, along with his high-powered legal experience, afforded him access to the highest executives in California industry and finance, a perquisite he would use when environmental projects required it.[1]

Steele served on the TRPA Governing Board from 1980 to 1983 and later was general counsel for the League to Save Lake Tahoe. Although extremely partisan in his positions regarding protecting Tahoe, he was politically astute and seen as credible by those who advocated property rights as well. In 1989 he contacted the disparate groups that had argued over Tahoe issues through the years and proposed an idea, collaborating on an undetermined issue that all might agree would benefit the lake. If they could agree on such an issue, they would be able to wield considerable influence. The Planning and Conservation League, a Sacramento-based group that promotes legislation to protect the California environment, hosted a meeting of those who agreed to take part. Representatives of the Attorney General's Office, the League to Save Lake

Tahoe, the Tahoe-Sierra Preservation Council, and the two biggest industries in the Tahoe business community—the Gaming Alliance and the California Ski Industry Association—participated. The group was later dubbed the "Unholy Alliance."

Group members agreed that improving transportation in the basin would benefit the environment, the economy, and the community, and this led to the formation of the "Tahoe Transportation Coalition." The alliance gained the support of the four Tahoe chambers of commerce, the lodging association, and the visitors' bureau. They raised some thirty-five thousand dollars and in June 1992 funded bringing in experts for a four-day workshop that produced a report dealing with improving roads and public transportation. The effectiveness of the process gave the coalition visibility and credibility.

Those involved came to realize the problem of having no regular funding source for sustaining projects within the basin and no one coordinating legislative advocacy in Washington, DC, and they organized a federal legislative agenda. Three individuals played primary roles in the group: Steve Teshara, the former director of the preservation council, representing the Gaming Alliance; Stan Hansen, Heavenly Valley senior vice president, representing the ski industry; and Rochelle Nason, early in her eighteen-year tenure as executive director of the League to Save Lake Tahoe. They enlisted the business and environmental communities and major resort industries to form a lobbying coalition that traveled to Washington, DC, on a somewhat regular biannual schedule. The league provided the funding for the first few years, and Dan Potash, the league's lobbying consultant, helped with coordination between the group and various congressional decision makers.

For the next ten years, the group, which broadened its base and eventually renamed itself the "Lake Tahoe Transportation and Water Quality Coalition," met to find areas of agreement for projects for which they might seek congressional appropriations.[2]

The Tahoe group's success came because, instead of looking for agreements about general issues regarding land use and planning, they identified projects over which they could gain consensus and sought to secure funding for them. Typically, a large group of stakeholders would meet once a month to develop a legislative agenda. A number of sources noted that the California Tahoe

Conservancy's Dennis Machida played an important role building relationships that allowed the coalition to succeed.[3] The effort became truly effective when James Baetge, beginning six years as executive director of TRPA in 1994, embraced the effort, and TRPA representatives took part in carrying the proposals to Washington.

In the mid-1990s, dealing with newly elected members of US Congress, unfamiliar with the lake's issues and the uniqueness of the bistate agency, the Tahoe group discussed the idea that perhaps California and Nevada needed to publicly reaffirm their commitment to the health of the lake. Nevada senator Harry Reid carried the idea of honoring the national treasure to President Clinton, who agreed to attend. After many months of planning, in July 1997 Lake Tahoe hosted the "Presidential Summit."[4]

Rochelle Nason pointed out how galvanizing the event was, saying, "It was very exciting and very heartening that people came together like they did." President Clinton brought numerous members of his administration, including Vice President Al Gore. Also in attendance were US senators Harry Reid and Richard Bryan of Nevada and Dianne Feinstein of California, as well as California and Nevada state and local officials.[5]

Along with cabinet-level forums held regarding specific issues—water and air quality, forest restoration, and transportation—one of the main goals of the summit was to create a partnership among private interests, local agencies, and the federal agencies. Senator Bryan said, "It was bipartisan consensus-building from the ground up." In touting the fact that the summit caused a number of key agreements to be signed, Steve Teshara later commented, "It wasn't arguing about what was in the regional plan or not. . . . [W]e were focused on getting things done on the ground."[6]

The Saturday morning of the summit, Clinton and Gore, arriving in separate helicopters for security reasons, accompanied scientists Goldman and Richards to do experiments aboard the *John LeConte*. The president and vice president saw how the Secchi dish was utilized and collected plankton samples. They also listened as Goldman described the increase of 300 percent in algal concentrations and the loss of one-third of the lake's clarity since his studies began. Giving worldwide publicity to the problems, the president issued a call to action.[7]

In 1979 President Carter had signed an executive order directing federal agencies to work together on Lake Tahoe issues. President Clinton now presented his own executive order, creating a federal interagency partnership that created links between the federal, state, and local agencies and the private sector. He also doubled the money agencies spent in the basin, pledging $26 million in new spending over the next two years.

James Baetge came up with the idea that all the projects needed to achieve and maintain TRPA's environmental thresholds would be contained in one Environmental Improvement Program (EIP). At the summit, he held up a large book and described how the program would be implemented through the newly announced partnership of agencies, private interests, and the Washoe Tribe. As no projects were yet approved, he was holding an empty book. But when the program was officially adopted in March 1998, it quickly filled. Expertise was galvanized on projects from the West Shore transit startup, costing $250,000, to the Federal Highway Administration's $4 million treatment of roadway runoff before its discharge into the lake. Over the next fifteen years, TRPA oversaw $1.55 billion being spent to complete 366 EIP projects, with 166 ongoing in 2012.[8]

The summit had naysayers like California representative John Doolittle: "[Clinton] is a good talker and the speech sounded good. But as Richard Nixon said, 'It's not what you say, it's what you do.'" A spokesman for California Republican governor Pete Wilson, who was conspicuously absent, was also critical, saying, "When you unwrap the bow and look at the details, its mostly packaging." But the partisan sniping proved to be only that, as the summit provided far-reaching outcomes, including renewed strategies to finance the lake's environmental health, partnerships that included all the key actors, and a commitment by federal representatives to hold annual "Lake Tahoe Summit" conferences, hosted by federal representatives.[9]

Throughout the original summit, the efforts of Tahoe's advocacy group were apparent. Stan Hansen told reporters the results had come from long hours of presummit negotiating. He said the steering committee had two mottoes: the league's "Keep Tahoe blue" and the property-rights advocates' "Remember the private sector." Both of them, he pointed out, were reflected in the presidential order developing federal-local partnerships.

Vice President Gore saw the results and commented, "In this special place, the business community and the environmentalists have resolved their conflicts and come together with one voice." Clinton noted the two reasons he had come to the summit: to point out the importance of Tahoe and to show the nation a place where "everybody is working together in common cause." He said, "We don't have to choose between the environment and the economy. That's a dumb choice."[10]

One result of the summit was support for the US Senate's Lake Tahoe Restoration Act. By the year 2000, the act's sponsors, Senators Feinstein and Barbara Boxer of California and Nevada's Reid and Bryan, gained the act's passage. It authorized $300 million in expenditures in the partnership that coordinated federal efforts with state and local entities. In response to the president's directives, Secretary of Agriculture Dan Glickman established the Lake Tahoe Federal Advisory Commission, comprising individuals from across the Lake Tahoe stakeholders' spectrum. It included representatives of property rights, the environment, gaming, science and research, state and local governments, TRPA, and the Washoe Tribe, all of whom had input on which EIP projects should be funded.[11]

Of the $1.55 billion spent on Tahoe restoration and conservation projects, the State of California contributed $621 million, or 40 percent, a large portion managed by the California Tahoe Conservancy. The federal government provided 32 percent, $490 million, much of it coming from the amended Southern Nevada Public Land Management Act of 1998, which, like the Burton-Santini law eighteen years earlier, sold BLM land in Clark County, generating moneys for use in southern Nevada while providing for work at Tahoe. Private entities contributed funding in the form of fees from programs like Best Management Practices and restoration projects, providing $286 million, or 18 percent. The State of Nevada put in $93 million, 6 percent, primarily through general obligation bonds. The local governments contributed $65 million, or 4 percent, in mitigation fees for building and development.[12]

The local coalition's era of collaboration was at the forefront of the national "greening of business" movement of the mid-1990s. Local coalition organizer Teshara said, "[The effort] was a true national model of how you would organize collaboration." Clinton's secretary of the interior, Bruce Babbitt, concurred, saying, "The cooperative way in which Lake Tahoe communities are working together is a showcase for innovative, collaborative approaches to restoring large-scale ecosystems."[13]

In 2004 and 2005, the coalition unraveled. The original organizer, Dwight Steele, died in 2002, and Dennis Machida, who had played such an important role in encouraging people to work together, died suddenly in March 2005.

When the TRPA Regional Plan was approved in 1987, it had a twenty-year time frame and called for a review and update by 2007. The agency's attempt to meet the deadline begun in 2004, an effort dubbed Pathway 2000, drove a wedge between the partners in the coalition. Under John Singlaub, a former BLM manager who took over as executive director of TRPA in January 2004, the agency decided that the previously agreed-upon environmental threshold carrying capacities would not necessarily guide the next regional plan. This was anathema to the conservation community now composed of seven grassroots groups from around the basin. Their leaders believed weakening the thresholds would irrevocably damage the lake.

Despite the protestations, the agency attempted to bring together all the basin stakeholders to formulate new standards. What was termed the "Pathways" process failed. As groups with environmental interests and those with economic concerns looked to plan for the future, old battles were rekindled. Singlaub was surprised at how fervent they were. "[Stakeholders] wanted to be sure it was clear we had polarized agendas," he said.[14]

The agency attempted to include all interested parties in the collaboration. This brought in dozens of representatives of councils, boards, agencies, and private organizations and firms, and it created too large a working group. Organization was unwieldy, and subcommittees broke into factions.[15]

The League to Save Tahoe wanted to maintain the thresholds and the Bailey land-classification system, evaluating the capacity for building parcel by parcel. Private-property advocates argued that Bailey was outdated and should be replaced, perhaps by a framework that would involve watershed management encompassing the entire basin. They thought to boost local economies by focusing on redevelopment, utilizing new technologies to better manage urbanized areas and allow for growth. The league feared redevelopment meant larger projects attracting more visitors, creating more pollution. With the acrimony, the transportation and water-quality coalition, which for years accommodated both perspectives, fell apart.[16]

Despite the political infighting, science seemed to be making notable gains. Professor Goldman's Tahoe Research Group had evolved into the Tahoe Environmental Research Center, or TERC. They were within a couple years of building a new Platinum Leed–certified research center at Incline Village, with three research vessels, including one named for Goldman's associate, the *Bob Richards*. At TERC six research institutes and nine agencies joined together to form the Tahoe Science Consortium, all contributing to the goal of preserving or restoring the lake's unique environmental values.

After years of measurements in the sixty-foot range, for four consecutive years beginning in 2001, the lake's water clarity was measured at more than seventy feet. In 2005 Professor Goldman proclaimed, "With all the work that's going on in the Basin, we feel we're beginning to win the battle against declining clarity in Lake Tahoe." A serious setback in late July 2007 threatened to annul his conclusion.[17]

Tahoe had suffered several years of drought, and the snowpack in 2007 was only 29 percent of normal. On a windy Sunday afternoon, several 911 calls reported smoke in Meyers, on the South Shore. There was a prescribed burn in the area, and dispatchers who took the calls did not immediately alert the nearby fire stations. The smoke was not a controlled burn, but an illegal campfire not completely extinguished.

Carried by winds, the fire raged for a week. It destroyed 254 homes and displaced more than a thousand people, causing $160 million in loss of property. Stands of majestic cedars, rare mosses, and northern goshawk territory had been annihilated in the 3,072-acre burn. Brook trout were found belly up in the river.[18]

Surprisingly, the effects of the fire on lake clarity were largely mitigated. Federal, state, and local governments combined resources to immediately remove structural debris and implement erosion-control measures. Throughout the summer and fall, planes were used to seed the burn area, while crews mulched and installed features to revitalize streams and control runoff. By October 2007, the cooperating agencies completed near-term measures and formulated review and maintenance procedures to be implemented over the following ten years. A study in 2012 found little harm, suggesting "the system is pretty resilient to the effects of fires and it will self-heal in a matter of a few years."[19]

A direct positive result of the Angora fire was the implementation of a forest-treatment program to reduce wildfire hazards. Tahoe fire districts and TRPA mutually agreed to guidelines for home owners. From 2008 to 2011, the Tahoe Fire and Fuels Team reduced potential fuels using understory burns, thinning and pile burning, and mastication to treat 4,679 acres, with an additional 7,318 acres in planning.[20]

While thinning was going on in areas close to population centers, far up the mountains above West Shore volunteers were planting berry bushes. Tahoe Bear League members, Washoe Indian elders, children, the Forest Service, and local nurseries had joined in an effort to keep bears away from neighborhoods. Several hundred black bears are believed to live in the Tahoe Basin, including some weighing up to six and seven hundred pounds. They are not often aggressive, and, although humans have been mauled to death in other states, no human has ever been killed by a black bear in California or Nevada. Nevertheless, with the great influx of humans, they can be worrisome. Unless hibernating, they eat continuously, and they will return to places where they have once found food or garbage.

In September 1998, a renter in Homewood stored garbage at a cabin, and a neighbor was frightened by a bear attempting to get it. The renter contacted the California Department of Fish and Game and subsequently hired one of the department's contract trappers, who killed the wrong bear and one of her cubs. A second cub was rescued from the top of a tree.

Within weeks three women, Kathy Travernier and Linda Brown, two local teachers, and Ann Bryant, who was doing wildlife rehabilitation work, organized the Bear League. Their goal was to avoid any more unnecessary killing. Bryant became the league's executive director; Travernier and Brown served on the organization's board. The Bear League arranged seminars, educating the public about averting problems associated with living in bear country, and by 2005 they had nine hundred members. Leery at first, Fish and Game officials soon took to the idea of community members being involved. By 2010 the Bear

League had more than fifteen hundred members and two hundred volunteers who fielded calls and responded to all kinds of emergencies involving bears.[21]

Not everyone calls the Bear League in encounters with bears. In July 2012, a bear named Sunny, living in the West Shore's Homewood area for years, and something of a mascot for the Bear League, was shot and killed on the lakeshore. Although fifteen thousand dollars in rewards was offered, and amid fears of vigilantism toward "a person of interest," the crime went unsolved.[22]

A West Shore property-rights case also signaled renewed problems between the League to Save Lake Tahoe and TRPA. Between 1993 and 2008, the league brought only one lawsuit against TRPA, a marina expansion case settled when the league's concerns were addressed. During those years of substantive collaboration and general agreement, league executive director Nason received the California Governor's Environmental and Economic Leadership Award and an EPA Outstanding Environmental Achievement Award. But the cooperative nature of the relationship between Nason's environmental group and the agency was set aside when a luxury timeshare project was approved to replace an old campground at Tahoe Vista.

The league filed suit over the land-coverage verification process TRPA used. The agency, in attempting to improve customer service by streamlining the permitting process, did not follow its usual oversight procedures. The league's protest said TRPA was weakening its watershed protection. When the development company agreed to significantly modify its coverage, the lawsuit was dropped. But TRPA insisted on continuing its streamlined approached, while the league demanded the agency reinstate its oversight procedures.[23]

The relationship between the two groups had moved to a contentious phase reminiscent of earlier eras. League officials believed any attempt to weaken standards needed to be supported by scientific documentation. They demanded that the updated TRPA Compact adhere to the concept that the agency's role is to plan to achieve the threshold carrying capacities. After the false start of Pathways, and the resultant strained relations, agreements on a revised compact could not be reached.

Nevada attorney general Ross Miller, a board member, said, "Those are complicated issues, but the problem in getting [the revised compact] passed is the same problem of getting anything through, which is that the voting structure as it exists almost requires a unanimous consensus among both states." In discussing the failure, Nason disagreed with Miller's assessment. She believed the inability of the TRPA staff to bring specific proposals for the compact forward was that the Californians on the TRPA Board would not allow an easing of environmental regulations. So year after year passed without a compact update, and resources became more limited.[24]

Finally, at a governing board meeting in January 2011, Joanna Marchetta, in the second year of her term as TRPA executive director, proposed to limit the revised compact's focus. With financial resources dwindling, she said there was a need to concentrate on the most critical issues. These included water quality, land-use issues, transportation, invasive species and catastrophic threats, air quality, and sustainability.[25]

Even with the limited goals, the board would not pass the revised compact until December 2012. In the meantime, the league insisted that the same rules apply to all proposed projects. They strongly objected to exemptions and decision making being done on a case-by-case basis.[26]

Under siege from the environmental activists, the agency was about to be attacked by the Nevada Legislature. Harking back to other sessions, the 2011 Nevada Senate formulated a law to withdraw from the agency. This time sponsors wrote the law so it would automatically take effect in 2015 if their demands were not met. Both state houses passed the bill, and a newly elected governor signed it.

Charles Goldman's limnological studies in the 1960s led directly to the formation of TRPA. Since then, the agency's utilization of science has been critical in protecting the lake. But as experiments produced additional data in the twenty-first century, TRPA changed its emphasis in attempting to solve the water-clarity problem. Research regarding clarity emphasized the effects of nitrates and phosphorus feeding algae until a number of scientists turned their attention to another contributor to losses: fine sediment, basically the tiniest particles of pulverized granite.

Beginning in 1978, researchers gathered data on stream-bank erosion and sediment input, looking at a few streams in various watersheds. In 2008 a study charted sediment inputs from each of the basin's sixty-three watersheds in order to better identify the chief polluting sources and their magnitude. The focus also shifted to sediment that carried into the water from urban areas, roads, and parking lots. Decision makers postulated that in critical areas, filtration systems and catch basins that captured storm-water sediment before it reached the lake would improve water clarity immeasurably.[1]

In 2011 TRPA changed its method of regulating projects from the Bailey system, approving proposals lot by lot, to a "Total Maximum Daily Load" plan that would measure fine sediment, phosphorus, and nitrogen entering the lake on a basin-wide basis. It would involve management agencies and state departments of transportation assisting local municipalities with pollutant-load reduction works intended to trap the contaminants. The undertakings were to be implemented at nine urban centers, and the local jurisdictions would be charged with reducing fine sediment emissions by 32 percent over the next fifteen years.

John Reuter, associate director of the Tahoe Environmental Research Center, cautioned that in Tahoe's steep granitic basin, with periodic flash flooding, officials should proceed slowly. Acknowledging that it is an interesting concept, he said, "Before agencies just approve a lot of new projects with this as the key, it would be nice if we knew more. . . . They may work. They may not work."[2]

Conservation activists wanted TRPA to heed Reuter's caution. Their concerns included the length of time TRPA would allow for the reduction of pollutants and how local governments would pay their share of the improvements.

Disregarding the objections, TRPA forged ahead with its strategic vision of rebuilding in urban areas to improve lake-water quality. Speaking in 2011, executive director Marchetta said that the lake's famed blue waters could be reclaimed. "The solution is clear," she told Nevada legislators. "We need to remake our town centers through environmental redevelopment that would be both environmentally and economically beneficial."[3]

The agency had concluded that balancing economic, environmental, and social concerns was necessary for restoring the lake's health. It pointed to studies revealing that urban upland, which made up only 15 percent of the basin's landmass, produced 72 percent of the pollution entering the lake. Using that data, the board determined that a top priority should be making old buildings ecofriendly. With all levels of government cutting spending, TRPA sought partnerships with private entities to strengthen the linkage between its environmental restoration program and a revitalized basin economy. The agency offered to allow developers to expand facilities if they created more environmentally sustainable buildings. The agency gained the support of the business community, but the conservation community was unconvinced.[4]

The TRPA plan would allow buildings up to six stories high to replace the old commercial area buildings, as well as more apartment buildings in neighborhoods. "Smart growth is an excellent strategy for urbanized areas where growth is inevitable," said the league's Nason. "But it is not smart to apply it to Tahoe, a sensitive area that is threatened by growth and overuse."[5]

When he quit as TRPA executive director in 2009, a weary Singlaub had commented, "The part that is frustrating for me is not being able to convince the environmental community that redevelopment and environmental improvements paid for by the private sector is best for the Lake. When I say that, they paint me as pro development."[6]

The League to Save Tahoe and the Tahoe Area Sierra Club had also challenged Singlaub when the TRPA shorezone plan was issued in 2008. In the plan's amendments, TRPA sought a position between those seeking boat moorings and those opposed to new shorezone structures. The proposed amendments allowed a maximum build-out of 1,800 new private buoys and the construction of 138 new piers, 6 new boat ramps, and 235 new boat slips. In January 2007, John Garamendi, serving as California's lieutenant governor, had written a letter to the agency opposing new moorings as blocking public access and restricting public recreation. At a public meeting, Jerome Waldie, a former US congressman and a member of TRPA's Governing Board, asked why the staff was recommending any new piers. Director Singlaub said that the decision, recommended after negotiations by California and Nevada agencies, was "a political and policy decision."[7]

In a letter opposing the plan's amendments, the Tahoe Area Sierra Club's Michael Donahoe questioned the scientific conclusions used to justify adding buoys and piers. Noting that TRPA's environmental impact statement reported that emissions of particles were projected to increase with growth in boating activity and that particulate offsets might have to be achieved through "an as-yet undetermined method," he commented that TRPA did not know what might be needed, and "therefore cannot determine whether feasible, successful mitigation measures will even exist." He also pointed out that TRPA decisions were required to support environmental thresholds, not political desires, and that maintaining the status quo was unacceptable, as new science indicated pollution must decrease by 55 percent to achieve clarity standards.[8]

With some shoreline home-owner advocates saying not enough piers were being allowed, a TRPA official declared that because everybody disliked the plan, they must be close to getting it right. The TRPA Governing Board approved the plan, and, a month later, in November 2008, the environmental activist groups filed a lawsuit challenging the amendments.

In September 2010, US District Court senior judge Lawrence Karlton ruled in favor of the league and the Tahoe Area Sierra Club. He found several provisions in the proposed amendments capricious and believed that they would be ineffective in achieving agency thresholds. "It is not enough that the amendments do not make the problem worse," he said. "TRPA must ensure that the ordinances, as amended, implement the regional plan in a way that will actually achieve the thresholds." Donahoe commented that Judge Karlton had affirmed TRPA's "duty to not only protect Lake Tahoe from further degradation but also to restore this national treasure to its former health and natural beauty."[9]

The new director, Marchetta, strongly disagreed. She decried the fact that a California federal judge had thrown out a policy that had taken twenty-two years to forge. "The balance set by reasonable compromise between the two states was unacceptable to the environmental special interests," she said. "One must wonder whether those special interests ever intend compromise to be the outcome." TRPA lost a motion to alter or amend the judgment of the decision and then appealed. In March 2012, a Ninth Circuit Court of Appeals ruling gave the agency directions on the parameters for its environmental analysis documents. It would require a reevaluation of the previous baseline for determining the number of moorings and more fully account for the effects of boat pollution. A TRPA spokesperson commented optimistically, "It gives us an opportunity to bring all the parties to the table and reach a conclusion."[10]

The next battle between the conservation groups and TRPA led to another effort by Nevada to pull out of the bistate pact. When the League to Save Tahoe opposed a proposed North Shore project, an article in the *Seattle Times* described the dispute as "green vs. green." The proposal was to tear down the old Tahoe Biltmore Lodge and Casino at Crystal Bay and replace it with Boulder Bay, a $140 million ecofriendly resort and wellness center. TRPA had invited Roger Wittenberg, an inventor as well as a developer, to submit the project proposal, as it would focus attention on their program of redeveloping aging urban sites.

Wittenberg spoke of the project as making "the next quantum leap forward," reducing sediment flow from the site to the lake by 90 percent. The new resort would be eight structures. Hotel units would go from Biltmore's 111 to 275; there would be 59 whole ownership units, 14 affordable housing units, and 10 off-site units designed for employee housing. The gaming area would be reduced from 22,400 square feet to 10,000.

The resort would use snowmelt to irrigate landscaping and for its flush toilets. It would feature an underground water-treatment facility to reduce erosion and recycled products throughout, including Wittenberg-invented TREX—decking made from plastic bags and sawdust. Insulation would be made from scrap paper and cardboard. Native grasses on some rooftops would absorb and filter water.[11]

Even with Boulder Bay's gold-standard Best Management Practices, the league's Nason argued against the development. Admitting they were in a tough situation because the hotel seemed to represent "a lot of good," Nason voiced disapproval of the height variance the project required, arguing that a person buying a property should use due diligence and build in accordance with the rules. She also questioned the size of the complex and how increased patronage would not increase traffic, and thereby air pollution.[12]

The traffic question was never fully answered, although the environmental document said vehicle miles would be reduced by having restaurants, shops, and spa on site, and one of the mitigation requirements was for Boulder Bay to put money into public transit. When the misgivings about traffic became an official call by California's attorney general for a revised traffic study, the project stalled.[13]

Boulder Bay was finally approved at the end of April 2011. The height was grandfathered in at roughly the same as the old Biltmore. Officials hoped allowing the height variance utilizing a grandfather clause would avoid setting a precedent, as a proposed project at Homewood, on the West Shore, was now also requesting its building be higher than the compact's ordinance allowed. The traffic study had been redone and again showed that the redevelopment would produce a reduction in vehicle travel and emissions. Although the TRPA Governing Board believed its twelve-to-two approval vote reflected the agency's willingness to partner with private-property owners to support economic as well as environmental revitalization, the delay had already instigated the next Nevada Legislature movement to pull the state out of the agency.[14]

There had been five similar bills, although this latest effort, SB 271, differed from the others. It came with the proviso that TRPA had to update its regional plan and in doing so take certain specified steps to change it or trigger the state's automatic withdrawal.[15]

In its early form, the bill would have reduced all voting from a majority of each state to a simple majority and demanded changes by October 1, 2013. In its amended final form, the bill moved the deadline back to 2015 and required a different number of votes for different issues. It would change voting for routine business from a majority of each state to a simple majority. To allow variances or amend or repeal threshold carrying capacities, or amend the regional plan, rather than the majority of each state, any nine votes would suffice. To approve projects, nine votes would be needed as well as four of seven members from the state where the project was located. Failure of the governing body to comply with the proposed voting procedures or other of the bill's stipulations would initiate Nevada's withdrawal unless the governor extended the deadline until October 1, 2017.[16]

Since the Nixon administration approved policies to protect the environment in the early 1970s, the national Republican Party, advocating a reduced role for the government, has often fought against environmental regulations. In many instances, Republican politicians have opposed what they perceive as the unnecessary inclusion of environmental concerns in economic affairs. This has been generally true in Nevada, although Democrats had a voter-registration edge of ninety thousand in 2011–12, giving them an eleven-to-ten majority in the state senate and a majority of twenty-seven to fifteen in the assembly.

In the case of SB 271, Democrat John J. Lee from Las Vegas, chair of the Nevada Senate Committee on Government Affairs, was the lead sponsor. Republican James A. Settelmeyer, a rancher from Douglas County, was the cosponsor. Like their counterparts, three Republican joint sponsors in the assembly, the senate sponsors said they had the best interests of the environment in mind but believed TRPA was obstructionist. They introduced anecdotal testimony attacking the bistate organization's policies: reports of home owners prevented by the agency from building a deck, paving a driveway, adding a bathroom, or even painting their house.

In the hearing on SB 271, held before his committee on April 1, 2011, Lee had a bigger issue as well. He said he was not advocating for the Boulder Bay project but mentioned it several times and used it as the primary example of California "and others" playing "political gamesmanship to obstruct due process of projects based in Nevada."

Rochelle Nason testified in opposition to the bill, saying at times that the league disapproved of TRPA's actions but supported its ultimate goals. She urged the legislators not to "throw the baby out with the bathwater." She pointed out that overbuilt impervious surfaces were damaging the basin's ecosystem and now needed to be restricted. Lee took the opportunity to accuse the league of controlling the California TRPA votes and "utilizing every power possible to control Nevada."

Nason responded that the league was following the same policies they had pursued since the 1960s, supporting science-based standards to protect the lake. Pointing to the tremendous financial investment the government had made, she said, "We cannot have unregulated damage to the Lake Tahoe watershed while we are asking taxpayers nationally and throughout California and Nevada to invest in the restoration of other mistakes."

TRPA's Joanna Marchetta testified that she shared the frustrations of those opposed to the agency. She spoke of her strategic vision of streamlining the regulatory process, remaking town centers through environmental redevelopment, and ceding more of the small-project decision making back to local governments.

Senator Settelmeyer seemed to be in support of TRPA's rebuilding approach, speaking of the Park family wanting to proceed with building a lodge (presumably the large-scale development project at Edgewood Golf Course initiated soon thereafter). Settelmeyer, sounding like Marchetta, proposed they replace small, antiquated hotels and motels. "It would be best," he said, "to have a willing buyer and willing seller to buy the smaller hotels and motels and build larger projects." He later acknowledged that the agency had improved under Marchetta's leadership, but believed the compact had failed and needed new procedural protocols.[17]

As with Nevada's other attempts to withdraw from the agency, lobbyists representing Tahoe businesses, Douglas County commissioners, the South Tahoe City Council, and conservative California state legislators representing El Dorado and Placer Counties all supported the effort. Each announced their support while the bill was being considered.[18]

At the next government affairs meeting, a senator suggested that further discussion of SB 271 was needed. Lee said he was not going to hear the bill twice, adding, "It was clear in the bill hearing that the League to Save Lake Tahoe controls Lake Tahoe." This belief must have reflected, in part at least, his motivation for pursuing the bill, although it was not broached in committee testimony other than his own accusation when Nason was testifying. On May 27, 2011, the Senate passed the bill by a vote of nineteen to two, and it was sent to the assembly.[19]

The hearing in the assembly's Government Affairs Committee took place on June 1 and 2. Three representatives from the Lake Tahoe Gaming Alliance testified. They read the proposed amendments to the bill to the committee and responded to questions regarding the intent of specific sections.

Just as during the senate hearing, every Nevada legislator who spoke of withdrawing the state from the bistate compact also spoke of their intent to protect the lake. Whereas Lee and the state senators had proposed reestablishing the Nevada TRPA to replace the bistate agency, the members of the assembly proclaimed that they did not want to abandon TRPA but rather wished to get the attention of the California Legislature and the TRPA Board.

The first two individuals to speak were lobbyists William and Nick Vassiliadis, father-and-son owners of R&R Partners, which, as Nevada's largest advertising agency, employs hundreds. William Vassiliadis is commonly referred to as the most powerful unelected person in Nevada. R&R Partners represent entities from hospitals to Las Vegas Strip casinos and markets Las Vegas to the world—a three-year deal in 2009 was worth more than ninety million dollars. William advises the state's senators and governors, runs campaigns, and acts as a political consultant.[20]

In this instance, the father-son team was representing the Lake Tahoe Gaming Alliance and other businesses at the lake. Nick Vassiliadis "walked through the bill," reading from the amendments to be changed. After discussing economic problems at Tahoe, William Vassiliadis said, "Clearly, we do not want to affect the quality or the clarity of the lake. The most important reason that people come to Lake Tahoe, which benefits the businesses that we represent, is that lake. It is the cleanliness, it is the landscape, and it is the beauty of Lake Tahoe." But he went on to say that Nevada businesses had to be convinced Nevada officials were looking out for them. "Our clients do not want to withdraw [from

TRPA]," he declared, "and I do not believe Nevada policymakers want to withdraw, but at some point Nevada needs to have some self determination."

Secretary of State Ross Miller, with long-standing political ties to William Vassiliadis, had modified the initial proposal. He spoke of now "enthusiastically" supporting it. The trigger date for withdrawal had been moved from 2013 to 2015, and Miller's amendment focused it on what he thought of as the basic problem with the organization, the restrictive voting structure. Nick Vassiliadis said that Miller's changes to the amendment were intended to "make it more agreeable between us, Nevada, and California." Miller disavowed supporting the threat of the state's withdrawal, stating, "I believed then, and I still believe, that simply withdrawing from the Compact does not make a bit of sense. It is irresponsible, it is shortsighted, and that is why previous attempts to withdraw have failed."[21]

Leo M. Drozdoff, Nevada's director of conservation and natural resources, said he was prepared to support the bill after the changes made by the secretary of state. Because it now allowed three more legislative sessions for Nevada's officials to decide, he and California's secretary of resources, John Laird, would be allowed to work out the differences between the two states. He reported, "Secretary Laird has given me assurance and vice versa that we are going to spend a lot of time working together to see if we can organize our differences and figure out the best way to move forward."

Two scientists urged the legislators to vote against SB 271. They stressed that the complex issues they confront did not have state boundaries and that the bistate compact provided stronger protection than a single-state governance model. One of those who testified, limnologist Sudeep Chandra, having just returned from a trip to a high mountain lake in Guatemala, said that in work around the world, they were advocating government structures like TRPA be adopted.

Members of the environmental community asked for the removal of the bill's ultimatum. Rochelle Nason said that although backers of the bill might not want the state to actually withdraw from the bistate compact, passing it might leave no other option. She remarked, "If action is not taken as specified by entities over which you have no control, then Nevada will withdraw."

Kyle Davis, representing the Nevada Conservation League and Education

Fund, argued that the negotiation tactic written into the bill was unproductive. "Essentially what this bill does is state that California must make these three specific changes as exactly outlined in this bill, and a regional plan must be adopted by a specific date otherwise we will pull out of the Compact. . . . It says California must do things exactly as we say otherwise the deal is off."

Toward the end of the second day of the hearing, chairwoman Marilyn Kirkpatrick expressed a fear that she said she was trying to avoid saying on the record. If the bill did not pass, she said, "I think we look pretty stupid for bringing something to the Legislature that we cannot all agree on, when we really want to do whatever is best for Lake Tahoe. I think it sends an even bigger message to California that the Nevada Legislature cannot agree on anything, so they can walk all over us—that is what I fear."

William Vassiliadis gave closing remarks. He said that the importance of the bill was that it would compel both sides to discuss the issues and find a balance. He argued that Nevada had nothing to lose. "If I am wrong, if progress has not been made, and this body decides to do so, any negative outcome that is at the heart of the opposition's concerns can be avoided. The potential benefits to Nevada are worth giving an opportunity to. . . . I maintain faith that this legislative body would take the preventative steps necessary to protect Nevada. In the interim, why not afford this bill the opportunity to be effective and reconsider it during the following sessions? There is a potential for six years, three total sessions, for reconsideration."[22]

The bill passed the Nevada Assembly on June 7, 2011, by a vote of twenty-eight to fourteen. Every Republican voted for it, as did every Democrat from Las Vegas and southern Nevada. All the Democrats from the North voted against it. An editorial in a Reno periodical said that some lawmakers saw the process as a "free" vote, one that would please big campaign contributors without doing any immediate policy damage. One Las Vegas legislator said that "the two-step plan was genius," as a later legislature would have to decide on withdrawing from TRPA. Several legislators who voted for the bill said Nevada would never pull out and that if there had been a straight vote on that issue, the measure would have failed.[23]

In November 2011, the TRPA Board changed its rules of procedure for voting. It used the Nevada proposition of any eight votes for routine business, but maintained four votes from each state for rules, threshold carrying capacities, or changes to the compact. It could have been foreseen that California would oppose the proposal that any nine of fourteen votes would amend or repeal important parts of the pact. Such a procedure might reestablish the coalition from the 1970s of Nevada board members and local California representatives. The voting process had been changed in the 1980s version of the compact precisely because such an alignment had failed to control development in the agency's early years.

A year later, in Nevada's primary election, John Lee, SB 271's main proponent, lost his bid for renomination, garnering only 37 percent of the votes after raising some $208,000 for his campaign. His opponent, a political novice, raised only $13,000 but received 63 percent of the votes after being backed by a coalition that included the Sierra Club and the Nevada Conservation League. The environmental groups had targeted Lee. Kyle Davis, of the Conservation League, said their goal of repealing SB 271 in the next legislative session prompted their involvement. "When we made the decision to try to defeat Lee in this election we were hopeful it would improve our chances to repeal this legislation," he said.[24]

Unsurprisingly, California lawmakers had a forceful response to overtures regarding the Nevada bill. Settelmeyer, Lee, and a lame-duck assemblyman were to carry the threatened withdrawal forward and negotiate compact changes. Calling SB 271 "unnecessarily inflammatory and deeply counterproductive," California Senate president pro tem Darrell Steinberg wrote Lee, pointing out that an act of Congress was required to dissolve the bistate compact.

Overlooking the fact that California's representatives had stopped attending TRPA meetings in 1979 when the state threatened agency withdrawal, Steinberg wrote, "One can only imagine how leaders in Nevada would react if California were to take similar action. It is both surprising and disappointing to see a national treasure as important as Lake Tahoe become a political hostage to the agenda of special interest groups who have little interest in the many values the region provides."

Steinberg notified Lee that the Californians would not meet in the summer of 2012, as the Nevadans requested, because the California Legislature was in session. By then the lame-duck Lee had abdicated his role in Nevada's approach to bistate relations.[25]

With Lee out of office, Nevada conservation activists hoped to convince legislators to overturn SB 271, a battle that carried into the 2013 session.

In its early years, TRPA was designed to be weak and ineffective. Environmental groups and the courts needed to take action to slow the lake's degradation. Its compact amended, TRPA became an awkward tool, slow to issue approvals and at times inefficient and petty. Not only did the agency deny building rights on sensitive lands, but it also came to restrict owners' prerogatives on developed properties and on land deemed buildable.

Today conservation activists are apprehensive that in attempting to loosen regulations and pursue restoration projects, the agency may be losing sight of its primary responsibility. The TRPA Draft 2011 Environmental Threshold Report revealed that of thirty-six indicators traditionally used in threshold evaluations, only nine are in attainment, eighteen are not being attained, and the other nine are unknown. Lack of funding has reduced or eliminated monitoring networks that reveal the status of some threshold attainment, yet, activists protest, the agency's approval of new developments will attract more visitors and create "more coverage, more cars, and more environmental impacts."[1] Despite inadequacies and the controversies that surround TRPA, it is clear that if it had not superseded local jurisdictions, with the associated pressures from developers, the decline in the lake's health would be significantly more pronounced.

At the August 2011 Tahoe Summit, Nevada governor Brian Sandoval, who had recently signed SB 271, and California governor Jerry Brown announced a joint commitment to produce a TRPA Regional Plan Update by the end of 2012. In April 2011, TRPA had introduced a draft RPU with a significant number of contentious issues. There had been little commentary on what executive director Marchetta described as the heart of the proposals: offering incentives for removal of buildings from stream environment zones, clustering buildings in town centers that would reduce land coverage and create walkable spaces, and developing pollution-reducing transportation systems.[2]

Critics found the items intended to support those proposals more problematic. At sessions held for public comment on the plan in the spring of 2012, individuals raised a number of questions about them. One challenge was over a proposal to allow condominiums or hotels on recreation land adjoining ski runs. The theory behind the recreation-lands idea was to encourage visitors to leave their cars parked once arriving at their destination. Pointing out the impact of building on such an immense number of sites—some ninety areas would be affected—E. Clement Shute, a former League to Save Lake Tahoe attorney for more than twenty years, now a TRPA Board member, agreed that regarding that issue, "there is plenty of room for debate."[3]

Along with environmentalists' reactions, the Draft RPU triggered an immediate response from another of the agency's usual watchdogs. The California Attorney General's Office pointed to examples of proposals that might lead to serious legal problems: the delegation of large projects to local governments, weakened coverage requirements, and the allowance of significant amounts of new development. But in a change of tone from previous critiques, Deputy Attorney General Daniel Siegel said that the plan's shortcomings could be solved if people worked together. "We think that these defects can be fixed in a way that meets the needs of the various stakeholders. They can be fixed in a way that gives local governments more say in the process. They can be fixed in a way that encourages environmentally sound redevelopment projects, and they can be fixed in a way that protects the lake."[4]

Owing to Brown's and Sandoval's commitment, the Draft RPU initiated a new procedure for addressing the unsettled policies. California's natural resources secretary, John Laird, and Nevada's Leo Drozdoff organized a stakeholders group to find solutions. E. Clement Schute chaired the committee. Referred to in the press as the "Gang of Ten," the group included diverse individuals: Dr. Darcie Goodman-Collins, the new executive director of the League to Save Lake Tahoe; Kyle Davis of the Nevada Conservation League; two county government representatives; TRPA Governing Board member Steve Robinson, a Nevada lobbyist representing that state's Department of Natural Resources; South Tahoe mayor Claire Fortier, an outspoken critic of the agency; a representative of basin businesses who had previously represented the casino alliance; as well as Laird and Drozdoff. The group considered seventeen disputed policies in the RPU, including a number of items challenged by board member Shute.

The process took hundreds of hours to reach agreements. Shute said that none of the stakeholders got all they wanted but that each felt they were heard. At the end of July 2012, they sent their recommendations to the TRPA Governing Board.[5]

An example of the kinds of compromises the Gang of Ten developed was the change to allow development on land designated for recreation. One problem, as Shute had pointed out, was the sheer number of recreation areas. In an effort to restrict affected locales, the group proposed establishing a new "Resort Recreation" designation and limiting new development to those districts. Building on approved parcels would be subject to retiring developments in other areas. Responding to developers' concerns, the group supported such a designation for two areas previously requesting such projects, Heavenly California Base and Edgewood Mountain.[6]

Fortier commented that the process created trust between the environmental community and local governments, calling it "a base for ongoing conversations that have stymied progress in Tahoe for decades." The league's Goodman-Collins believed the biggest threats in the RPU had been addressed. She expressed the sentiment that although the new plan in and of itself will not save the lake, there are enough safeguards that it does not put the lake at risk. When the work was completed, both TRPA director Marchetta and TRPA Governing Board chair Norma Santiago complimented the leadership of the two states, and the compromises were accepted as a package.[7]

In December 2012, the TRPA Board voted to approve the updated compact with the compromises. Shortly thereafter, the Sierra Club and another grassroots organization, Friends of the West Shore, filed a lawsuit against TRPA in federal court. The environmentalists objected that the magnitude of corporate resort developments allowed in the new compact and the authority given the counties to permit "bigger, higher, denser growth" will hinder the attainment of the thresholds in the agency's charter. Marchetta countered that incentives mixed with a streamlined permit process are necessary for renewal that realizes environmental improvements. A TRPA spokesperson added that the agency will continue to put the new pact into effect until a judge instructs them to do otherwise.[8]

Along with the lawsuit, TRPA's lack of funding is a daunting problem in implementing the new plan. In 2011 California's Senators Feinstein and Boxer and Nevada's Reid failed to get an austerity-minded Congress to reauthorize the expiring Lake Tahoe Restoration Act, which would have provided $415 million over ten years.[9]

Without government moneys, the agency believes the only option available to improve the environment is through their proposal to promote private redevelopment that they tout as "green." In August 2012, the TRPA Board unanimously approved a large renovation at Edgewood Golf Course, which fronts the lake at Stateline on South Shore. It included building Edgewood Tahoe Lodge and the development of the nearby 254 acres, creating a walkable center for visitors that TRPA is promoting.

Edgewood has gained fame for hosting the nation's premier annual celebrity golf tournament, the nationally televised Tahoe Celebrity Golf Championship. The new lodge at the golf course is to be a LEED-certified destination resort, featuring 194 hotel rooms, a health spa, and a bistro-style restaurant.

In exchange for development approval, the builders will modify management to reduce golf course fertilizer entering the lake. They also propose to upgrade water quality in the Stateline Storm Water Association pond system that discharges into Edgewood Creek and Lake Tahoe. Improvements to Edgewood Creek that enhance riparian and wetland function and create fish habitat are included in the plan, as is rehabilitation of Friday's Station dam, across Highway 50, that will control discharge of fine sediments into the lake. The improvements are projected to stop fifty thousand pounds of fine sediment from flowing into the lake annually.[10]

Tahoe Area Sierra Club representative Laurel Ames, involved in local environmental politics since the 1960s, opposed the Edgewood plan. She is concerned about the increased traffic the project will generate and worried that the storm-water system that runs down the Edgewood property will be overwhelmed by increased runoff. The builders maintain that making the development into a walkable area mitigates the traffic impact and that the storm-water system was designed to accept the increase. The project has not been challenged in court. The same is not true of another example of TRPA's new policy: Homewood Mountain Resort Ski Area.

Earthjustice, representing the Tahoe Area Sierra Club and the Friends of the West Shore, filed suit in January 2012 to stop the Homewood development. The plan included a 75-room five-star hotel, 143 condominiums, 48 ski-out chalets, 16 townhouses, 30 penthouse units, fifteen thousand square feet of retail space, and 13 workforce apartments. Describing it as a "mass of buildings that climb 77 feet up the face of the Homewood ski slope," the Sierra Club and Friends of the West Shore protested that "it would not fit with the community, and it would not protect the lake."[11]

TRPA argued that by bulldozing most of the fifty-year-old resort and installing new drainage systems and other environmental improvements, 150,000 pounds of sediment would be diverted from the lake. In January 2013, in a 114-page ruling, a California district court concluded that the project's environmental review needed to explore economic ramifications of building a smaller development, specifically a revised study with a 15 percent reduction.[12]

The company's decision to pursue adjusting the study precludes the involvement of the California Tahoe Conservancy. The CTC has resolved eleven previous land-use lawsuits by purchasing parcels from willing sellers. Over the course of twenty years, the CTC, funded by California taxpayers, won the approval of property-rights advocates as well as the conservation community. Under the direction of Dennis Machida, the agency paid fair market prices to acquire nearly five thousand environmentally sensitive properties. The agency's erosion-control, wetlands-restoration, and wildlife-habitat improvement programs included innumerable projects throughout the California portion of the basin. On the North Shore, to protect a watershed as well as provide public lake access, the agency bought and rehabilitated several lakefront properties. These acquisitions included Kings Beach Plaza, two portions of beachfront land at Carnelian Bay, the Beach Club at the intersection of Highways 28 and 267, and Commons Beach at Tahoe City. The agency has also funded recreation projects such as construction of parts of the Tahoe Rim Trail, encircling the lake along its mountains' crest lines, and the publication of a Tahoe water-trail map featuring campgrounds, other lodging, eateries, and public beaches for kayakers taking multiple days to circumnavigate the lake.[13]

Although most are limited by reduced funding, other groups, including federal and state agencies, local boards, scientific institutions, and environmental organizations, continue efforts to restore and sustain the Lake Tahoe Basin. The UC Davis–sponsored research center TERC and its associated Tahoe Science Consortium provide comprehensive findings from research, monitoring, and modeling. The Forest Service maintains its pursuit of improvements to damaged public lands. The Lahontan Regional Water Quality Control Board and the EPA continue to monitor water- and air-quality policies.

The League to Save Lake Tahoe is seeking to add a supplementary component to its work advocating for the environment: community engagement. Director Goodman-Collins, with a bachelor's degree in aquatic biology and a PhD in environmental science and management, was born and raised in South Lake Tahoe. By stimulating dialogue, she hopes to involve local governments and citizens in helping to fulfill the organization's mission of environmental stewardship. She is also working to enlist corporate partners and businesses whose employees can join in league forest-stewardship projects.

Goodman-Collins, with three scientists now on staff, is also seeking a distinct shift in focus to more fully involve the league in the conversations regarding scientific management of the basin. Working with the researchers from TERC and its associated institutes and agencies, she intends to ensure that science gets translated into policy.

Goodman-Collins is also proposing to assist TRPA in procuring funding for monitoring networks that reveal levels of thresholds' attainment, which can run into the millions of dollars annually. Another of her ideas is to create citizen-monitoring programs where communities adopt subdivision and road-drainage pipes to monitor outflows that lead into the lake.[14]

There is another group working specifically on the drainage-pipe problem. Since 2010 the Tahoe Pipe Club has been advocating for a change in the method of treating water pollution in the basin watershed. Their goals have included identifying and publicizing locations where pollutant-carrying storm water flows through pipes into the lake or its tributaries. Rather than allowing pipes to continue conveying storm water, the group is advocating for an infiltration-based approach whereby storm water is cleaned by percolating through the basin's natural soil.

The Pipe Club has been collecting water samples from urban runoff and measuring its turbidity, illustrating roadway storm-water toxicity. The group posts provocative videos on YouTube, showing murky discharges that end up in the lake.

The Tahoe Pipe Club is said to be composed of scientists, engineers, and business owners. While other club directives deal with storm water and urban drains, mirroring a 1999 movie, the Pipe Club's first rule is you do not talk about the club and the second rule is you do not talk about the club. Members believe anonymity must be preserved, as at least one club founder's job may be jeopardized by their involvement.[15]

Although approving of the Pipe Club's messaging technique, Laurie Kemper, assistant executive director of Lahontan Water Control, notes that land availability for infiltration is a problem in some areas and that high groundwater levels would render it ineffective in others. Lahontan has, in fact, teamed with Caltrans to find areas where infiltration can be used, and there are Caltrans-installed drains along Highway 50 that now dump into infiltration basins.[16]

Along with the Pipe Club's videos, news releases regarding Tahoe's health in 2013 have been alternately discouraging and heartening. Photos in a recent TERC press release showed a catch taken from the lake: a four-and-a-half-pound goldfish, so large the researcher holding it needed to use two hands. The fish, one of a school, was exhibited as an example of invasive species that have been released in the warm waters of Tahoe Keys and are making their way into the shallows of the lake. They are a serious problem, as they excrete nutrients that promote algal growth, and there are so many that wildlife managers plan to tag some with tracking devices to devise strategies for their removal.

Recent positive news included the release of a CTC draft plan for restoration of six hundred acres of the Upper Truckee River marsh; another comeback by Lahontan cutthroat trout, albeit at the other end of the Truckee River in Pyramid Lake; and the most recent annual Secchi dish measurement that averaged 75.3 feet, the clearest in ten years.

News, good or bad, regarding the interaction between humans and the lake's natural ecosystems needs to be qualified. The health of a body as large as Tahoe is slow to reveal the results of changes. Regarding water clarity, for example, variability is extremely high from season to season and year to year, and the effects of current-day decisions regarding restorative actions will not be known for many years.

One other seemingly encouraging piece of news regarding compromise turned bleak as it evolved. In the 2013 legislative session, the Nevada Senate passed a bill to rescind SB 271 that required the state to withdraw from TRPA. Nevada governor Sandoval immediately threatened to veto the new bill in order to maintain the withdrawal threat.

When SB 271 was passed in 2011, proponents said it was intended to force a new compact that eased building regulations and instituted voting procedures to facilitate development. Although still not reflecting the Nevadans' proposal on voting, Nevada Democratic legislators believed the new TRPA Compact to be a balanced compromise; Republican officials did not agree.

In 2010 Nevada voters elected Sandoval, the third consecutive Republican governor since 1999. In declaring his intent to sustain SB 271, Sandoval was seeking to further loosen TRPA control over development projects. The senate had voted along party lines, and the assembly, with a large Democratic majority, appeared poised to vote to rescind it as well until Sandoval's veto threat stopped the process.

Steve Robinson, a Sandoval appointee to the TRPA Board, was also a contract lobbyist and former government affairs director for R&R Partners, the William Vassiliadis firm that pushed through SB 271 in 2011. Although Robinson was not involved in lobbying for SB 271 when it passed, he spoke in favor of retaining it at the 2013 legislative hearings when its repeal was being considered.

Arguing that the option to withdraw needed to remain in place, Robinson, a member of the stakeholders' compromise committee—the Gang of Ten— said that in the collaborative effort to update the TRPA Compact, "the specter of the possibility of Nevada's withdrawal was absolutely essential to changing the hearts and the minds of those on both sides." In the 2013 session, Sandoval's conservation and natural resources director, Leo Drozdoff, speaking for the governor, concurred, saying that rescinding SB 271 threatened recent progress, as the approved plan had not been fully implemented and conservation groups were suing to block it.[17]

The vote to rescind SB 271 showed that the Democrats disagreed. One Democratic senator said the legislature needed to recognize what California and the agency had accomplished. An assemblyman said, "It's time to come back together." But the Democrats did not have the votes to override a gubernatorial veto.[18]

When Sandoval made his position known, California legislators responded in kind. The California Senate introduced a bill that would pull it out of the bistate agency on January 1, 2014, if Nevada's SB 271 was not rescinded. California would replace TRPA by reestablishing its regulatory body, CTRPA.

California bill sponsors contended that their bill merely prepared for the eventuality of a Nevada withdrawal. Democratic senator Fran Pavley said, "[The intent] is to have a backup plan in case it is needed in California in the event Nevada decides to withdraw from the Tahoe compact as provided in its current law."[19]

Several conservation groups, concerned over TRPA's shifting of authority to local jurisdictions and perceived weakening of pollution controls, welcomed the conflict as a way to reestablish CTRPA, whose tough stands severely limited development in the 1970s and 1980s.

This state of affairs caused an unexpected reaction from local governments. The South Tahoe City Council and Douglas County Board of Commissioners held a joint meeting in April 2013, with representatives voicing opposition to Governor Sandoval's position for two reasons. First, they worried that in threatening to dissolve TRPA, Sandoval would cost the area tens of millions of dollars in future federal funding. Second, they feared a reinstituted CTRPA's harsh restrictions. The South Lake Tahoe mayor said he was surprising himself by announcing that TRPA needed to be kept together. "[Reconstituting CTRPA would] put the Tahoe economy back in the dark ages. This is how wars get started," he declared. The local committees' members concurred, and they passed a motion to compose a joint letter from the affected jurisdictions, urging state officials to honor their bistate commitments.[20]

Drama, regarding the future of TRPA, built for a month. The biennial Nevada Legislature meets for only 120 days, after which it is required to adjourn. With less than a week left in the 2013 session, Sandoval and California's governor, Brown, issued a joint statement. They and their representatives had met, and the Californians agreed to pass legislation supporting a couple of Nevada's proposals. The Nevadans dropped their demand that TRPA voting procedures be changed, stipulating simply that in the future, the regional plan must reflect changing economic conditions and that a party challenging the plan has the burden of proof in showing that the agency is not in conformance. This last term appeared to be largely a face-saving measure, as in civil cases it is always the duty of the plaintiff to prove or disprove disputed facts. A California negotiator said they agreed to include the condition because the Nevada Legislature "felt strongly about it." Nevada's Drozdoff, conceding that plaintiffs always start with the burden of proof, commented that by including the statement, they might create "a little bit of an extra burden . . . something that federal courts will at least have to look at."[21]

Shortly before adjourning until 2015, the Nevada Legislature rescinded SB 271, ending their threatened withdrawal. Agreeing to encourage the US Congress to approve the updated TRPA Compact's changes, the California Legislature abandoned its plan to reestablish CTRPA.[22]

TRPA had again survived, although elements of its updated plan are yet to be decided by the federal court. The conservationists' lawsuit, being considered in 2013, objects to the delegation of authority to local governments and the size of new developments. The court is weighing whether the new policies will hinder the attainment of environmental thresholds required in the agency's charter. As in the mid-1980s, a finding that the new plan is detrimental to its avowed goals might well require a radical change in the agency's direction.

CONCLUSION

On a recent trip, following the scenic seventy-two-mile highway around Lake Tahoe, I visited South Shore's Tallac Estates and West Shore's Ed Z'berg Sugar Pine Point State Park. Each harbored majestic old-growth pines. These stands contrast vividly with Tahoe's preponderant second-growth forests, calling to mind the nineteenth-century trade-off of ecodestruction for Comstock riches.

In that era, conflicts between multiple governing authorities saved the lake from becoming a reservoir for industries, farms, and cities below the Sierra. Ironically, the same discordant approach to governance nearly caused the lake's ruin in the twentieth century. This was apparent driving past Rubicon Point in the Northwest and through Incline Village in the Northeast, where housing developments, approved by county governments, are cut into steep, erosive mountainsides. Inching along in lines of traffic through the Stateline casino corridors at North and South Shores; viewing Heavenly Valley's face, scarred with ski runs; and visiting the vast subdivision at Tahoe Keys, the dredged marsh that previously protected the lake from polluting silt, further illustrated the effects of mismanagement on the basin's ecosystems.

Withal, in circling the lake, its distinctive characteristic is its transcendent beauty. It is apparent why in 1970, after Charles Goldman and environmental activists sounded alarms regarding damage being done by the sheer numbers of visitors, Congress empowered TRPA to protect it. It explains as well the passion that continues to generate political infighting and lawsuits.

At a glance, ecological politics today resemble those of the 1960s and 1970s. The Tahoe Pipe Club's website and videos call attention to turbid discharges into the lake much like the 1963 *McGauhey Report*. TERC news releases can be compared to Goldman's pronouncements about serious biological challenges. Scientists continue to look for better ways to maintain water purity and control other problems, now including the effects of invasive species and climate change. Money is scarce for improvements. Conservation organizations are suing to stop a TRPA-approved project and to invalidate the agency's updated compact. Local government officials and residents continue to disparage TRPA, accusing it of infringements, and the State of Nevada's threat to withdraw from the agency caused California to do the same.

Although it may seem that the new manifestation of the same historical cycle might ultimately doom the lake, there is room for cautious optimism. A change in attitude from earlier eras is suggested by the Tahoe Pipe Club's announcement that business owners are included in its fight for improvements in water clarity. Nevada's Gaming Alliance still wields considerable power as regards the lake, as seen in the SB 271 debate, but the growth of Indian casinos in California and a continually evolving ecological awareness have chipped away at the industry's influence. Many Tahoe business leaders have become proponents of outdoor, recreation-based tourism. Chambers of Commerce on each side of the lake support the TRPA's proposals that would clean up blighted areas and create walkable town centers that de-emphasize the use of cars.

Casey Blann, vice president of Kirkwood Ski Area and chair of the South Shore Chamber, penned an editorial in July 2012, encouraging residents to participate in building a healthier community. "Let's make Lake Tahoe more walkable and bikeable," he wrote, "and maybe it will be a place where our kids can return to work, play and raise a family."[1]

Bob Kingman, a longtime CTC staff member now working for the Sierra Nevada Conservancy, detects an expanding "sense of place" that has provided a unity of purpose at Tahoe. In the summer of 2012, he spoke about new planning efforts. "It is encouraging seeing the transition to a more sustainable, resource-based economy," said Kingman, "one that recognizes the health of the environment is critical to the health of the community—that the two are inextricably joined."[2]

With few exceptions, local leaders were late to the realization that urbanization reduced the lake's health, thereby devaluing basin properties and businesses. Some still claim that land and business owners should be allowed to develop their properties unregulated or regulated by local jurisdictions only. But more now realize the damage that would have been done had TRPA regulations not been tightened in 1987. Two additional Douglas County–approved hotel-casinos would have been built, as would businesses, condominium complexes, and subdivisions pursued by the City of South Lake Tahoe and the other counties. Now projects are required to account for ecoprotection along with economic viability.

Steve Teshara, who has spent his career representing Tahoe businesses— including eleven years with the Gaming Alliance—said that after the intense litigation, when TRPA's 1987 plan was instituted, a portion of the business community felt that "[regional government] is here; we better deal with it." It was at that point that he, Heavenly Valley's Stan Hansen, and the League to Save Lake Tahoe's Rochelle Nason began collaborating to raise money for improvements in the basin. Teshara believes it is past time to reorganize the partnership between business interests and the conservation community, and he is actively engaged in pursuing that effort.[3]

Roger Wittenberg, who as the principal owner and chief executive officer of Boulder Bay had to negotiate the minefield of regulations to get the reengineering of the Biltmore Casino passed, spoke to the Nevada Legislature in 2011 as it considered withdrawing from TRPA. Although critical of the uncertainty regarding authorization after going through the arduous and time-consuming approval process, Wittenberg supported "keeping the TRPA whole." He also complimented the conservation community, saying, "Organizations like the League to Save Lake Tahoe have done an excellent job over the years in protecting the very thing that you are worried about."[4]

Along with the widespread consensus over the importance of the basin's ecological value, there are other reasons for a forward-looking assessment of its health. Scientific efforts to restore and sustain it have improved due to the accumulation of physical and biogeochemical data and advances in technological engineering. Improvements in the watershed have ongoing effects. The purchase of sensitive private lands has eliminated potential threats, and new development is limited by these acquisitions: in 1980 some 65 percent of Tahoe Basin land was publicly owned; today public agencies manage 87 percent.[5]

At the same time, the battle over conflicting visions and TRPA's new direction continues to engender protests from both sides of the political spectrum. As demonstrated in Nevada's latest threat to withdraw from the agency, conservative politicians seek to ease restrictions they say are hindering development and the economy. They question previous scientific applications and the viability of current research, and they continue to advocate for developers' rights.

On the other hand, conservationists, supported by progressive state legislators, raise critical questions about the proposed changes to the status quo. Will large-scale, high-density projects lead to further urban sprawl? How is it possible to mitigate the effects of developments that will attract more visitors, increasing traffic pollution? In replacing the Bailey land-capabilities system, can the Total Maximum Daily Load concept be relied upon to protect lake clarity?

Planning adviser Robert Twiss speaks for much of the conservation community when he voices concern about TRPA's plan to delegate authority to local governments. In the past, the local governments were hesitant to enforce regulations that developers perceived as onerous. Twiss points out that, with its limited capacity, the entire basin is affected by development in any particular community, and remedies for communities' overbuilding would come after the fact, too late for protecting the ecosystem.

Environmental activist Ames, in observing the new push toward redevelopment, expresses an agonizing concern regarding the lack of safeguards. "We'll see," she concludes. "But while we see, the lake is in jeopardy."[6]

The historical record of Lake Tahoe's management illustrates the need for an entity to oversee local governments and enforce regional environmental standards. Despite its ongoing struggles and many breakdowns, TRPA has had successes. In particular by codifying science, it has slowed the deterioration of the lake's transparency. But the agency's failures illustrate the necessary role that conservationists and the courts play in ensuring that attainment of the lake's environmental thresholds remains a priority.

The future of Tahoe's health remains tenuous. The only certainty is that, owing to its value as an irreplaceable treasure, battles to control, manage, conserve, and profit from it will continue far into the twenty-first century.

NOTES

‖‖

INTRODUCTION

1. Deterioration in the water's clarity was determined by a lake-bottom sediment core study a century later. Thomas Bachand, *Lake Tahoe: A Fragile Beauty,* 174; University of California, Davis, Docent's Manual, "Reading History," 45.

2. Larry Schmidt, "Comstock Logging Impacts in the Tahoe Basin," unpublished manuscript (2012).

ONE ▓ CLEAR-CUTTING THE GRANDEUR

1. Barbara Lekisch, *Tahoe Place Names: The Origin and History of Names in the Lake Tahoe Basin,* 18–19, 72; Susan Lindstrom, "Submerged Tree Stumps as Indicators of Mid-Holocene Aridity in the Lake Tahoe Basin," 146–57.

2. David C. Antonucci, *Fairest Picture: Mark Twain at Lake Tahoe,* 8.

3. Stuart Bruchey and Eleanor Bruchey, eds., "Report of the Public Lands Commission Created by the Act of March 3, 1879," 606; Samuel Bowles, *Across the Continent: A Summer's Journey to the Rocky Mountains, the Mormons, and the Pacific States with Speaker Colfax,* 165.

4. Lekisch, *Tahoe Place Names,* 11, 88; Douglas H. Strong, *Tahoe: From Timber Barons to Ecologists,* 20, 32.

5. William Ashburner to Samuel Bowles, November 1865, in Bowles, *Across the Continent,* 449.

6. *Territorial Enterprise,* March 25, 1875; *Nevada State Journal,* September 6, 1878, as cited in Bob McQuivey, "Summary of Lake Tahoe Basin Resources (1854–1976)."

7. For discussions of the Comstock's role in building the West, see Michael J. Makley, *The Infamous King of the Comstock: William Sharon and the Gilded Age in the West* and *John Mackay: Silver King in the Gilded Age.*

8. Bruchey and Bruchey, "Report of the Public Lands Commission," 424, 36, 88.

9. Despite the abuses, the act was not repealed until 1955, by which time some 2,899,000 acres had been patented in California. Samuel Trask Dana and Myron Krueger, *California Lands: Ownership, Use, and Management,* 42–43.

10. Makley, *Infamous King of the Comstock,* 34–35.

11. William S. Bliss, "Biography of D. L. Bliss," n.d., Hubert Howe Bancroft Collection; Grace Dangberg, *Conflict on the Carson: A Study of Water Litigation in Western Nevada,* 310.

12. Lekisch, *Tahoe Place Names,* 55, 75; Douglas H. Strong, *Tahoe: An Environmental History,* 25.

13. Bruchey and Bruchey, "Report of the Public Lands Commission," 606. As to the issue of purchasing timberlands, see the testimony of Judge J. W. North, Nevada's first surveyor-general, in ibid., 131–32; Makley, *Infamous King of the Comstock,* 38, 70; and John S. Hittell, *The Commerce and Industries of the Pacific Coast,* 420.

14. Bruchey and Bruchey, "Report of the Public Lands Commission," 606, 607.

15. E. B. Scott, *The Saga of Lake Tahoe,* 171–72; Lekisch, *Tahoe Place Names,* 48.

16. Lekisch, *Tahoe Place Names,* 8; Susan Lindstrom with contributions from Penny Rucks and Peter Wigand, "A Contextual Overview of Human Land Use and Environmental Conditions," in *Lake Tahoe Watershed Assessment,* edited by Dennis D. Murphy and Christopher M. Knopp, 21–127, 65.

17. Sessions S. Wheeler with William W. Bliss, *Tahoe Heritage: The Bliss Family of Glenbrook, Nevada,* 34–35; Scott, *Saga of Lake Tahoe,* 212, 215.

18. Grant H. Smith, *The History of the Comstock Lode, 1850–1920,* 120, 256; Makley, *Infamous King of the Comstock,* 38; Makley, *John Mackay,* 61.

19. Scott, *Saga of Lake Tahoe,* 305–8.

20. Bruchey and Bruchey, "Report of the Public Lands Commission," 606; Scott, *Saga of Lake Tahoe,* 14.

21. Smith, *History of the Comstock Lode,* 247; George H. Goddard in Scott, *Saga of Lake Tahoe,* 181.

TWO ■ TRADES

1. Steve Raymond, *The Year of the Trout,* 205–19.

2. *Bulletin of the United States Fish Commission, Volume 15 for 1895,* Marshall McDonald, Commissioner (Washington, DC: US Government Printing Office, 1896), 433.

3. Scott, *Saga of Lake Tahoe,* 51, 154, 165, 327, 329; *San Francisco Call,* January 24, 1913.

4. In 1899 a public campaign led to the designation of the acreage the Lake Tahoe Forest Reserve. In 1926 the secretary of agriculture designated some of this land as recreation area, and much of it became the Desolation Valley Wilderness Area by an act of Congress in 1969. Richard J. Fink, "Public Land Acquisition for Environmental Protection: Structuring a Program for the Lake Tahoe Basin," 498.

5. Lekisch, *Tahoe Place Names,* 28; Jeffrey P. Schaffer, *Desolation Wilderness and the South Lake Tahoe Basin: A Guide to Lake Tahoe's Finest Hiking Area,* 144–47; *Truckee Republican,* May 20, 1903, June 24, 1905; *San Francisco Call,* May 16, 1909.

6. *Bulletin of the United States Fish Commission, Volume 15 for 1895,* 433; *Biennial Report of the Fish Commissioner of the State of Nevada for the Years 1895 and 1896,* as cited in Bob McQuivey, comp., "Summary of Lake Tahoe Basin Resources (1854–1976)."

7. Matthew Stephen Makley, "These Will Be Strong: A History of the Washoe People," 34–35.

8. John Charles Frémont, *Narratives of Exploration and Adventure,* 341.

9. *Virginia Daily Union,* January 15, 1864, March 28, April 14, 1865.

10. Strong, *Tahoe: From Timber Barons to Ecologists,* 13; *Carson Daily Appeal,* April 20 1867; *Daily Alta California,* July 3, 1870.

11. *Carson Morning Appeal,* June 6, 1883.

12. *Territorial Enterprise,* November 7, 1869; Scott, *Saga of Lake Tahoe,* 232, 443–45; Gordon Richards, "Demise of the Lahontan Cutthroat Trout."

13. *Daily Alta California,* April 12, 1866.

14. *Sacramento Daily Union,* April 27, 1872.

15. *San Francisco Call,* August 28, 1895.

16. *Daily Alta California,* July 8, 1890; *Sacramento Daily Union,* August 20, 1874.

17. *Daily Alta California,* June 17, 1871.

18. See, for example, *Daily Alta California,* December 11, 1871, May 31, 1873, June 17, 1877; *Sacramento Daily Union,* February 22, 1875, June 8, 1878; and *Nevada Daily Tribune,* April 18, 1881.

19. Scott, *Saga of Lake Tahoe,* 105; *Carson Morning Appeal,* June 6, 1883, as cited in McQuivey, "Summary of Lake Tahoe Basin Resources."

20. *Daily Alta California,* June 21, 1870. See also *Sacramento Daily Union,* February 22, May 29, 1875, June 8, 1878.

21. *Sacramento Daily Union,* January 26, 1884; Scott, *Saga of Lake Tahoe,* 156.

22. *Sacramento Daily Union,* February 22, 1875; Martha C. Knack and Omer C. Stewart, *As Long as the River Shall Run: An Ethnohistory of Pyramid Lake Indian Reservation,* 161–78.

23. *Sacramento Daily Union,* February 22, 1875.

24. *Reno Evening Gazette,* September 16, 1879; *Sacramento Daily Union,* July 15, November 28, 1887.

25. Richards, "Demise of the Lahontan Cutthroat Trout"; *Sacramento Daily Union,* January 26, 1884, July 15, November 28, 1887.

26. *Sacramento Daily Union,* February 14, May 19, 1887, January 22, February 8, 1889; F. P. Deering and J. H. Deering Jr., *Supplement to Deering's Codes and Statutes of California,* 468.

27. *Sacramento Daily Union,* September 12, April 18, 1889, August 3, 1895.

28. Richards, "Demise of the Lahontan Cutthroat Trout"; State of Nevada Division of Water Resources, "Truckee River Chronology, Part III, Twentieth Century."

29. *San Francisco Call,* May 24, 25, 1912; *Truckee Republican,* November 16, 1916.

30. *Gardnerville Record-Courier,* August 1, 1924, May 15, 1925, as cited in McQuivey, "Summary of Lake Tahoe Basin Resources."

THREE ■ USING THE LAKE

1. *San Francisco Daily Alta,* July 10, 1870.

2. Von Schmidt's first plan was to take the water the other way, to Nevada. In 1863 he

proposed a plan to the Virginia City Board of Aldermen that a pipeline be constructed to bring Tahoe's water out of the Sierra, across Washoe Valley, to their town. The aldermen rejected the proposal out of hand. Because the valley's elevation was forty-five hundred feet and Virginia City's was six thousand, they thought the engineering, if possible, too expensive. Donald J. Pisani, "'Why Shouldn't California Have the Grandest Aqueduct in the World?': Alexis Von Schmidt's Lake Tahoe Scheme," 348.

3. A. W. Von Schmidt, *Report to the Lake Tahoe and San Francisco Water Works Company, on Its Sources of Supply: Proposed Line of Works; Estimated Cost and Income,* 3–9.

4. Ibid., 4–5; Donald J. Pisani, *From the Family Farm to Agribusiness: The Irrigation Crusade in California and the West, 1850–1931,* 23.

5. *Territorial Enterprise,* January 17, 1878.

6. George Hinkle and Bliss Hinkle, *Sierra-Nevada Lakes,* 308.

7. William D. Rowley, "Visions of a Watered West," 142–45; Donald J. Pisani, "Federal Reclamation and Water Rights in Nevada," 540–43.

8. Hinkle and Hinkle, *Sierra-Nevada Lakes,* 336–37.

9. State of Nevada Division of Water Resources, "Truckee River Chronology."

10. Knack and Stewart, *As Long as the River Shall Run,* 284–85, 373–76.

11. Hinkle and Hinkle, *Sierra-Nevada Lakes,* 337–38. After building the Derby Dam, in July 1905 the service attempted to build another dam just below the Lake Tahoe Dam to establish its own control of the lake's water. Twenty property owners, including Oakland mayor Warren Olney, a founding member of the Sierra Club, and John D. Spreckles, the developer of San Diego and a multimillionaire, petitioned the governor of California, an action that again stopped the government from proceeding. Pisani, "Federal Reclamation and Water Rights in Nevada," 544.

12. State of Nevada Division of Water Resources, "Truckee River Chronology."

13. Timothy Egan, *The Big Burn: Teddy Roosevelt and the Fire That Saved America,* 95.

14. Hinkle and Hinkle, *Sierra-Nevada Lakes,* 338–39.

15. Ibid., 339–40; Strong, *Tahoe: From Timber Barons to Ecologists,* 54.

16. State of Nevada Division of Water Resources, "Truckee River Chronology."

17. *San Francisco Call,* January 24, 1913.

18. Hinkle and Hinkle, *Sierra-Nevada Lakes,* 340; State of Nevada Division of Water Resources, "Truckee River Chronology."

19. Hinkle and Hinkle, *Sierra-Nevada Lakes,* 341.

20. Knack and Stewart, *As Long as the River Shall Run,* 288; State of Nevada Division of Water Resources, "Truckee River Chronology."

21. State of Nevada Division of Water Resources, "Truckee River Chronology"; Scott, *Saga of Lake Tahoe,* 2:239–41.

22. "Farad Diversion Dam Replacement Project Draft Environmental Impact

Report," Appendix B, B2; Truckee River Agreement, http://www.troa.net/documents/TRA_1935/; State of Nevada Division of Water Resources, "Truckee River Chronology."

23. Knack and Stewart, *As Long as the River Shall Run,* 334; Leah J. Wilds, *Water Politics in Northern Nevada: A Century of Struggle,* 32–36.

24. Knack and Stewart, *As Long as the River Shall Run,* 335–38; Wilds, *Water Politics in Northern Nevada,* 61–66. These agreements dramatically reduced the number of battles over the river, but did not extinguish them. As late as 2009, the US Ninth Circuit Court of Appeals overruled a lower court's decision, finding that groundwater was significant to the Truckee River flow and hence part of the tribe's decreed rights. *USA, et al. v. Orr Water Ditch Co., et al.,* no. 07-17001 D.C., No. CV-73-00018-LDG Opinion (2009).

25. Truckee-Carson-Pyramid Lake Water Settlement, S. 3084, http://www.focuswest.org/law/pl101-618II.cfm.

FOUR ■ THE BOOM

1. Scott, *Saga of Lake Tahoe,* 2:18, 21, 197, 280.

2. Michael J. Makley, *A Short History of Lake Tahoe,* 59.

3. Russell R. Elliott, with the assistance of William D. Rowley, *History of Nevada,* 278–79, 284–85, 327.

4. Scott, *Saga of Lake Tahoe,* 53, 161; Scott, *Saga of Lake Tahoe,* 2:138.

5. Scott, *Saga of Lake Tahoe,* 2:46–47, 128.

6. Makley, *Short History of Lake Tahoe,* 90, 92, 102.

7. Robert Frohlich, *Mountain Dreamers: Visionaries of Sierra Nevada Skiing,* 37–39, 46, 68–71.

8. Ibid., 46–48. The year-round residency figure comes from Tahoe Regional Planning Agency and Forest Service, US Department of Agriculture, "Soils of the Lake Tahoe Region: A Guide for Planning," 2.

9. Tahoe Regional Planning Agency and Forest Service, US Department of Agriculture, "Vegetation of the Lake Tahoe Region: A Guide for Planning," 17–22.

10. *Tahoe Daily Tribune,* June 24, 1965.

11. Andrew Schmidt, *The Role of the United States Forest Service and Other Federal Agencies in the Evolving Political, Social, and Economic Microcosm of the Lake Tahoe Region: An Historical Brief,* 173, 176–78.

12. Ibid., 178–80; Ray Knisley taped interview by Andy Schmidt, Carson City, NV, April 12, 1979, tape in possession of Larry Schmidt, Minden, NV; Earl E. Bachman to Andy Schmidt, March 12, 1979; Doug Leisz, taped interview by Michael Makley and Larry Schmidt, Placerville, CA, March 12, 2012, tape in possession of the author.

13. Fink, "Public Land Acquisition," 519n240; *Sacramento Bee,* February 16, 1971.

14. A. Schmidt, *Role of the United States Forest Service,* 178.

15. *Sacramento Bee,* August 16, 1958; *Tahoe Daily Tribune,* January 1, April 7, 1960.

16. Bachand, *Lake Tahoe*, 15; Charles R. Goldman, "Science a Decisive Factor in Destroying Tahoe Clarity," 45; *Tahoe Daily Tribune*, May 28, 1971; Strong, *Tahoe: From Timber Barons to Ecologists*, 59.

17. Ivan Sack, taped interview by Andy Schmidt, Reno, March 26, 1979, tape in possession of Larry Schmidt, Minden, NV.

18. *Sacramento Bee*, May 20, 1971; A. Schmidt, *Role of the United States Forest Service*, 21–22; Gary E. Elliot, *Senator Alan Bible and the Politics of the New West*, 191, 199.

19. Antony R. Orme, "Toward a Shore-Zone Plan for Lake Tahoe," 10; Alan D. Jassby et al., "Origins and Scale Dependence of Temporal Variability in the Transparency of Lake Tahoe, California-Nevada," 284.

20. *Nevada State Journal*, June 22, 1960.

21. Orme, "Shore-Zone System for Lake Tahoe," 14; Bob Richards, taped interview by Michael Makley, Tahoe City, CA, July 11, 2012, tape in possession of the author.

22. Carl R. Pagter and Cameron W. Wolfe Jr., "Lake Tahoe: The Future of a National Asset; Land Use, Water, and Pollution," 570–72; *Sacramento Bee*, June 7, 1971.

23. Pagter and Wolfe, "Lake Tahoe," 570–72.

24. John LeConte, "Physical Studies of Lake Tahoe—I," 512–13.

25. Richards, taped interview, July 11, 2012; University of California, Davis, Docent's Manual, "Reading History," 45; Jassby et al., "Origins and Scale Dependence," 283–85.

26. University of California, Davis, "Secchi Depth Data at Lake Tahoe, 1968–2011"; Bachand, *Lake Tahoe*, 173–74; *Christian Science Monitor*, January 2, 1973; Fink, "Public Land Acquisition," 539n369.

27. *Sacramento Bee*, September 12, 1957.

28. Sack, taped interview, March 26, 1979.

29. Strong, *Tahoe: An Environmental History*, 132; Bachand, *Lake Tahoe*, 15–16. For information on oligotrophic lakes, as differentiated from eutrophic lakes, see Tahoe Regional Planning Agency and Forest Service, US Department of Agriculture, "Limnology and Water Quality of the Lake Tahoe Region: A Guide for Planning," 6.

30. The *McGaughey Report* was officially titled *Comprehensive Study on Protection of Water Resources of Lake Tahoe Basin Through Controlled Waste Disposal*. Bachand, *Lake Tahoe*, 15; P. H. McGauhey et al., "Summary and Conclusions," June 1963, 1, 2, California State Library. Charles R. Goldman and Ralf C. Carter, "An Investigation by Rapid Carbon-14 Bioassay of Factors Affecting the Cultural Eutrophication of Lake Tahoe, California-Nevada," 1044–45, 1058; Rick Hydrick, "Definitions of Blue: The History of the South Tahoe Public Utility District," unpublished manuscript, n.d., chap. 1, pp. 1, 4–5.

31. A. Schmidt, *Role of the United States Forest Service*, 23–25.

FIVE ■ OPPOSING GOALS

1. *Tahoe Daily Tribune*, December 1, 1965.

2. Strong, *Tahoe: An Environmental History*, 126.

3. *Tahoe Daily Tribune*, December 9, 1965.

4. *Tahoe Daily Tribune,* December 10, 1965. Sixteen months later, the *Sacramento Bee* reprinted an article from the *Los Angeles Times,* claiming that "as much as 2 million gallons of sewage effluent has been pumped into the lake daily" (*Sacramento Bee,* April 18, 1967).

5. *Tahoe Daily Tribune,* December 13, 1965. .

6. *Tahoe Daily Tribune,* December 16, 1965.

7. Andy Schmidt, "In Retrospect: A Synopsis of Key Dates, Actions, and Events," 3–4, unpublished manuscript, in possession of Larry Schmidt, Minden, NV; *Tahoe Daily Tribune,* December 16, 1965.

8. Strong, *Tahoe: An Environmental History,* 141.

9. Ibid., 86–87.

10. *Tahoe Daily Tribune,* March 19, March 22, 1960.

11. *Sacramento Bee,* July 25, 1973; *Tahoe Daily Tribune,* November 12, 1965.

12. Strong, *Tahoe: An Environmental History,* 88.

13. League to Save Lake Tahoe, *Bulletin,* no. 3 (February 1968): 3–4.

14. Leisz, taped interview, March 12, 2012 (see chap. 4, n. 12); A. Schmidt, *Role of the United States Forest Service,* 34–35; *Sacramento Bee,* July 25, 1973.

15. *Sacramento Bee,* April 18, 1967, June 2, 1971; California Department of Parks and Recreation, "State Parks Seeks Special Honor for Leading Environmental lawmaker," news release, March 19, 2003; Henry J. Vaux, "The Regulation of Private Forest Practices in California: A Case in Policy Evolution," 130.

16. Strong, *Tahoe: An Environmental History,* 138, 140–41; A. Schmidt, *Role of the United States Forest Service,* 36; Mark T. Imperial and Derek Kauneckis, "Moving from Conflict to Collaboration: Watershed Governance in Lake Tahoe," 1021–22.

17. Nevada State Legislature, "Minutes of Hearing Held on AB 1, AB 2, and SB 9," Special Session, February 12, 1968.

18. Ibid.; *Sierra Sun,* July 22, 2008.

19. Strong, *Tahoe: From Timber Barons to Ecologists,* 67.

20. Ibid.; Kenneth Hanf and Geoffrey Wandesforde-Smith, "Institutional Design and Environmental Management: The Tahoe Regional Planning Agency," 5–6; interview with Paul Laxalt, October 9, 2001, Miller Center, University of Virginia, http://millercenter.org/president/reagan/oralhistory/paul-laxalt.

21. Interview with Laxalt.

22. "Coe Swobe Interview," *Nevada Silver and Blue: The Magazine of the University of Nevada, Reno,* July 2007.

23. A. Schmidt, *Role of the United States Forest Service,* 36–38; Strong, *Tahoe: From Timber Barons to Ecologists,* 67–69, Strong, *Tahoe: An Environmental History,* 143–44; Leisz, taped interview, March 12, 2012.

24. A. Schmidt, *Role of the United States Forest Service,* 38.

25. Strong, *Tahoe: An Environmental History,* 143–44.

SIX ■ IMPOSSIBLE CONDITIONS

1. Public Law 91-148, 91st Cong., S. 118, December 18, 1969, 1.

2. Leisz, taped interview, March 12, 2012 (see chap. 4, n. 12); Hanf and Wandesforde-Smith, "Institutional Design and Environmental Management," 15.

3. J. Allen Bray, tape recording by Andy Schmidt, Oakland, May 15, 1979, in possession of Larry Schmidt

4. A. Schmidt, *Role of the United States Forest Service*, 59–60.

5. Fink, "Public Land Acquisition," 513–14.

6. Strong, *Tahoe: An Environmental History*, 149–50; Knisley, tape recording, April 12, 1979 (see chap. 4, n. 12). For a comprehensive discussion of TRPA's structure and early political failures, see Hanf and Wandesforde-Smith, "Institutional Design and Environmental Management."

7. Western Federal Regional Council Interagency Task Force, *Lake Tahoe Environmental Assessment*, 32–33; A. Schmidt, *Role of the United States Forest Service*, 54–56; Strong, *Tahoe: An Environmental History*, 150.

8. *Sacramento Bee*, July 10, 1970; *Tahoe Daily Tribune*, August 10, 1970.

9. Strong, *Tahoe: From Timber Barons to Ecologists*, 71–72; A. Schmidt, *Role of the United States Forest Service*, 92–93; Robert H. Twiss, "Planning and Land Regulation at Lake Tahoe: Five Decades of Experience"; *Sacramento Bee*, March 12, 1971.

10. *Sacramento Bee*, January 29, March 24, 1971; *Tahoe Daily Tribune*, February 4, 1971.

11. Knisley, tape recording, April 12, 1979.

12. William R. Eadington, "The Casino Gaming Industry: A Study of Political Economy," 26.

13. *Nevada State Journal*, February 21, March 17, 1970; *Tahoe Daily Tribune*, June 8, 1972; *Sacramento Bee*, May 12, 1971.

14. *Tahoe Daily Tribune*, January 26, 1971; *Sacramento Bee*, May 14, 1971.

15. *Sacramento Bee*, May 10, 1971.

16. *Sacramento Bee*, December 31, 1970; *Tahoe Today*, supplement to *Tahoe Daily Tribune and Sierra Sun*, February–March 1971; A. Schmidt, *Role of the United States Forest Service*, 63.

17. Robert G. Bailey, taped interview by Michael Makley, Fort Collins, CO, June 12, 2012, tape in possession of the author.

18. Robert Twiss, taped interview by Michael Makley, Markleeville, CA, July 26, 2012, tape in possession of the author; A. Schmidt, *Role of the United States Forest Service*, 69–70; Twiss, "Planning and Land Regulation," 5–6.

19. Ian L. McHarg and Frederick R. Steiner, eds., *To Heal the Earth: Selected Writing of Ian L. McHarg*, 146–53.

20. Twiss, "Planning and Land Regulation," 5–6; Bailey, taped interview, June 12, 2012; Twiss, taped interview, July 26, 2012.

21. Bailey, taped interview, June 12, 2012.

22. *Sacramento Bee,* May 13, 1971; A. Schmidt, *Role of the United States Forest Service,* 69–70; Twiss, taped interview, July 26, 2012; Laurel W. Ames, "The Real Life Adventures of a Planning Agency," 16.

23. Ames, "Real Life Adventures," 16; Strong, *Tahoe: An Environmental History,* 153; Bray, tape recording, May 15, 1979.

24. A. Schmidt, *Role of the United States Forest Service,* 73–74.

25. Twiss, taped interview, July 26, 2012; A. Schmidt, *Role of the United States Forest Service,* 74.

26. A. Schmidt, *Role of the United States Forest Service,* 75–76.

27. Ames, "Real Life Adventures," 16; Robert G. Bailey, *Land-Capability Classification of the Lake Tahoe Basin, California-Nevada: A Guide for Planning,* 23–25.

28. *San Francisco Examiner,* May 23, 1971; A. Schmidt, *Role of the United States Forest Service,* 75–76; Hanf and Wandesforde-Smith, "Institutional Design and Environmental Management," 30–32, 37; Strong, *Tahoe: An Environmental History,* 151–53.

29. *Tahoe Daily Tribune,* June 3, 1971; *Sacramento Bee,* May 20, June 2, 1971.

SEVEN ■ CHANGING DIRECTION

1. *Nevada State Journal,* June 16, 1971; *Tahoe Daily Tribune,* June 16, 17, 1971; *Sacramento Bee,* June 26, 1971.

2. *Tahoe Daily Tribune,* June 14, 16, 22, 1971; Hanf and Wandesforde-Smith, "Institutional Design and Environmental Management," 32; A. Schmidt, *Role of the United States Forest Service,* 76.

3. Ames, "Real Life Adventures," 16; *Tahoe Daily Tribune,* June 22, 1971.

4. Derek Kauneckis, Leslie Koziol, and Mark Imperial, "Tahoe Regional Planning Agency: The Evolution of Collaboration"; A. Schmidt, *Role of the United States Forest Service,* 76–77, 81, 110–11; *Tahoe Daily Tribune,* July 8, 1971; Knisley, tape recording, April 12, 1979 (see chap. 4, n. 12); Bray, tape recording, May 15, 1979 (see chap. 6, n. 3).

5. *Sacramento Bee,* July 25, 1971; *Tahoe Daily Tribune,* August 5, 1971; A. Schmidt, *Role of the United States Forest Service,* 110–11.

6. A. Schmidt, *Role of the United States Forest Service,* 134–35; *Tahoe Daily Tribune,* March 22, August 9, 1971; *In the Supreme Court of the State of California, In Bank,* Sac. 7896, August 17, 1971, 15, 36, 46.

7. *Sacramento Bee,* June 17, June 24, 1971; Twiss, taped interview, July 26, 2012 (see chap. 6, n. 18).

8. Bray, tape recording, May 15, 1979; *Tahoe Daily Tribune,* November 10, 1971.

9. Andrew Schmidt, "Statement by the Forest Service Planning Team to the Governing Body of the Tahoe Regional Planning Agency," Crystal Bay, NV, September 10, 1971, Andrew Schmidt files, in possession of Larry Schmidt.

10. A. Schmidt, *Role of the United States Forest Service,* 81–82; Ames, "Real Life Adventures," 16–17.

11. Wilbur Twining to J. K. Smith, August 31, 1971; *San Francisco Examiner,* September 1, 1971.

12. *Sacramento Bee,* September 23, 1971.

13. Twiss, taped interview, July 26, 2012.

14. *Sacramento Bee,* September 23, 30, 1971.

15. *Tahoe Daily Tribune,* September 23, 1971; Twiss, taped interview, July 26, 2012.

16. Dwight C. Steele for the Sierra Club, "Statement Before the Governing Body of the Tahoe Regional Planning Agency," December 8, 1971, Dwight C. Steele Papers, Bancroft Library, Berkeley, CA; Ames, "Real Life Adventures," 17.

17. *Tahoe Daily Tribune,* December 14, 23, 1971; A. Schmidt, *Role of the United States Forest Service,* 82–85.

EIGHT ■ APPROVING DEVELOPMENT

1. *Tahoe Daily Tribune,* July 26, 1971.

2. A. Schmidt, *Role of the United States Forest Service,* 93.

3. *Sacramento Bee,* October 24, 1971.

4. *Tahoe Daily Tribune,* December 2, 1971; A. Schmidt, *Role of the United States Forest Service,* 93; *Sacramento Bee,* October 26, 1971.

5. *Tahoe Daily Tribune,* September 5, 7, 9, 1972; *Sacramento Bee,* October 13, 1972.

6. *Sacramento Bee,* April 18, 19, 1973.

7. *Lake County Estates, Inc. v.* TRPA, 99 S. Ct. 1171 (1979); *Lake Country Estates v. Tahoe Planning Agcy.,* 440 U.S. 391 (1979); *Tahoe Daily Tribune,* June 8, 1984.

8. Elliot, *Senator Alan Bible,* 199; Public Law 91-425, 91st Cong., S. 2208, September 26, 1970.

9. *Sacramento Bee,* February 4, 1971.

10. *San Francisco Chronicle,* August 2, 1971; *Sacramento Bee,* August 1, 1971; Federal Water Pollution Control Act Amendments of 1971, S. 2770, 92nd Cong., 1st sess. (Washington, DC: US Government Printing Office, 1971), 22–23.

11. *Sacramento Bee,* August 31, 1972.

12. *Sacramento Bee,* November 10, 1971, September 21, 1972.

13. A. R. Schmidt to Jack Deinema, May 2, 1972; *Oakland Tribune,* March 8, 1972.

14. A. Schmidt, *Role of the United States Forest Service,* 121; *Tahoe Daily Tribune,* January 17, 18, 1973.

15. *Sacramento Bee,* March 4, March 28, April 12, 1973.

16. John Wise, *The Lake Tahoe Study,* 49, 54.

17. Thomas F. Cargill and William R. Eadington, "Nevada's Gaming Revenues: Time Characteristics and Forecasting," 1222; A. Schmidt, *Role of the United States Forest Service,* 95–97.

18. A. Schmidt, *Role of the United States Forest Service,* 95, 103.

19. *Tahoe Daily Tribune,* March 15, 1973; *Sacramento Bee,* March 15, May 3, 1973.

20. *Sacramento Bee,* April 1, 19, 1973.

21. *Tahoe Daily Tribune*, September 19, 1973; *Sacramento Bee*, April 17, June 14, 1973.

22. *Nevada State Journal*, June 22, 1973.

23. Knisley, tape recording, April 12, 1979 (see chap. 4, n. 12); *Sacramento Bee*, June 15, 1973; *Tahoe Daily Tribune*, June 28, July 20, 1973.

24. *Tahoe Daily Tribune*, June 28, July 20, 1973; *Sacramento Bee*, May 24, July 1, July 24, 1973; *Nevada State Journal*, July 22, 1973.

25. *Sacramento Bee*, August 24, 1973.

26. Bray, tape recording, May 15, 1979 (see chap. 6, n. 3).

27. *Sacramento Bee*, October 2, 1973.

28. *Sacramento Bee*, July 24, September 21, November 27, 28, 1973; A. Schmidt, *Role of the United States Forest Service*, 138–39.

29. *Tahoe Daily Tribune*, October 22, 24, November 22, 1973.

30. *Tahoe Daily Tribune*, November 8, 30, 1973; *Sacramento Bee*, November 29, 1973.

31. *Tahoe Daily Tribune*, March 20, October 29, December 6, 1973; *Sacramento Bee*, December 7, 1973.

32. A. Schmidt, *Role of the United States Forest Service*, appendix, "In Retrospect: A Synopsis of Key Dates, Actions, and Events," 8.

33. Strong, *Tahoe: An Environmental History*, 164; Knisley, tape recording, April 12, 1979.

34. Strong, *Tahoe: An Environmental History*, 165.

NINE ■ INFLUENCES

1. *Tahoe Daily Tribune*, December 6, 18, 1972; *Sacramento Bee*, December 19, 1972.

2. *Tahoe Daily Tribune*, August 27, 1973; *Sacramento Bee*, August 29, 1973.

3. *Tahoe Daily Tribune*, February 5, 1974; Strong, *Tahoe: An Environmental History*, 168–69.

4. A. Schmidt, *Role of the United States Forest Service*, 108.

5. *Tahoe Daily Tribune*, May 12, 1971; A. Schmidt, *Role of the United States Forest Service*, 183.

6. Leisz, taped interview, March 12, 2012 (see chap. 4, n. 12); A. Schmidt, *Role of the United States Forest Service*, 183–84.

7. Leisz, taped interview, March 12, 2012.

8. A. Schmidt, *Role of the United States Forest Service*, 183–84; typescript of an oral history with Douglas Leisz conducted in 2004 by US Department of Agriculture, Forest Service Region Five in collaboration with the Regional Oral History Office, the Bancroft Library, University of California, 83–84; Dawn Levy and John Sanford, "Technology Pioneer William R. Hewlett Dead at 87," *Stanford Report*, January 12, 2001.

9. Forest Service: Region 5, "The California Log," November 17, 1972, US Forest Service, Pacific Southwest Regional Office, Heritage Resources Section, San Francisco.

10. Goldman and Carter, "An Investigation by Rapid Carbon-14," 1044; Richards, taped interview, July 11, 2012 (see chap. 4, n. 21).

11. Richards, taped interview, July 11, 2012.

12. University of California History Digital Archives, "Presidents: John LeConte"; LeConte, "Physical Studies of Lake Tahoe," 512–13.

13. Richards, taped interview, July 11, 2012.

14. Lake Tahoe Area Research Coordination Board, "Research Needs for the Lake Tahoe Basin."

15. Governor's Message to Legislature, *Appendix to Journals of Senate and Assembly of the Fifty-Eighth Session of the State of Nevada* (Carson City, NV, 1976), 1:7–8; Elmo J. DeRicco, "Presentation Before Nevada State Senate Committee on Environment and Public Resources," March 11, 1975.

16. Governor's Message to Legislature, *Appendix to Journals of Senate and Assembly of the Fifty-Ninth Session of the State of Nevada* (Carson City, NV, 1978), 13–14.

17. Cargill and Eadington, "Nevada's Gaming Revenues," 1222.

18. Elliott, *History of Nevada,* 335; Hal Rothman, *Neon Metropolis: How Las Vegas Started the Twenty-First Century,* 20–23; Eadington, "Casino Gaming Industry," 26.

19. Cargill and Eadington, "Nevada's Gaming Revenues," 1223.

20. Fink, "Public Land Acquisition," 502.

21. *Sacramento Bee,* October 12, 14, November 18, 1978.

22. *Sacramento Bee,* July 27, 1982.

23. Bill Morgan, taped interview by Michael Makley, Woodfords, CA, August 23, 2011, tape in possession of the author.

TEN ■ WAR BETWEEN THE STATES

1. *Sacramento Bee,* September 13, 1978.

2. Robert E. Stewart, taped interview by Michael Makley, Carson City, NV, May 19, 2012, tape in possession of the author.

3. *Sacramento Bee,* August 26, September 13, 1978.

4. Charles McCabe, "Himself," *San Francisco Chronicle,* September 25, 1978.

5. *Sacramento Bee,* January 23, 1979.

6. *Sacramento Bee,* January 28, 1979.

7. *Sacramento Bee,* November 18, 1978.

8. *Sacramento Bee,* January 13, 1979; *Nevada State Journal,* February 7, 1979.

9. Elliott, *History of Nevada,* 365; *Sacramento Bee,* January 19, 24, 1979, July 27, 1982.

10. Steele, unpublished chronology, 23 (see chap. 7, n. 16); *Sacramento Bee,* December 1, 22, 1978.

11. *Sacramento Bee,* December 22, 1978.

12. *Sacramento Bee,* January 19, February 9, 21, 1979.

13. *Sacramento Bee,* January 25, 1979.

14. *Nevada State Journal,* January 20, 1979; *Sacramento Bee,* March 15, 1979.

15. *Sacramento Bee,* March 21, May 22, 23, 25, 1979.

16. *Sacramento Bee,* April 13, May 29, 1979.

17. *Sacramento Bee,* May 14, 1979.

18. Larry E. Anderson, "Nationalizing Lake Tahoe," 688–89; *Sacramento Bee,* May 8, 28, 1979.

19. For the complete CTRPA transportation plan, see Tahoe Regional Planning Agency Staff Summary and Recommendation, "CTRPA Transportation Plan," March 1977, Draft and Draft EIR, California State Archives, Sacramento.

20. *Sacramento Bee,* February 7, 17, 1979.

21. *Sacramento Bee,* March 2, 1979.

22. *Sacramento Bee,* May 5, 1979, March 24, 1980.

23. *Sacramento Bee,* May 16, 30, 1979; *Mountain Democrat-Times,* June 1, 1979.

24. Board of Supervisors Minutes, County of El Dorado, May 23, 1978, 232, http://www.edcgov.us/bosarchive/minutes/1978%200523.pdf; *Sacramento Bee,* February 1, 1997.

25. Tahoe Regional Planning Agency, "Pershing Settlement Agreement."

26. Makley, *Short History of Lake Tahoe,* 118–19.

27. *Sacramento Bee,* June 21, July 7, 10, August 10, 1979, January 23, June 27, 1980.

ELEVEN ■ SAGEBRUSH AND A SUBMARINE

1. *Sacramento Bee,* June 5, 15, 1979.

2. *Sacramento Bee,* July 30, 1979.

3. Elliot, *History of Nevada,* 342; *US News and World Report,* December 1, 1980.

4. *Lexington (NC) Dispatch,* July 7, 1980; *Prescott (AZ) Courier,* November 11, 1980.

5. R. McGreggor Cawley, *Federal Land, Western Anger: The Sagebrush Rebellion and Environmental Politics,* 92–119; Elliot, *History of Nevada,* 342–43.

6. *Sacramento Bee,* June 29, August 5, October 19, 1979.

7. Andrew Schmidt, *An Historical Brief, 1980 Update,* 9, US Department of Agriculture, US Forest Service, Pacific Southwest Regional Office, Heritage Resources Section, San Francisco.

8. *Sacramento Bee,* January 9, August 5, 1980.

9. *Salinas Californian,* October 13, 1979.

10. *Sacramento Bee,* October 17, 18, 19, 21, 1979; *Salinas Californian,* October 22, 1979.

11. *Sacramento Bee,* September 23, October 20, 1979, February 28, 1980.

12. The DeVoto quote came from Charles F. Wilkinson, *Crossing the Next Meridian: Land, Water, and the Future of the West,* 245. For a discussion of the Sagebrush Rebellion in Nevada in this era, see Hal K. Rothman, *Nevada: The Making of Modern Nevada,* 141–45.

13. *Sacramento Bee,* November 10, 1979, January 1, 1980.

14. *Sacramento Bee,* January 17, April 9, September 27, 1980.

15. *Sacramento Bee,* March 8, 9, 1980.

16. *Sacramento Bee,* March 28, 1980.

17. *Sacramento Bee,* June 22, 1980; Richards, taped interview, July 11, 2012 (see chap. 4, n. 21).

18. Morgan, taped interview, August 23, 2011 (see chap. 9, n. 23); Strong, *Tahoe: An Environmental History*, n. 210; Nevada State Legislature, Background Paper 85-2, "The Tahoe Regional Planning Agency After Amendment of the Bistate Compact in 1980," February 1985, 11, http://www.leg.state.nv.us/Division/Research/Publications /Bkground/BP85-02.pdf.

19. *Sacramento Bee*, August 8, 1980, July 23, 1981; Bill Johnson, taped interview, by Michael Makley, Woodfords, CA, May 30, 2012, tape in possession of the author; Glen Smith for W. A. Morgan, "Report on Land Use Issues at Lake Tahoe," May 1, 1980, US Forest Service, Lake Tahoe Basin Management Unit, South Lake Tahoe, CA.

20. *Sacramento Bee*, August 27, 1980; *Mountain Democrat-Times*, September 21, 1980.

21. A. Schmidt, *Historical Brief, 1980 Update*, 15; *Sacramento Bee*, August 24, 1980.

22. *Sacramento Bee*, September 13, 14, 1980; *Journal of the Assembly of the State of Nevada: Fourteenth Special Session, 1980* (Carson City, September 13, 1980), 19–22.

23. See 96th Cong., H.R. 8235, introduced September 30, 1980.

24. California Senate Bill no. 82, Garamendi, Tahoe Regional Planning, received by the governor September 3, 1980, 40–41; *Sacramento Bee*, September 6, November 8, 1980.

25. 96th Cong., 2nd sess., House of Representatives version H.R. 7306, September 10, 1980; Jim Williams, acting secretary of agriculture, Washington DC, to Honorable Henry M. Jackson, November 19, 1980; A. Schmidt, *Historical Brief, 1980 Update*, 12.

26. Interview with Laxalt, October 9, 2001 (see chap. 5, n. 20); Vic Fazio to Andrew R. Schmidt, October 6, 1980; *Sacramento Bee*, May 16, 1980.

27. *Sacramento Bee*, October 14, December 6, 1980; A. Schmidt, *Historical Brief, 1980 Update*, 14; Presidential Documents, Executive Order 12247 of October 15, 1980, "Federal Actions in the Lake Tahoe Region," *Federal Register* 45, no. 202 (October 16, 1980).

TWELVE ▪ NEW MINISTRATIONS, OLD FRUSTRATIONS

1. *Sacramento Bee*, April 17, November 20, 1979; *Lexington (NC) Dispatch*, July 7, 1980.

2. *Sacramento Bee*, February 26, March 14, 1981.

3. *Sacramento Bee*, January 24, 25, 1981; *Los Angeles Times*, January 30, 1981.

4. *Sacramento Bee*, February 3. Both issues were afterward resolved following usual channels. For a summary of the North Shore Club battle, see *Sacramento Bee*, July 10, 1981; the parking garage issue was covered in numerous articles throughout the 1980s.

5. *Sacramento Bee*, March 14, 1981.

6. *Los Angeles Times*, March 13, 1981.

7. *Sacramento Bee*, January 19, March 24, 25, 1982.

8. David Roberti and Willie L. Brown Jr. to Robert List, May 7, 1982; Governor Robert List to Senator Roberti, May 14, 1982.

9. *San Francisco Sunday Examiner & Chronicle*, August 1, 1982; *Sacramento Bee*, July 27, 1982.

10. *Sacramento Bee*, February 10, May 6, 1982.

11. *Sacramento Bee,* August 22, 1982.

12. Roberti and Brown to List, August 24, 1982; *Sacramento Bee,* August 27, 1982.

13. *Sacramento Bee,* October 6, November 19, 25, 1982.

14. Bill Morgan, telephone interview, by Michael Makley, May 8, 2010; Johnson, taped interview, May 30, 2012 (see chap. 11, n. 19).

15. *Sacramento Bee,* March 31, April 3, May 23, 1984; *Tahoe Daily Tribune,* April 4, 1984.

16. *Sacramento Bee,* January 23, 26, April 19, 22, May 14, 1983.

17. *Sacramento Bee,* March 22, 24, April 14, 16, 26, 1983.

18. *Sacramento Bee,* November 17, December 15, 1983.

19. See, for example, *Sacramento Bee,* May 26, 1982, November 9, 1983, July 4, 1984.

20. *Tahoe Daily Tribune,* April 3, May 1, 2, 1984.

21. *Sacramento Bee,* May 2, 1984.

22. *Sacramento Bee,* May 26, June 6, 1984; *Tahoe Daily Tribune,* May 14, 1984.

23. *Tahoe Daily Tribune,* June 12, 13, 15, 1984.

24. *Tahoe Daily Tribune,* June 20, 1984; *Sacramento Bee,* June 16, 28, 1984.

25. *Sacramento Bee,* June 26, July 13, 1984.

26. Vic Fazio, news release, "House Panel Approves $12 Million to Protect Lake Tahoe," Washington, DC, June 20, 1984; *Tahoe Daily Tribune,* June 8, 1984.

27. Fink, "Public Land Acquisition," 521, 524–25; California Tahoe Conservancy, "Progress Report, 1985–1991," 1–2, 5.

28. Bob Kingman, tape recorded interview by Michael Makley, Auburn, CA, September 11, 2012, tape in possession of the author.

29. Johnson, taped interview, May 30, 2012.

30. *Sacramento Bee,* March 1, 1985.

31. *Sacramento Bee,* March 14, 1985.

32. *Sacramento Bee,* March 15, 31, April 11, 1985.

THIRTEEN ■ ELUSIVE AGREEMENTS

1. Kauneckis, Koziol, and Imperial, "Tahoe Regional Planning Agency," 34; Morgan, taped interview, August 23, 2011 (see chap. 9, n. 23).

2. Morgan, taped interview, August 23, 2011.

3. Christopher M. Weible, "Stakeholder Perceptions of Scientists: Lake Tahoe Environmental Policy from 1984 to 2001." The quote on science is from Steve Teshara, taped interview by Michael Makley, Lake Tahoe, NV, July 31, 2012, tape in possession of the author.

4. See Paul Sabatier, Susan Hunter, and Susan McLaughlin, "The Devil Shift: Perceptions and Misperceptions of Opponents," 450–52, 461, 470.

5. Morgan, taped interview, August 23, 2011; *Sacramento Bee,* July 23, 25, 1985.

6. *Los Angeles Times,* August 3, 1985.

7. Kauneckis, Koziol, and Imperial, "Tahoe Regional Planning Agency," 34; Morgan, taped interview, August 23, 2011.

8. *Sacramento Bee,* January 24, 1986; Fink, "Public Land Acquisition," 543–44.

9. Kauneckis, Koziol, and Imperial, "Tahoe Regional Planning Agency," 36; Morgan, taped interview, August 23, 2011.

10. California Tahoe Conservancy, "Progress Report, 1985–1991," 27; Kauneckis, Koziol, and Imperial, "Tahoe Regional Planning Agency," 39–40; Morgan, taped interview, August 23, 2011.

11. *Sacramento Bee,* January 23, February 23, 1986; Morgan, taped interview, August 23, 2011.

12. *Sacramento Bee,* April 16, June 27, 1986; Morgan, taped interview, August 23, 2011.

13. *Sacramento Bee,* April 8, June 26, 1987.

14. Rothman, *Nevada,* 141; Fink, "Public Land Acquisition," 521–22; Steele, unpublished chronology, 44 (see chap. 7, n. 16).

15. *Sacramento Bee,* April 8, June 26, 1987.

16. *Sacramento Bee,* May 28, 29, June 8, 1987.

17. *Sacramento Bee,* May 28, June 26, 1987; Steele, unpublished chronology, 45, 47.

18. Kauneckis, Koziol, and Imperial, "Tahoe Regional Planning Agency," 34–35.

FOURTEEN ■ LITIGATING THE ISSUES

1. Daniel R. Walsh to Governor Mike O'Callaghan, November 14, 1975; Daniel R. Walsh to Members of the TRPA Governing Board, November 14, 1975; *Kelly v. TRPA,* 109 Nev. 638, 639 (1993).

2. *Kelly v. TRPA,* 109 Nev. 638, 639 (1993); Twiss, taped interview, July 26, 2012 (see chap. 6, n. 18).

3. Richard J. Lazarus, "Litigating *Suitum v. Tahoe Regional Planning Agency* in the United States Supreme Court," 183–86; Jon Christensen, *High Country News,* July 7, 1997.

4. Lazarus, "Litigating *Suitum,*" 197–99.

5. Ibid., 199–201, 186n22.

6. Ibid., 187–220; Legislative Analyst's Office, "California Legislative Update: Tahoe Area Development Lawsuits Could Have Far Reaching Impacts."

7. Jordan C. Kahn, "Lake Tahoe Clarity and Takings Jurisprudence: The Supreme Court Advances Land Use Planning in Tahoe-Sierra," 45–46; *Tahoe-Sierra v. TRPA,* 34 F.Supp. 2d 1226 (D. Nev. 1999).

8. Kahn, "Lake Tahoe Clarity and Takings Jurisprudence," 46–49, 50–51; Twiss, taped interview, July 26, 2012; Edward J. Sullivan, "A Brief History of the Takings Clause."

9. Kahn, "Lake Tahoe Clarity and Takings Jurisprudence," 52–57.

FIFTEEN ■ DAMAGES AND COURTS

1. Frohlich, *Mountain Dreamers,* 44–51; Makley, *Short History of Lake Tahoe,* 96–98, 150–51.

2. Makley, *Short History of Lake Tahoe,* 150.

3. Unless otherwise noted, the account of this case follows *Hewlett v. Squaw Valley Ski Corp.,* 54 Cal. App. 4th 499-Cal: Court of Appeal, 3rd Appellate Dist., April 22, 1997.

4. Makley, *Short History of Lake Tahoe*, 96–98; *Los Angeles Times*, October 31, 1991.

5. *Los Angeles Times*, October 31, 1991; Makley, *Short History of Lake Tahoe*, 150–51; *Hewlett v. Squaw Valley Ski Corp.*, April 22, 1997.

6. Ibid.

7. *Las Vegas Review Journal*, June 25, 2000.

8. John Brissenden, interview by Michael Makley, Hope Valley, CA, August 14, 2012; *People of the State of California v. Squaw Valley Ski Corporation*, California Superior Court, Case No. SCV 12916, http://oag.ca.gov/system/files/attachments/press _releases/02-007.pdf.

9. Scott Ferguson, telephone interview by Michael Makley, August 15, 2012; *People of the State of California v. Squaw Valley Ski Corporation*, California Superior Court, Case No. SCV 12916, Consent Agreement and Stipulation for Entry of Final Judgment: Order, July 8, 2005.

10. Ski Area Citizen's Coalition, Top Ten, http://www.skiareacitizens.com/index .php?nav=top_ten.

11. Levy and Sanford, "Technology Pioneer William R. Hewlett Dead at 87," *Stanford Report*, January 12, 2001.

12. Brian Wallace to Steve Chilton, August 24, 1992, Washoe Tribe of Nevada and California files, Gardnerville, NV.

13. Matthew S. Makley and Michael J. Makley, *Cave Rock: Climbers, Courts, and a Washoe Indian Sacred Place*, 23–24. See also Don Handelman, "The Development of a Washoe Shaman"; and Edgar E. Siskin Papers, Collection No. 90-68, Box No. 1, Special Collections Department, University of Nevada, Reno. The statement regarding traditional Washoes and the tunnels comes from discussions with numerous tribal members.

14. Makley and Makley, *Cave Rock*, 4–5, 46–47.

15. *Tahoe Daily Tribune*, May 28, 1997.

16. "Proposal from Climbers at Discussion Session 3," handout given to participants at Cave Rock Collaboration Effort Meeting no. 3, March 17, 1998, copy in possession of the author.

17. Brian Wallace, interview with Michael Makley, video recording, Carson City, NV, June 14, 1998, video in possession of the author.

18. Juan Palma, "Cave Rock Management Direction Proposed Action," January 13, 1999, US Forest Service, Lake Tahoe Basin Management Unit, Sacramento.

19. Jones and Stokes Associates, Inc., *Cave Rock Management Plan: Final Environmental Impact Statement*, appendix B, n.p.

20. Maribeth Gustafson, telephone interview with Michael J. Makley, January 9, 2009.

21. LTBMU, "Summary: Cave Rock Management Plan Final Environmental Impact Statement," 10, US Forest Service, Lake Tahoe Basin Management Unit, South Lake Tahoe, CA.

22. Maribeth Gustafson, LTBMU, "Record of Decision for Cave Rock Management Direction," July 8, 2003.

23. Richard Herz, "Legal Protection for Indigenous Cultures: Sacred Sites and Communal Rights," 705–6; *Lyng v. Northwest Indian Cemetery Protective Association,* syllabus, Supreme Court of the United States, Supreme Court Collection, Cornell University Law School, http://www.law.cornell.edu/supct/html/histories /USSC_CR_0485_0439_ZS.hml.

24. Associated Press, "Government Proceeds with Indian Cattle Auction," May 31, 2002; *United States and Pyramid Lake Paiute Tribe of Indians v. Alpine Land and Reservoir Company,* 340 F.3d 903 (Ninth Cir. 2003); Ryan Slattery, "Men Who Stole Petroglyphs Sentenced to Prison."

25. "Cave Rock Management Direction: Hearing in US District Court, Nevada," February 1, 2005, http://www.fs.fed.us/r3/spf/tribal/documents/caveroc-020205.rtf.

26. "For Publication United States Court of Appeal for the Ninth Circuit," August 27, 2007, http://www.fs.fed.us/r5/tribalrelations/caverock.php?more=9ccoaoocr.

27. For a more complete discussion of the entire Cave Rock issue, see Makley and Makley, *Cave Rock.*

SIXTEEN ▦ THE SUMMIT

1. *San Francisco Chronicle,* July 17, 2002; Twiss, taped interview, July 26, 2012 (see chap. 6, n. 18).

2. Teshara, taped interview, July 31, 2012 (see chap. 13, n. 3).

3. Kingman, taped interview, September 11, 2012 (see chap. 12, n. 28); Laurel Ames, taped phone interview by Michael Makley, September 14, 2012, tape in possession of the author; Mike Chrisman in the *San Francisco Chronicle,* March 10, 2005.

4. Teshara, taped interview, July 31, 2012.

5. Susan D. Rock, "Looking Back: The Best of Each Decade," *Tahoe Quarterly* (Spring 2007), http://www.tahoequarterly.com/; *Lake Tahoe Traveler,* "Best of Each Decade."

6. Teshara, taped interview, July 31, 2012.

7. *Tahoe Daily Tribune,* July 27, 1997.

8. Teshara, taped interview, July 31, 2012; "Tahoe Regional Planning Agency, Environmental Improvement Program: Highlights & Accomplishments," August 2011, http://www.trpa.org.

9. *Tahoe Daily Tribune,* July 27, 1997.

10. *Tahoe Daily Tribune,* July 27, 1997.

11. H.R. 3388 (106th), Lake Tahoe Restoration Act, November 13, 2000, http://www .govtrack.us/congress/bills/106/hr3388; Teshara, taped interview, July 31, 2012.

12. TRPA, Tahoe Regional Planning Agency, "Environmental Improvement Program: Highlights and Accomplishments."

13. Teshara, taped interview, July 31, 2012; California Biodiversity News, "Presidential Forum Spotlights Lake Tahoe's Great Environmental Challenges."

14. Teshara, taped interview, July 31, 2012; *Lake Tahoe News,* May 4, 2009.

15. Laurel Ames, taped interview by Michael Makley, South Lake Tahoe, CA, July 10, 2012, tape in possession of the author.

16. Rochelle Nason, guest column, *Tahoe Daily Tribune,* June 20, 2010; Tetra Tech, "Lake Tahoe Watershed Plan."

17. TERC and TRPA news release, "New Analysis Shows Important Slowdown in Lake Tahoe Clarity Loss," May 12, 2008, http://www.trpa.org/documents/press_room/2008/Clarity_Release_5-12-08.PDF.

18. *Lake Tahoe News,* May 4, 2009.

19. *San Francisco Chronicle,* August 9, 2012.

20. TRPA, news release, June 27, 2007, http://www.trpa.org/documents/press_room/Tree_Rules_6-27-07.pdf.

21. Makley, *Short History of Lake Tahoe,* 151–54; "Bear Education, Aversion, Response," http://www.savebears.org/.

22. *North Lake Tahoe Bonanza,* August 24, 2012.

23. *Tahoe Daily Tribune,* June 20, 2010.

24. Minutes of the Meeting of the Assembly Committee on Government Affairs, Seventy-Sixth Session, June 1, 2011, http://www.leg.state.nv.us/Session/76th2011/Minutes/Assembly/JUD/Final/1393.pdf.

25. *North Lake Tahoe Bonanza,* February 1, 2011.

26. *Tahoe Daily Tribune,* June 20, 2010.

SEVENTEEN ▪ CONFLICTING HOPES

1. Andrew Simon, "Fine-Sediment Loadings to Lake Tahoe."

2. *Los Angeles Times,* July 27, 2011.

3. Ames, taped interview, July 10, 2012 (see chap. 16, n. 15); Nevada Senate Committee on Government Affairs, Hearing on SB 271—NV Withdrawal from TRPA Compact, April 1, 2011, http://www.leg.state.nv.us/Session/76th2011/Minutes/Senate/GA/Final/641.pdf.

4. Tetra Tech, "Lake Tahoe EIP 2010–2020: An Economic Analysis of Private Source Stormwater BMP Expenditures on Redevelopment Projects"; Joanne Marchetta, *Tahoe Mountain News,* May 2010.

5. Makley, *Short History of Lake Tahoe,* 156–57.

6. *Lake Tahoe News,* May 4, 2009.

7. *Moonshine Ink,* June 12, 2008, http://www.moonshineink.com/sections/spot/test-driving-trpas-preferred-alternative.

8. Michael Donahoe to Tahoe Regional Planning Agency Governing Board Members and Staff, July 3, 2008; *Moonshine Ink,* June 12, 2008.

9. *Mountain Democrat-Times,* September 23, 2010.

10. Joanne S. Marchetta, "Fireside Chat"; United States District Court for the Eastern District of California, *League to Save Lake Tahoe and Sierra Club v. Tahoe Regional Planning Agency,* No. CIV. S-08-2828 LKK/GGH; *Tahoe Daily Tribune,* March 3, 2012.

11. *Seattle Times,* December 26, 2009; *Lake Tahoe News,* April 28, 2011.

12. Nevada Senate Committee on Government Affairs, Hearing on SB 271, April 1, 2011.

13. *Lake Tahoe News,* April 28, 2011.

14. *Sierra Sun,* April 27, 2011.

15. *Reno Gazette-Journal,* March 24, 2011.

16. Nevada Senate Bill No. 271—Senators Lee and Settelmeyer, March 18, 2011 (reprinted with amendments adopted on June 6, 2011), http://www.leg.state.nv.us /Session/76th2011/Bills/SB/SB271.pdf.

17. Nevada Senate Committee on Government Affairs, Hearing on SB 271, April 1, 2011.

18. *Tahoe Daily Tribune,* April 8, April 13, 2011; *Sierra Sun,* April 27, 2011.

19. Nevada Senate Committee on Government Affairs, Hearing on SB 271, April 11, May 26, 2011.

20. *New York Times,* June 4, 2004; VEGASINC, "In Politics, Top Executives at R&R Partners Wear Different Stripes," October 17, 2011, http://www.vegasinc.com/news/2011 /oct/17/.

21. Minutes of the Meeting of the Assembly Committee on Government Affairs, Seventy-Sixth Session, June 1, 2011; SB 271, Amendment Proposed by the Office of the Secretary of State, June 1, 2011, http://www.leg.state.nv.us/Session/76th2011/Minutes /Assembly/JUD/Final/1393.pdf.

22. Minutes of the Meeting of the Assembly Committee on Government Affairs, Seventy-Sixth Session, June 1, 2, 4, 2011 http://www.leg.state.nv.us/Session/76th2011/Minutes/ Assembly/JUD/Final/1393.pdf, http://www.leg.state.nv.us/session/76th2011/minutes /senate/fin/final/1428.pdf, https://leg.state.nv.us/Session/76th2011/Minutes/Assembly /GA/Final/1452.pdf, respectively.

23. *Reno News and Review,* August 23, 2012.

24. *Lake Tahoe News,* June 27, 2012.

25. *Gardnerville (NV) Record Courier,* June 1, 2012; Tahoe Project, Nevada Senate Bill 271 Interview with Senator John Lee, n.d., http://tahoeproject.org.

EIGHTEEN ▪ GREEN VERSUS GREEN

1. Laurel Ames, Tahoe Area Sierra Club, "Comments on the Draft 2011 Environmental Threshold Report," July 25, 2012, 7, 8–9, 13, 147; University of California, Davis, Tahoe Environmental Research Center, "Lake Tahoe Clarity"; *Tahoe Daily Tribune,* April 21, 2011.

2. *Reno Gazette-Journal,* August 17, 2011; Marchetta, "Fireside Chat."

3. *Lake Tahoe News,* May 24, 2012.

4. *Reno Gazette-Journal,* May 27, 2012; *Lake Tahoe News,* May 24, 2012; Tahoe Project, "Tahoe Regional Plan: California Attorney General's Office April Statement."

5. John Laird and Leo M. Drozdoff to Chair Norma Santiago and Members of the Governing Board, July 26, 2012; *Reno Gazette-Journal,* August 28, 2012; Tahoe Regional Planning Agency, news release, August 23, 2012; *Lake Tahoe News,* August 10, 2012.

6. California-Nevada Consultation: Regional Plan Update Recommendations, July

25, 2012, 5, http://www.trpa.org/documents/rp_update/Bi-State_Consult/Final%20
Consultation%20Document.pdf.

7. Tahoe Regional Planning Agency, news release, August 23, 2012; Darcie Goodman-Collins, taped interview by Michael Makley, South Lake Tahoe, CA, September 27,
2012, tape in possession of the author.

8. *Tahoe Daily Tribune,* February 11, 13, 2013.

9. *Reno Gazette-Journal,* August 17, 2011; Barbara Boxer, Report to Accompany S.
432, Lake Tahoe Restoration Act of 2011, 112th Cong., 2nd sess., February 7, 2012.

10. Ames, taped phone interview, September 14, 2012; Tahoe Project, "Edgewood
Tahoe Lodge Permit Approved"; Ames, taped interview, July 10, 2012.

11. Ames, taped phone interview, September 14, 2012; *Gardnerville (NV) Record-
Courier,* January 13, 2012.

12. *Reno Gazette-Journal,* January 7, 2013.

13. California State Conservancy, *California Tahoe Conservancy: 20th Anniversary
Report,* 23; Kingman, taped interview, September 11, 2012 (see chap. 16, n. 3); Makley,
Short History of Lake Tahoe, 161–62.

14. Goodman-Collins, taped interview, September 27, 2012; Tahoe Project, "Interview with Dr. Darcie Goodman-Collins (1 & 2)."

15. Tahoe Pipe Club, "Save Tahoe Clarity."

16. *Moonshine Ink,* May 11, 2012.

17. *Las Vegas Sun,* April 11, 2013; *Tahoe Daily Tribune,* May 15, 2013.

18. *Sacramento Bee,* March 11, 2013.

19. *San Diego Union,* April 11, 2013.

20. *Gardnerville (NV) Record-Courier,* April 24, 2013.

21. *Nevada Journal,* May 15, 2013.

22. *Tahoe Daily Tribune,* May 15, 2013; *San Jose (CA) Mercury,* May 15, 2013; *Nevada
Journal,* May 15, 2013.

CONCLUSION

1. *Lake Tahoe News,* July 21, 2012.

2. Kingman, taped interview, September 11, 2012 (see chap. 16, n. 3).

3. Teshara, taped interview, July 31, 2012 (see chap. 13, n. 3).

4. Minutes of the Meeting of the Assembly Committee on Government Affairs, Seventy-Sixth Session, June 1, 2011, http://www.leg.state.nv.us/Session/76th2011/Minutes
/Assembly/JUD/Final/1393.pdf.

5. Strong, *Tahoe: An Environmental History,* 84; Tahoe Fund, "Protecting Lake Tahoe."

6. Twiss, taped interview, July 26, 2012 (see chap. 6, n. 18); Ames, taped interview,
July 10, 2012 (see chap. 16, n. 15).

BIBLIOGRAPHY

ARCHIVES AND MANUSCRIPT COLLECTIONS

Bancroft, Hubert Howe. Collection. Bancroft Library, University of California, Berkeley.

d'Azevedo, Warren. Papers. Collection 97-04. Box 6. Special Collections Department, University of Nevada, Reno.

Governors' Records, 1861–2010. Records of the Nevada State Legislature: Journals of the Assembly and Senate, Legislative Bills, 1864–2005.

Nevada State Library and Archives, Carson City, Nevada.

Siskin, Edgar E. Papers. Collection 90-68. Box 1. Special Collections Department, University of Nevada, Reno.

Special Collections Department, University of Nevada, Reno.

PERIODICALS

Carson Morning Appeal (Carson City, NV)
Christian Science Monitor
Daily Alta California (San Francisco)
Gardnerville (NV) Record-Courier
High Country News (Paonia, CO)
Lake Tahoe News (South Lake Tahoe, CA)
Las Vegas Review Journal
Lexington (NC) Dispatch
Los Angeles Times
Moonshine Ink (Truckee, CA)
Mountain Democrat-Times (Placerville, CA)
Nevada Daily Tribune (Carson City)
Nevada State Journal (Carson City)
New York Times
North Lake Tahoe Bonanza (Tahoe City, CA)
Prescott (AZ) Courier
Reno Evening Gazette
Reno Gazette-Journal
Reno News & Review
Sacramento Bee
Sacramento Daily Union
Salinas Californian

San Diego Union
San Francisco Call
San Francisco Chronicle
San Francisco Examiner
San Francisco Sunday Examiner & Chronicle
San Jose (CA) Mercury
Seattle Times
Sierra Sun (Tahoe City, CA)
Tahoe Daily Tribune (South Lake Tahoe, CA)
Tahoe Quarterly (Incline Village, NV)
Territorial Enterprise (Virginia City, NV)
Truckee (CA) Republican
US News and World Report
Virginia Daily Union (Virginia City, NV)

OTHER SOURCES

Ames, Laurel W. "The Real Life Adventures of a Planning Agency." *California Journal* 3, no. 1 (1972): 12, 16–17.

Anderson, Larry E. "Nationalizing Lake Tahoe." *Santa Clara Law Review* 19, no. 3 (1979): 681–717.

Antonucci, David C. *Fairest Picture: Mark Twain at Lake Tahoe.* Lake Tahoe: Art of Learning, 2011.

Bachand, Thomas. *Lake Tahoe: A Fragile Beauty.* San Francisco: Chronicle Books, 2008.

Bailey, Robert G. *Land-Capability Classification of the Lake Tahoe Basin, California-Nevada: A Guide for Planning.* South Lake Tahoe, CA: Forest Service, US Department of Agriculture, 1974.

Bowles, Samuel. *Across the Continent: A Summer's Journey to the Rocky Mountains, the Mormons, and the Pacific States with Speaker Colfax.* 1865. Reprint, Ann Arbor, MI: University Microfilms, 1966.

Bruchey, Stuart, and Eleanor Buchey, eds. "Report of the Public Lands Commission Created by the Act of March 3, 1879." In *Use and Abuse of America's Natural Resources.* 1880. Reprint, New York: Arno Press, 1972.

California Biodiversity News. "Presidential Forum Spotlights Lake Tahoe's Great Environmental Challenges." Fall 1997. http://biodiversity.ca.gov/newsletter/v5n1/presidential.html.

California State Conservancy. *California Tahoe Conservancy: 20th Anniversary Report.* Sacramento: California Tahoe Conservancy, 2005.

California Tahoe Conservancy. "Progress Report, 1985–1991." Sacramento: California Tahoe Conservancy, 1991.

Cargill, Thomas F., and William R. Eadington. "Nevada's Gaming Revenues: Time Characteristics and Forecasting." *Management Science* 24, no. 12 (1978): 1221–30.

Cawley, R. McGreggor. *Federal Land, Western Anger: The Sagebrush Rebellion and Environmental Politics.* Lawrence: University Press of Kansas, 1993.

Dana, Samuel Trask, and Myron Krueger. *California Lands: Ownership, Use, and Management.* Washington, DC: American Forestry Association, 1958.

Dangberg, Grace. *Conflict on the Carson: A Study of Water Litigation in Western Nevada.* Minden, NV: Carson Valley Historical Society, 1975.

Deering, F. P., and J. H. Deering Jr. *Supplement to Deering's Codes and Statutes of California.* San Francisco: Bancroft-Whitney, 1889.

DeRicco, Elmo J. "Presentation Before Nevada State Senate Committee on Environment and Public Resources." Carson City, NV, March 11, 1975.

Eadington, William R. "The Casino Gaming Industry: A Study of Political Economy." *Annals of the American Academy of Political and Social Science* 474 (July 1984): 23–35.

Egan, Timothy. *The Big Burn: Teddy Roosevelt and the Fire That Saved America.* Boston: Houghton Mifflin Harcourt, 2009.

Elliot, Gary E. *Senator Alan Bible and the Politics of the New West.* Reno: University of Nevada Press, 1994.

Elliott, Russell R., with the assistance of William D. Rowley. *History of Nevada.* 1973. Reprint, Lincoln: University of Nebraska Press, 1987.

Fink, Richard J. "Public Land Acquisition for Environmental Protection: Structuring a Program for the Lake Tahoe Basin." *Ecology Law Quarterly* 18, no. 3 (1991): 488–557.

Frémont, John Charles. *Narratives of Exploration and Adventure.* Edited by Allan Nevins. New York: Longmans, Green, 1956.

Frohlich, Robert. *Mountain Dreamers: Visionaries of Sierra Nevada Skiing.* Truckee, CA: Coldstream Press, 1997.

Goldman, Charles R. "Science a Decisive Factor in Destroying Tahoe Clarity." *California Agriculture* 60, no. 2 (2006): 45–46.

Goldman, Charles R., and Ralf C. Carter. "An Investigation by Rapid Carbon-14 Bioassay of Factors Affecting the Cultural Eutrophication of Lake Tahoe, California-Nevada." *Journal (Water Pollution Control Federation)* 37, no. 7 (1965): 1044–59.

Handelman, Don. "The Development of a Washoe Shaman." In *Native Californians: A Theoretical Retrospective,* edited by John Lowell Bean and Thomas Blackburn. Menlo Park, CA: Ballena Press, 1976.

Hanf, Kenneth, and Geoffrey Wandesforde-Smith. "Institutional Design and Environmental Management: The Tahoe Regional Planning Agency." Research report no. 24. Institute of Government Affairs, University of California, Davis, August 1972.

Herz, Richard. "Legal Protection for Indigenous Cultures: Sacred Sites and Communal Rights." *Virginia Law Review* 79, no. 3 (1993): 691–716.

Hinkle, George, and Bliss Hinkle. *Sierra-Nevada Lakes.* 1949. Reprint, Reno: University of Nevada Press, 1987.

Hittell, John S. *The Commerce and Industries of the Pacific Coast.* San Francisco: A. L. Bancroft, 1882.

Imperial, Mark T., and Derek Kauneckis. "Moving from Conflict to Collaboration: Watershed Governance in Lake Tahoe." *Natural Resources Journal* 43 (Fall 2003): 1009–1955.

Jassby, Alan D., Charles R. Goldman, John E. Reuter, and Robert C. Richards. "Origins and Scale Dependence of Temporal Variability in the Transparency of Lake Tahoe, California-Nevada." *Limnology and Oceanography* 44, no. 2 (1999): 282–94.

Jones and Stokes Associates, Inc. *Cave Rock Management Plan: Final Environmental Impact Statement.* Sacramento: Jones and Stokes, 2002.

Kahn, Jordan C. "Lake Tahoe Clarity and Takings Jurisprudence: The Supreme Court Advances Land Use Planning in Tahoe-Sierra." *Environmental Law and Policy Journal* 26 (2002): 33–63.

Kauneckis, Derek, Leslie Koziol, and Mark Imperial. "Tahoe Regional Planning Agency: The Evolution of Collaboration." School of Public and Environmental Affairs, Indiana University, Bloomington, August 2000. http://people.uncw.edu/imperialm/Instructor/Papers/NAPA_TRPA_Case.pdf.

Knack, Martha C., and Omer C. Stewart. *As Long as the River Shall Run: An Ethnohistory of Pyramid Lake Indian Reservation.* 1984. Reprint, Reno: University of Nevada Press, 1999.

Lake Tahoe Area Research Coordination Board. *Research Needs for the Lake Tahoe Basin.* South Lake Tahoe, CA: Lake Tahoe Area Research Coordination Board, 1974.

Lazarus, Richard J. "Litigating *Suitum v. Tahoe Regional Planning Agency* in the United States Supreme Court." *Journal of Land Use & Environmental Law* 12, no. 2 (1997): 179–220.

LeConte, John. "Physical Studies of Lake Tahoe—I." *Overland Monthly and Out West Magazine (1868–1935)* 2, no. 11 (November 1883): 506–17. American Periodicals Series. http://terc.ucdavis.edu/publications/LeConte_PhysicalStudiesOfLake Tahoe_I_1883.pdf.

Legislative Analyst's Office. "California Legislative Update: Tahoe Area Development Lawsuits Could Have Far Reaching Impacts." August 1999. http://www.lao.ca.gov/1999/cal_update/aug_99_trpa.html.

Lekisch, Barbara. *Tahoe Place Names: The Origin and History of Names in the Lake Tahoe Basin.* Lafayette, CA: Great West Books, 1988.

Lindstrom, Susan. "Submerged Tree Stumps as Indicators of Mid-Holocene Aridity in the Lake Tahoe Basin." *Journal of California and Great Basin Anthropology* 12, no. 2 (1990).

Makley, Matthew S. "These Will Be Strong: A History of the Washoe People." PhD diss., Arizona State University, 2007.

Makley, Matthew S., and Michael J. Makley. *Cave Rock: Climbers, Courts, and a Washoe Indian Sacred Place.* Reno: University of Nevada Press, 2010.

Makley, Michael J. *The Infamous King of the Comstock: William Sharon and the Gilded Age in the West.* Reno: University of Nevada Press, 2006.

———. *John Mackay: Silver King in the Gilded Age.* Reno: University of Nevada Press, 2009.

———. *A Short History of Lake Tahoe.* Reno: University of Nevada Press, 2011.

Marchetta, Joanne S. "Fireside Chat." Sierra Nevada College, April 18, 2011. http://www .trpa.org/documents/press_room/2011/SNC_Fireside_Chat_4-18-2011.pdf.

McGaughey, P. H., and Lake Tahoe Area Council. *Comprehensive Study on Protection of Water Resources of Lake Tahoe Basin Through Controlled Waste Disposal.* Lake Tahoe, CA: Engineering-Science, 1963.

McHarg, Ian L., and Frederick R. Steiner, eds. *To Heal the Earth: Selected Writing of Ian L. McHarg.* Washington, DC: Island Press, 1998.

McQuivey, Bob, comp. "Summary of Lake Tahoe Basin Resources (1854–1976)." January 16, 2006. http://ndep.nv.gov/bwqp/file/tahoemcquivey_oct06.pdf.

Murphy, Dennis D., and Christopher M. Knopp, eds. *Lake Tahoe Watershed Assessment.* Vol. 1. Albany, CA: Pacific Southwest Research Station, US Department of Agriculture, 2000.

Orme, Antony R. "The Shore-Zone System for Lake Tahoe." Report for the Tahoe Regional Planning Agency, Stateline, NV, May 1971.

———. "Toward a Shore-Zone Plan for Lake Tahoe." Report for the Tahoe Regional Planning Agency, Stateline, NV, Summer 1972.

Pagter, Carl R., and Cameron W. Wolfe Jr. "Lake Tahoe: The Future of a National Asset; Land Use, Water, and Pollution." *California Law Review* 52, no. 3 (1964): 563–622.

Pisani, Donald J. "Federal Reclamation and Water Rights in Nevada." *Agricultural History* 51, no. 3 (1977): 540–59.

———. *From the Family Farm to Agribusiness: The Irrigation Crusade in California and the West, 1850–1931.* Berkeley: University of California Press, 1984.

———. "'Why Shouldn't California Have the Grandest Aqueduct in the World?': Alexis Von Schmidt's Lake Tahoe Scheme." *California Historical Quarterly* 53, no. 4 (1974): 347–60.

Raymond, Steve. *The Year of the Trout.* Seattle: Sasquatch Books, 1995.

Richards, Gordon. "Demise of the Lahontan Cutthroat Trout." Truckee Donner Historical Society. http://truckeehistory.org/.

Rothman, Hal K. *Neon Metropolis: How Las Vegas Started the Twenty-First Century.* New York: Routledge, 2003.

———. *Nevada: The Making of Modern Nevada.* Reno: University of Nevada Press, 2010.

Rowley, William D. "Visions of a Watered West." *Agricultural History,* no. 76 (Spring 2002): 142–53.

Sabatier, Paul, Susan Hunter, and Susan McLaughlin. "The Devil Shift: Perceptions and Misperceptions of Opponents." *Western Political Quarterly* 40, no. 3 (1987): 449–76.

Schaffer, Jeffrey P. *Desolation Wilderness and the South Lake Tahoe Basin: A Guide to Lake Tahoe's Finest Hiking Area.* 1980. Reprint, Berkeley: Wilderness Press, 2003.

Schmidt, Andrew. *The Role of the United States Forest Service and Other Federal Agencies in the Evolving Political, Social, and Economic Microcosm of the Lake Tahoe Region: An Historical Brief.* San Francisco: US Department of Agriculture, Forest Service, 1979.

Scott, E. B. *The Saga of Lake Tahoe.* Crystal Bay, Lake Tahoe: Sierra-Tahoe Publishing, 1957.

———. *The Saga of Lake Tahoe.* Vol. 2. Crystal Bay, Lake Tahoe: Sierra-Tahoe Publishing, 1973.

Simon, Andrew. "Fine-Sediment Loadings to Lake Tahoe." *Journal of the American Water Resources Association* 44, no. 3 (2008). http://naldc.nal.usda.gov /download/17990/PDF.

Slattery, Ryan. "Men Who Stole Petroglyphs Sentenced to Prison." *Indian Country Today,* September 27, 2004. http://www.coloradoaim.org/blog/2004/09/articles -september-28.html.

Smith, Grant H. *The History of the Comstock Lode, 1850–1920.* 1943. Reprint, Reno: University of Nevada Press, 1998.

State of Nevada Division of Water Resources. "Truckee River Chronology, Part III, Twentieth Century." http://water.nv.gov/mapping/chronologies/truckee/part3.cfm.

Strong, Douglas H. *Tahoe: An Environmental History.* Lincoln: University of Nebraska Press, 1984.

———. *Tahoe: From Timber Barons to Ecologists.* Lincoln: University of Nebraska Press, 1999.

Sullivan, Edward J. "A Brief History of the Takings Clause." http://law.wustl.edu /landuselaw/Articles/Brief_Hx_Taking.htm.

Tahoe Fund. "Protecting Lake Tahoe." http://www.tahoefund.org/about-tahoe /help-protect-lake-tahoe.

Tahoe Pipe Club. "Save Tahoe Clarity." http://www.tahoepipeclub.com/.

Tahoe Project. "Edgewood Tahoe Lodge Permit Approved." August 24, 2012. http:// tahoeproject.org.

———. "Interview with Dr. Darcie Goodman-Collins (1 & 2)." July 25, 2012. http://tahoeproject.org/.

———. "Tahoe Regional Plan: California Attorney General's Office April Statement." April 26, 2011. http://tahoeproject.org.

Tahoe Regional Planning Agency. "Environmental Improvement Program: Highlights and Accomplishments." August 2011. http://www.trpa.org/documents /docdwnlds/EIP/Update/EIP_4PG_2011_FNL.pdf.

———. "Pershing Settlement Agreement." April 15, 1997. http://www.trpa.org /documents/agendas/archive/gb_agendas/1997/1997-april.pdf.

Tahoe Regional Planning Agency and Forest Service, US Department of Agriculture. "Limnology and Water Quality of the Lake Tahoe Region: A Guide for Planning." South Lake Tahoe, July 1971.

———. "Soils of the Lake Tahoe Region: A Guide for Planning." South Lake Tahoe, July 1971.

———. "Vegetation of the Lake Tahoe Region: A Guide for Planning." South Lake Tahoe, June 1971.

Tetra Tech. "Lake Tahoe EIP, 2010–2020: An Economic Analysis of Private Source Stormwater BMP Expenditures on Redevelopment Projects." March 2010. http://nltra.org/documents/pdfs/Redevelopment%20econ.pdf.

———. "Lake Tahoe Watershed Plan." N.d. http://www.tetratech.com/us/lake-tahoe-watershed-plan.html.

Twiss, Robert H. "Planning and Land Regulation at Lake Tahoe: Five Decades of Experience." http://www.law.berkeley.edu/files/twiss_planning.pdf.

University of California, Davis. "Secchi Depth Data at Lake Tahoe, 1968–2011." http://terc.ucdavis.edu/research/SecchiData.pdf.

University of California, Davis, Docent's Manual. "Reading History." http://terc.ucdavis.edu/documents/DocentManual_Chap5_AdditionalResources.pdf.

University of California, Davis, Tahoe Environmental Research Center. "Lake Tahoe Clarity." February 29, 2012. http://terc.ucdavis.edu/research/clarity.html.

University of California History Digital Archives. "Presidents: John LeConte." http://sunsite.berkeley.edu/~ucalhist/general_history/overview/presidents/index.html.

Vaux, Henry J. "The Regulation of Private Forest Practices in California: A Case in Policy Evolution." *Journal of Forest History* 30, no. 3 (1986): 128–34.

Von Schmidt, A. W. *Report to the Lake Tahoe and San Francisco Water Works Company, on Its Sources of Supply: Proposed Line of Works; Estimated Cost and Income.* San Francisco: Alta California Printing House, 1871.

Weible, Christopher M. "Stakeholder Perceptions of Scientists: Lake Tahoe Environmental Policy from 1984 to 2001." School of Public Policy, Georgia Institute of Technology, September 11, 2007. http://www.ucdenver.edu/academics/colleges/SPA/FacultyStaff/Faculty/Documents/Weible_TahoePerceptSci_EM07.pdf.

Western Federal Regional Council Interagency Task Force. *Lake Tahoe Environmental Assessment.* Washington, DC: US Government Printing Office, 1979.

Wheeler, Sessions S., with William W. Bliss. *Tahoe Heritage: The Bliss Family of Glenbrook, Nevada.* Reno: University of Nevada Press, 1984.

Wilds, Leah J. *Water Politics in Northern Nevada: A Century of Struggle.* Reno: University of Nevada Press, 2010.

Wilkinson, Charles F. *Crossing the Next Meridian: Land, Water, and the Future of the West.* Washington, DC: Island Press, 1991.

Wise, John. *The Lake Tahoe Study.* Washington, DC: National Service Center for Environmental Publications, 1976.

INDEX

|||||||||||||||||||||||||||||||||||||||||||||||||||||||||||||||||||||||||||||||||||||||||||||||||||||||||||||||||||||||||||||||||||||||||||||||||||||||||||||||||||||||||||||||||

Morgan, William "Bill," 94, 110, 125–29, 130–33, 155
Morrison, Angeline, 6
Morton, Rogers, 76–78
Mountain States Legal Foundation, 106
Mount Tamalpais State Park, 29
Muir, John, 29
Muir Woods National Monument, 29
Murphy, Brad, 47–48
Muskie, Edmund, 75, 76

Nagy, Les, 67
Nason, Rochelle: awards won by, 163; Boulder Bay criticism by, 169; Lake Tahoe Transportation and Water Quality Coalition role of, 156, 189; Nevada Legislature testimony of, 164, 171–73; Presidential Summit and, 157; TRPA and, 163, 164, 166, 171, 173
National Audubon Society, 142
National Cathedral, 152
National Conservation Association, 29
National Home Builders Association, 4, 142
National League of Cities, 112, 138, 142
National Park Service, 29, 58, 105
National Recreation Area (NRA), 93, 99, 108
National Register of Historic Places, 149
National Scenic Area (NSA), 112
National Science Foundation (NSF), 84, 89
Native people, 1, 6, 19, 30
Neal, Joe, 96, 98
Nelson, Gaylord, 57
Nevada Bureau of Environmental Health, 59
Nevada-California Lake Tahoe Association, 44
Nevada Conservation League, 173, 175, 178
Nevada Health Department, 38
Nevada Highway Department, 97
Nevada Legislature: California and, 31, 174; composition of, 91; gaming influence over, 100; Hoffman lobbying of, 122; land-bank responsibility of, 131; Morgan and, 126; regional study created by, 51; Tahoe conservancy rejected by, 123; TRPA composition and, 112; TRPA withdrawal and, 24, 164, 169; Warren proposal and, 96, 99–100

Nevada Senate, 132, 164, 170, 184
Nevada State Journal, 7, 42, 80
Nevada Supreme Court, 81, 134, 136
Nevada Tahoe Regional Planning Agency (NTRPA), 55–56
Nevada Tahoe Regional Planning Commission, 52
Newell, Frederick H., 28, 30
Newlands, Francis J., 26
Newlands Water Project, 22, 26–27, 30–31
New Mexico, 105
New York City, 139
1980 Plan, 48–49
Ninth Circuit Court of Appeals, 75, 101, 138, 140–43, 149, 153, 168, 195n24
Nixon, Richard M., 33, 57, 60, 68, 77, 158
Nixon administration, 73, 76, 86, 170
Northern California, 9, 25, 84, 109
North Lake Tahoe Chamber of Commerce, 53
North Shore, 12, 35, 45, 68, 77, 158
North Shore Club, 116
North Shore Stateline, 42, 187
Nunes, Don, 102

Oakland (CA), 25, 26
O'Callaghan, Mike: casinos and, 83; development opposed by, 79; environmental protection and, 91; federal environmental action supported by, 112; TRPA and, 60, 72; Warren proposal and, 96, 107
O'Connor, Sandra Day, 139, 152
Office of Management and Budget, 86, 113
Old Buckhorn Inn, 36
Olney, Warren, 194n11
Olsen, Ted, 142
Orme, Antony, 42, 64
Orr Ditch Decree, 32–33
Osgood Swamp, 123
Overton, Captain John Bear, 12–13

Pacific Legal Foundation (PLF), 137–39
Packard, David, 86
Paiute Indians: claims awards and, 33–34; cutthroat trout and, 16; Pyramid Lake and,

20, 27, 30–31, 33, 34, 115; Truckee River and, 27–28, 33–34
Palace Hotel, 17
Palma, Juan, 149–51, 153
Park Cattle Company, 78
Park family, 78, 171
Park Tahoe Hotel and Casino, 78–80, 99, 101
Pasadena, 8
Pavley, Fran, 185
Pelcyger, Bob, 34
Penn Central Railroad, 85
Penn Central Transportation Co. v. New York City, 139, 142
People of the State of California v. Squaw Valley Ski Corporation, 144
Pepper, James, 71
Pershing, Bob, 102–3
Pershing, Mrs., 103
Phillip Burton Wilderness, 109
Phipps, William, 19
Pilarcitos dam and tunnel, 25
Pinchot, Gifford, 29–30
Pioneer I, 107–8
Placer County (CA): court injunction from, 32; CTRPA and, 102, 104; fishing in, 22; Heikka and, 67; Henry and, 98, 102; irrigation and mining in, 24; 1980 Plan acceptance by, 49; Nunes and, 102; SB 271 and, 171; Squaw Valley and, 145–46, 148; summer homes in, 39; TRPA assessments and, 58; TRPA Board and, 119; TRPA lawsuits and, 68, 70
Planning and Conservation League, 155
Point Reyes National Seashore, 109
Pope-Baldwin recreation complex, 39, 50
Pope Beach, 39, 85
Pope family, 39
Potash, Dan, 156
Poulsen, Sandy, 37
Poulsen, Wayne, 37, 144
Preemption Act of 1841, 8
Presidential Summit, 157–59
Prewett, James E., 22
Pruitt, Robert, 49
Public Lands Commission, 8
Pyramid Lake: decline of, 30, 33; Ely pursuing

health of, 34; Lahontan cutthroat and, 14, 20, 183; Laxalt and, 34, 115; Newlands Water Project diverting water from, 31; Paiute fishery at, 20, 27, 30, 33–34; Paiute rights to, 33–34, 115; Truckee River and, 20, 30

Raley's shopping center (North Shore), 80, 81
Ralston, William, 7
R&R Partners, 172, 184
Reagan, Ronald: bistate compact and, 54; Carter's order rescinded by, 114, 116; Clean Water Act opposition of, 76; CTRPA and, 84; Garcia appointed by, 121; Gorsuch appointed by, 9, 115; land-acquisition cuts by, 118–19, 123; Laxalt and, 53–54, 114; Sagebrush Rebellion and, 106–7; Squaw Valley and, 145; TRPA and, 115–16, 117; Watt appointed by, 106, 115; Z'berg and, 53, 55, 61
Reclamation Act of 1902, 27
Reclamation Service, 28, 30, 31. *See also* Bureau of Reclamation
Redding, B. B., 19
Redstone Mining Company, 73–74
Redwood National Park, 109
Reed, Edward C., 132, 139, 140–41
Rehnquist Court, 152
Reid, Harry, 157
Reno, 14, 21, 26, 27, 30, 32, 37, 132, 174
Reno Evening Gazette, 13
Reno-Sparks, 92
Reno Tahoe International Airport, 144
Republican Party, 30, 107, 170
Resource Recovery Act, 57
Reuter, John, 165–66
Richards, Robert C. "Bob": Clinton, Gore, and, 157; laboratory of, 89; limnological data collection and, 43, 87–89, 90, 157; measurements and, 43, 157; research vessels and, 88, 90
Richardson, Cora, 39
Ridder, Tony, 107
Roberti, David, 117
Roberts, John G., 4, 142
Robinson, Steve, 178, 184
Roosevelt, Theodore, 15, 26, 27, 28–30

on, 50, 85; Hewlett and, 86; Homewood on,
169; Hooper and, 85; Kent and, 29; Meeks
Bay on, 85; parkland on, 50, 187; property
rights on, 163; topography of, 5, 15; transit
startup on, 158; TRG boat on, 88; USFS
rehabilitation of, 124
Whittell, George, 41
Wickersham, George, 29
Wickman, Sally, 36
William Kent Campground and Recreation
Area, 29
Wilson, James, 29
Wilson, Pete, 158
Wilson, Thomas "Spike," 98, 108, 124
Wilson, Woodrow, 26, 30–31
Winter Olympic Games (1960), 37, 144

Wise, John, 77
Wittenberg, Roger, 168–69, 189
Woods, Norm, 121, 133
World War II, 36, 39, 49
Wyoming, 105

Yerington, Henry M., 9–12
Yerington (NV), 96

Z'berg, Edwin: California Assembly service
by, 51–52; CTRPA and, 55, 84; Lake Tahoe
and, 51–52; Nevada contentions and, 52,
54–55; state park named for, 50, 187; TRPA
finance and, 61; TRPA formation and, 52–55;
vilification of, 55
Ziegler, David, 122, 132